Ethics, Accountability and the Social Professions

Ethics, Accountability and the Social Professions

Sarah Banks

Consultant Editor: Jo Campling

First published 2004 by
PALGRAVE MACMILLAN
Houndmills, Basingstoke, Hampshire RG21 6XS and
175 Fifth Avenue, New York, N.Y. 10010
Companies and representatives throughout the world

PALGRAVE MACMILLAN is the global academic imprint of the Palgrave
Macmillan division of St. Martin's Press, LLC and of Palgrave Macmillan Ltd.
Macmillan® is a registered trademark in the United States, United Kingdom
and other countries. Palgrave is a registered trademark in the European
Union and other countries.

ISBN 0–333–75166–3

This book is printed on paper suitable for recycling and made from fully
managed and sustained forest sources.

A catalogue record for this book is available from the British Library.

A catalog record for this book is available from the Library of Congress.

10   9   8   7   6   5   4   3   2   1
13 12 11 10 09 08 07 06 05 04

Printed and bound in Great Britain by
J.W. Arrowsmith Ltd, Bristol

For Mary and Fred Banks

Contents

List of figures and tables

Figures

Tables

Acknowledgements

Many people and organisations have contributed in different ways to the making of this book. I am particularly grateful to the Leverhulme Trust for a research fellowship during 2000–1, which enabled me to undertake interviews with practitioners and begin some of the writing.

I am grateful to Blackwell publishers for permission to reproduce the 'duck-rabbit' figure from Wittgenstein's *Philosophical Investigations* (1972, p. 194) in Chapter 3 of this book, and to Taylor & Francis (http://www.tandf.co.uk) for allowing me to draw substantially on an article published in the *European Journal of Social Work* (vol. 6, no. 2, 2003) in Chapter 4. The section on accountability in Chapter 6 draws on parts of a chapter (Banks, 2002) written for a Palgrave text, *Critical Practice in Social Work*.

I would also like to express my appreciation to all the practitioners who agreed to be interviewed. They and their employing agencies remain anonymous, but without their contributions the book would not have been written. I found the interviews and group discussions with practitioners extremely thought-provoking. The work that these managers, social workers, youth workers, community workers and other practitioners are doing is very challenging. I found their ability to reflect on their work, their values and identities and to face the issues and problems that constantly arise in daily practice impressive. I would also like to thank Vicki Battell, who undertook some of the individual interviews with members of a youth offending and community safety service.

The opportunity to work with colleagues who teach in the social education and care field in the European Social Ethics Project has also been a great source of stimulation to me. The material that forms Chapter 4 on codes of ethics was originally given as a paper at the World Congress of AIEJI (International Association of Social Educators) and CEESC (College of Social Educators of Catalunya) in Barcelona in June 2001, and I am grateful to colleagues for their comments. In addition to conversations with practitioners and academics, working with students undertaking professional education and training helps generate and maintain an interest in the subject. I am very grateful to the many groups of students who have contributed to discussions and debates on ethics. These particularly include the undergraduate community and youth work students at the University of Durham, but also the postgraduate social work students at Durham and York, and more recently engineering and medical students and tutors at Newcastle and Stockton. Their own experience of dilemmas, issues and problems has added greatly to my understanding of the richness and complexity of professional ethics as an area of study.

My recent encounters with moral philosophers have been largely through reading, but links with colleagues at Durham through various colloquia and seminars have been valuable. This has, perhaps, not been sufficient to bring my expertise in philosophical ethics as up-to-date as it might be. Although I owe a great debt to my teachers in the Department of Philosophy at the University of Edinburgh where I was an undergraduate, they cannot be held to account for my current shortcomings. However, they (particularly John Llewelyn and Roy Bhaskar) were responsible for stimulating my interest in ethics and the philosophy of social science.

This book has been a long time in the making, and I am grateful to many people for their support and forbearance. Jo Campling (consultant editor) and Catherine Gray (Palgrave editor) have been encouraging and patient. I am especially grateful to two anonymous referees for their very helpful comments on the first draft of this book, which resulted, I hope, in its improvement. Colleagues in the Community and Youth Work Studies Unit and Centre for Applied Social Studies at the University of Durham have been very supportive, particularly Linda Ray, who catalogued my offprint collection into Endnote. My family, neighbours and friends have been very understanding, often making thoughtful inquiries about progress and providing kind opportunities for short breaks and diversions. I am especially grateful to Yvonne Richardson, who has always believed in me and spurred me on, and to Robin Williams, who has lent me books, listened to progress reports, read chapters and sent encouraging and sometimes ambiguous messages, the last of which was: 'downhill'.

SARAH BANKS

Introduction: exploring professional ethics

Professional ethics as a topic of concern

> Our present concern with ethics distinguishes this age from others. (Davis, 1999, p. 3)

Many commentators have noted the recent growth of interest in ethics in the western world. Numerous factors have contributed to this, including: developments in biomedical science (especially genetics), leading to a questioning of the nature and value of human life and personal identity; a growing awareness of human-induced ecological changes and their interrelationship with global business interests; and increasing publicity given to 'scandals' surrounding senior figures in public life. According to Davis (1999, p. 20): 'the ethics boom is primarily a boom in "professional ethics" and other forms of "applied" (or "practical") ethics'.

This book is concerned with professional ethics. Its focus is particularly on the implications for professional ethics of changes in the organisation and practice of a group of related occupations that I will refer to as the social professions. Whilst the 'ethics boom' has generated a large and ever-growing literature in many areas of professional ethics, particularly in medical and health care ethics, much less hitherto has been written specifically on the professions working in the social welfare field. This book is one contribution to the exploration of ethics in relation to the social professions.

The social professions

I will use the term 'social professions' as shorthand to refer the occupations of social work, youth work and community work as defined

1

in the UK. These are related, but still distinct, occupational groups involved in care, social control, informal education and advocacy with a range of vulnerable, troublesome or 'disadvantaged' user/client groups. Whilst it may be argued that this is rather an *ad hoc* and amorphous grouping, it does reflect a recent tendency, particularly in the European literature, to group these types of occupations together (covering social care and informal education/social pedagogic work). It has no more internal logic than alternative groupings, such as 'the caring professions' (which tends to include social work and nursing) or the broader 'welfare professions' (which might include a range of occupations in the fields of health, social care, informal and formal education).

To a large degree, many of the same broad issues and challenges are faced by a whole range of 'welfare and caring' professions in many different countries. However, in order for the book to have a practice focus, without the need to note constantly the differences and similarities between too many different occupational groups and countries, I have chosen social, youth and community work in a UK context. More than anything else, the choice of these occupations reflects my own interests, as someone who has worked and taught in social work and community and youth work. These occupations also have common origins in nineteenth-century community-based philanthropy and moral education. Although in some respects they have now grown apart, with separate educational and regulatory systems, there are still considerable areas of overlap and interchange of ideas and practice. While there is a growing interchange between health and social work, especially in the fields of community care, mental health and hospital-based work, arguably the knowledge and skills base of nursing is fundamentally different from that of social work.

Some readers, particularly those in North America, Australasia or other countries of the southern world outside Europe, may not be familiar with the term 'the social professions', or may dispute whether it covers precisely those occupations I have suggested. I would ask readers to bear in mind that the term is not important in itself, but is rather used as a convenient shorthand to obviate the need continually to repeat the phrase: 'social, youth and community work'. It is also important to draw readers' attention to the fact that this is not another book about social work ethics – its occupational focus is broader than social work (in the sense used in English). Furthermore, a key focus of its subject matter is professional ethics (drawing on insights from moral philosophy) as well as professional practice (drawing on insights from practitioners and social welfare theorists).

The nature of professional ethics

Before moving on to outline the rationale for the book, it is important to point out that the term 'professional ethics' has at least two broad senses:

- the norms and standards of behaviour of members of specific occupational groups and the ethical issues and dilemmas that arise in their practice (a plural term, as in the phrase: 'The professional ethics for youth workers *were* ignored');
- the study of these norms and ethical issues (a singular term, as in: 'The social worker reported that professional ethics *was* her best subject at university).

This can generate confusion, since some commentators move quite cavalierly and seemingly unconsciously between the use of the term as singular and plural. Although somewhat cumbersome, at times in the book I will refer to 'professional ethics (as norms)' or 'professional ethics (as study)' if there seems to be a need for clarity. Although it is quite common for an area of study or body of knowledge (like 'geography' or 'law') to share the same name as the subject studied, the confusion in the case of ethics is compounded by the noun being singular when referring to 'the study of' and plural when referring to the subject matter studied.

According to Chadwick and Levitt (1997, p. 55), the second sense of professional ethics outlined above (as the study of moral norms) is a branch of applied ethics. The term 'applied ethics' tends to be used to refer to moral philosophy that is applied to practical or policy issues, as opposed to 'theoretical ethics' which focuses more on the development and evaluation of ethical theories or the analysis of general ethical concepts *per se*. But this distinction is somewhat artificial, as all ethics is about the practice of how human beings behave towards each other.

However, just as we talk about 'pure' and 'applied' mathematics, knowing that there is no hard and fast distinction, so we understand what is meant by 'applied ethics'. The intention in the applied subjects is to work more directly on problems and issues experienced in the real world, and perhaps even (although not always) to make a difference to people's understanding and actions in relation to these issues. As already mentioned, the biggest growth in the field of applied ethics in recent years has been in areas such as environmental ethics, bioethics and professional ethics. Here general ethical questions relating to the value of human life, the nature of justice and human rights, our duties towards other living beings or the meaning of 'autonomy' are discussed in the context of a specific subject matter. For example, in the field of environmental ethics, we may find questions arising about whether animals have rights, or whether people have a responsibility to future generations. In bioethics, questions around the rights and wrongs of genetic manipulation are high on the agenda – what right scientists have to 'interfere' with nature and what harms may be caused. In professional ethics, consideration may be given to the nature of confidentiality and when it should be broken or the limits of client autonomy and professional paternalism. This may involve analysis of the meaning and legitimacy of concepts like 'confidentiality', 'autonomy' or even 'professional ethics'. Alternatively, or in addition, it may entail the application of ethical theories, such as Kantian, utilitarian, virtue or care theories of ethics to professional practice.

The themes of the book: professionalism, ethics and change

The existence of an area of study known as 'professional ethics' suggests that it is possible to identify certain occupations as 'professions', and that there is something distinctive about the ethics (norms) of professional practice over and above the ethics of 'ordinary life'. The fact that we speak of 'medical ethics', 'engineering ethics', or 'social work ethics', for example, also implies that different occupational groups have different sets of norms and standards. To find written summaries of these norms and standards, usually we have to look no further than the codes of ethics or principles and rules of professional conduct published by the different occupational groups. These documents usually reflect a rather traditional view of professional ethics, which rests on certain key assumptions, including that:

1. distinct professional groups exist;
2. these groups have distinct sets of values/ethical principles and rules of professional conduct that are broadly accepted;

3. the first loyalty of the professional lies with the client/patient/ service user;
4. professional values come before those of the employing agency or society;
5. professionals make ethical judgements on the basis of ethical principles and rules accepted by the profession.

This book is concerned with the implications for this traditional notion of professional ethics of three broad trends:

1. *Professions and professional ethics* – There is a well-established tendency in the sociological literature to question the usefulness of the category of 'profession' and the legitimacy of 'professional ethics'.
2. *Ethical theory and professional ethics* – In the field of moral philosophy generally, including professional ethics, there is a growth of interest in theoretical approaches that question the dominance of ethical principles and reasoned approaches to making ethical judgements; instead emphasising the importance of emotion and care, sometimes appearing to collapse the 'personal'/'professional' distinction.
3. *The changing social professions and professional ethics* – There are many changes that have been taking place in the organisation and practice of the professions in the latter decades of the twentieth century, particularly under the banner of 'managerialism' with the stated aims of improving accountability and service delivery.

These trends will be explored in relation to the occupations of social work, youth work and community work, with examples drawn largely from a British context, but with relevance to other countries going through similar shifts in social and economic policy.

(1) Professions and professional ethics

The starting point for the book is the fact that in the some of the traditional sociological literature on the professions (from the early and mid twentieth century), the occupational groups in both the social care and health field were often referred to as 'semi', 'quasi' or 'aspirant' professions. If this designation is accepted, then it implies that certain aspects of traditional professional ethics might not apply to such occupations. For example, the social professions may have less autonomy to make their own decisions on the basis of professionally defined values insofar as they tend to work for, or on behalf of, state bureaucracies with social control functions. However, later theorists challenged what might be called an essentialist view of the professions (the idea that an occupation is a profession if and only if it possesses certain characteristics). They argue that the process of 'professionalisation' is a strategy on the part of occupational groups to gain status, wealth and power. Different occupational groups may adopt different strategies at different times, and there is no single set of essential criteria for what counts as being regarded as a 'profession'. The 'strategic' and 'historical/developmental' approaches to the study of the professions make it more legitimate to discuss professional ethics in the context of the social professions, as they can be seen to be occupations making bids for status. However, at the same time, the strategic approach also questions the credibility of separate 'professional' ethics (as norms) for any occupational group. For example, it has been argued that claims made for special sets of professional ethics embodying a selfless ideal of service are mere rhetorical devices designed to gain credibility. The question of whether any occupation, and in particular the social professions, can justifiably claim special sets of ethics, and if so, what these might comprise, is one of the questions explored in this book.

(2) Ethical theory and professional ethics

How this question about the distinctiveness of professional ethics is answered depends not only on how professions are construed, but what view of ethics is held. Those who regard ethical conduct as based on universally applicable principles, impartially applied by 'neutral' agents, would tend to argue that professionals are governed by norms no different from those by which the rest of us are bound. Professional ethics would be regarded either as unnecessary, or as a set of special obligations that is nevertheless established in accordance with prevailing moral norms. Those who regard ethical conduct as dependent on the character of moral agents (honesty, integrity, and so on) and as relative to the particular context and the nature of relationships and commitments we have to each other, have produced different arguments about the distinctiveness or otherwise of professional ethics. Some have argued that professional ethics are no different from personal ethics – indeed, that the role of a good professional is akin to that of a friend. Others have argued that professional relationships are derived from distinctive professional roles, albeit designed to promote human flourishing, and may entail behaviour that would be regarded as morally unacceptable in ordinary life (for example, lawyers may deliberately undermine the credibility of opposition witnesses in cases where they know the witness to be truthful). The legitimacy of professional ethics as a set of norms and as a subject of study in its own right does seem to depend on its distinctiveness. This can be questioned from a philosophical point of view, but also in the light of radical changes in the organisation and practice of occupations regarded as professions.

(3) The changing social professions and professional ethics

All professions working in the area of public services have faced serious challenges as the welfare state has undergone a 'restructuring' during the latter decades of the twentieth century. This has been an international phenomenon, although the rationale for the changes, and the implications for policy and practice have varied greatly between different countries. Two particular themes in relation to changes in the organisation and practice of the social professions in the UK are of concern in this book, namely: aspects of the trend towards increasing interprofessional working and what I will call 'the new accountability'.

(a) *'Interprofessional' working* refers to the developing trend for members of different professional groups to work together in teams, services, partnerships or taskforces to tackle particularly intractable problems or develop new services. Whilst developing over several decades, it has gathered momentum in the UK as the New Labour government elected in 1997 has placed a stress on 'joined up' policy and practice as part of its modernisation programme for all levels of government and public services (the 'modern management' agenda). Interprofessional working shades into 'inter-agency' working where the stress is on different agencies developing a unified strategic approach to tackle a particular problem (for example, through a regeneration partnership) and multiprofessional working, where professionals with distinct roles coordinate their work with service users to meet their needs better (for example, a hospital-based team for the elderly).

But true interprofessional working may entail some interchangeability of professional roles (for example, with pre-sentence reports being completed not just by probation officers or social workers, but by any member of a youth offending team, including police officers or youth workers). This appears to threaten the idea of distinct professional groups each with their special sets of guiding ideals and ethical principles.

(b) *'New accountability'* is a term I have adopted to encapsulate the growth of a whole host of accountability requirements in the form of procedures for doing tasks; predefined targets or outcomes for work; and monitoring systems to measure performance. These have developed with the growth of the 'new managerialism' or 'new public management' from the 1980s and 1990s, alongside the introduction of market-based approaches to social welfare, contracting arrangements for service delivery, managerial challenges to professional autonomy and the setting of centralised standards and targets for work. The background to these changes includes a serious questioning and restructuring of the 'welfare state', within which the social professions are firmly based, and a climate where the expertise, legitimacy, trustworthiness, effectiveness and efficiency of all professionals are increasingly questioned. Furthermore, the 'modern management' agenda of the late 1990s and early 2000s in the UK has intensified the accountability demands on public services. In being subjected to increasing levels of internal and external regulation and audit, it would seem that the autonomy of professional decision-making and room for discretion are being seriously curtailed. Since the key features of professional ethics traditionally are adherence to a set of principles and norms defined by a professional body (as opposed to an employer or auditing agency) and the ability of and opportunity for the individual practitioner to reflect on the ethics of certain choices and make informed decisions, it would seem that these trends pose a serious threat to professional ethics.

Exploring professional ethics

This book comprises a series of explorations on the theme of professional ethics in relation to the social professions from several different perspectives. It contains a set of interrelated chapters, each exploring certain key concepts, ideas, theories or aspects of professional practice, as mentioned above, which may shed light on the nature of professional ethics in theory and practice. It draws on literature and thinking in the fields of moral philosophy, the social sciences and the practice of social, youth and community work. Some chapters are more philosophical, some more sociological and some more practice-focused. One of the sub-themes of the book is the extent to which the treatments of the topic of professional ethics from different disciplinary standpoints interrelate, contradict or simply complement each other. Although we may expect to see the traditional disciplinary boundaries breaking down, in line with the current trend for interdisciplinary working, different disciplines nevertheless have different aims, norms and traditions that may mean their theories, findings or conclusions, while complementary, may not be directly comparable. So if the reader were to ask, what is the direct connection of **Chapter 2** (a philosophical exploration of the legitimacy of professional ethics, as distinct from the ethics of everyday life) with **Chapter 5** (a case study based on interviews with practitioners in an interprofessional context covering the issue of the distinctiveness of each profession's ethics), the answer might be simply: they are both explorations of professional ethics, but from different perspectives.

In **Chapter 3** of the book there is a more detailed discussion of the interrelationship between the social sciences and philosophy, and of the tendency for philosophy deliberately to divorce itself from everyday practice. This is not the main theme of the book, but I am raising the issue now merely to alert the reader to the rather different styles that may be encountered in the different sections of the book. Moral philosophers frequently have a substantial interest in the meanings of moral concepts such as 'good' or 'right' (sometimes called 'metaethics'), and/or in the development of moral theories about what is good or right ('normative ethics'). They may use examples from the professions to illuminate and elaborate their philosophical discussions. Social scientists or practitioners, whose main interest is in studying the actual daily practice and ethical dilemmas of professionals (sometimes referred to as 'descriptive ethics'), may refer to or use insights from moral philosophy in terms of clarifying the meanings of moral concepts, or may attempt to apply ethical theories to practice. So, for example, from the point of view of studying the practice of professionals in relation to ethics, **Chapter 2**, which offers an essentially philosophical argument about the distinctiveness of professional ethics, is important, as it argues for professional ethics as a legitimate topic of study. But it may be unimportant for a practitioner already convinced of the importance of professional ethics and interested in its relation to ethical theory and professional practice, who may therefore wish to skip this chapter.

Outline of the book

Following this introductory chapter, the main body of the book falls essentially into four parts, which focus on: historical and sociological perspectives on professions (**Chapter 1**); philosophical perspectives on professional ethics (**Chapters 2 and 3**); the move from philosophical principles to professional practice through codes of ethics (**Chapter 4**); and practitioner perspectives on changing practice (**Chapters 5 and 6**). **Chapter 7** is a brief concluding chapter which draws together some of the key ideas and issues.

Historical and sociological perspectives on professions

Chapter 1 is concerned to explore the nature of professions, professionalism and the process of professionalisation over time. It explores these issues in relation to professions in general, drawing on some of the sociological literature, and then in relation to the social professions in particular, drawing on some of the practice-related literature. Although there have been many texts discussing and debating the nature of professions and professionalism, the rationale for including this chapter is that the coherence of the notion of 'professional ethics' relies on there being some meaningful concept of 'profession'. So the arguments need to be rehearsed, and the social professions need to be placed in the context of professions in general.

This chapter explores different approaches to the study of professionalism, arguing that a historical/developmental approach enables a better understanding of the processes of change and development in occupational groups, as opposed to seeing professionalism in terms of the possession of a fixed set of essential features or traits. In the light of this, it then discusses the development of the occupations that make up the social professions, in a UK context, from their nineteenth-century origins in philanthropy and voluntarism, through their involvement in the welfare state, their embryonic professionalism and their recent place in the mixed economy of welfare and the new regulatory systems for occupational groups. A brief outline is given of the growth of managerialism and its interrelationship with professionalism. Three arguments are considered: (i) that a process of 'deprofessionalisation' is taking place; (ii) that there is scope for a 'new professionalism' based on a more participatory relationship with service users; and (iii) that the current changes in the organisation and practice of the social professions are just part of a continually evolving concept of professionalism. Although all three arguments have some purchase, and are not mutually exclusive, the third version is preferred.

Philosophical perspectives on professional ethics

Chapters 2 and 3 consider the contribution of moral philosophy to the study of professional ethics. First a clearing of the ground is undertaken, in terms of outlining the multiplicity of meanings of 'ethics' and 'professional ethics'. The rationale for including separate chapters on philosophical perspectives, as opposed to simply interweaving the main points within the rest of the book, is precisely because the aims, assumptions and questions asked in the philosophical treatments of professional ethics are not always the same as, or compatible with, those raised in the social science or practice-based literature. One view of philosophy is that it is the 'handmaiden' of the other disciplines, performing a kind of clearing of the ground (especially in terms of conceptual clarification) for other disciplines to perform their substantive work. Others would dispute this subservient role, and would emphasise its substantive contribution to matters of everyday practical importance. It is likely that it can perform both roles, with **Chapter 2** exemplifying more of the former (conceptual clarification), and **Chapter 3** the latter (normative ethical theory).

Chapter 2 considers the philosophical arguments in relation to the question of whether professional ethics (both as a set of norms and an area of study) are/is distinctive and their/its relationship with ordinary ethics (both as the ethics of everyday life and general moral theory). It focuses on issues of meaning and justification – an area of moral philosophy that has sometimes been called 'meta-ethics'. The chapter concludes that professional ethics (as a set of norms) cannot be regarded as completely free-floating and divorced either from the ethics of everyday life or from general ethical theory. But equally, they cannot simply be subsumed within ordinary ethics. Professional ethics are a sub-set of ordinary ethics, or an intensification of the relationship of trust in ordinary life. This chapter argues for the legitimacy of professional ethics, both as a distinctive set of norms, and as an area of study. It is, therefore, an important philosophical foundation for the rest of the book and ends by outlining three axes along which professional ethics is moving: contract–trust; ordinary ethics–distinct professional ethics; and deprofessionalisation–new professionalism. For those readers who are less interested in philosophical arguments and are prepared to take it as read that professional ethics are/is distinctive, then this chapter is not essential reading.

Chapter 3 begins by discussing some of the debates about the extent to which professional ethics (as the study of moral norms) is a subject in its own right, or part of moral philosophy or social science. We conclude that these disciplines have something to contribute and learn from each other, but may sometimes work with different assumptions about what counts as evidence or valid argument. A range of ethical theories or theoretical approaches developed by moral philosophers that may have relevance for professional ethics is then outlined. Insofar as it focuses on ethical theories that explain and/or prescribe the nature of the right or the good, this chapter is about that area of moral philosophy that has sometimes been called 'normative ethics'. The theoretical approaches to ethics covered are divided into two broad categories: impartial, detached approaches (stressing principles, rights and justice); and partial, situated approaches (stressing relationships, motives and emotions). Although these different approaches have often been characterised as mutually exclusive, it is argued that both are needed for a full picture of the sphere of the ethical. There is some discussion of those (mainly postmodernists) who argue for the 'end of ethics', in particular the end of universalist and foundational ethical theories. But in the realm of professional ethics it is suggested that a postmodernist approach is difficult to sustain. The main contribution of this chapter to the discussions in the rest of the book is the articulation of the two broad approaches to ethics summarised in Table 3.1: impartial and detached; partial and situated. These are picked up again in **Chapter 6** in relation to the theme of the 'new accountability' and its impact on practitioners' relationships with service users/participants.

From philosophical principles to professional practice

Chapter 4 essentially forms a bridge between the philosophically focused section of the book and the practitioner-based section. Its theme is codes of professional ethics, which ostensibly comprise some rather general ethical principles (linked with the broad ethical theories developed in moral philosophy) that can be applied to professional practice. Codes have been the subject of analysis and critique by moral philosophers, sociologists of the professions and practitioners/academics in the social professions themselves. Codes of ethics are also important as a topic for discussion as they have often been regarded as the embodiment of professional ethics (as norms).

This chapter analyses and discusses three examples of different types of codes of ethics developed for social workers in the USA, black social workers in South Africa and youth workers in the UK. According to some commentators, codes of ethics can be regarded as codes of moral philosophy (based on general principles derived from ethical theory) applied to professional practice. Alternatively, they can be viewed as codifications of existing good practice (taking practice as the starting point), or, more cynically, as part of an occupational bid for the power accruing from professional status (one badge of which is adherence to a code of ethics). Some philosophers have taken a rather literal approach to the analysis of professional codes of ethics (seeing them as flawed applications of ethical theory), whereas sociological critiques have analysed codes as the embodiment of the contradictory nature of professional life itself, seeing them as deliberately rhetorical, idealistic and aspirational. Some of the criticisms of codes of ethics, particularly those stemming from moral philosophers, are discussed and it is argued that quite often the criticisms rest on misunderstandings. Codes of ethics have complex and contradictory functions, which may include aspirational, rhetorical, educational and regulatory elements. In practice terms, the shift from codes as short 'oaths' to long 'rulebooks' is noted, in the light of some of the changes taking place in professions generally and the social professions in particular. Some of the recently revised codes have a greater stress on the regulatory functions and are very different from the earlier oaths. This development of the regulatory functions of codes links to the practice-related themes of the next section, which looks at the changes taking place in the organisation and practice of the social professions.

Practitioner perspectives on changing practice

Chapters 5 and 6 draw on interviews with senior practitioners and group discussions with members of teams/services working broadly in the field of social, youth and community work. The interviews were generally very loosely structured and open-ended, with a focus on the changing nature of professional practice and what it meant for the workers interviewed (see Appendix). Although the interviewees knew I was interested in ethics, and one of the questions asked was about examples of ethical dilemmas, the questions were not framed in order to elicit participants' views directly on the nature of professional ethics, or what professional values they held. Rather, they were asked to identify significant changes in the work in general, and their own work in particular, and what this meant for their practice. Specifically they were asked about their experience of and views on interprofessional working, and working to standards, targets, outcomes and procedures. Inevitably this led the discussion into matters of relationships with service users, resources, responsibilities, and so on. The interviews on which these chapters are based were designed to answer different kinds of questions from those raised in the earlier chapters of the book. The starting point of the interviews was professional practice, rather than professional ethics. In analysing the interviews, I looked for comments relevant to the broad predefined themes of interprofessional working, procedures/accountability and ethical tensions and dilemmas. I also used my pre-existing knowledge of and interest in ethical theory to identify themes relating to care, trust, equity, and so on. It should be noted that the interviews have been analysed and written up in order capture 'practitioner voices', providing illustrative and case-study material to illuminate the topic under discussion, rather than a systematic, empirical study of changing professional practice.

Chapter 5 discusses issues relating to interprofessional working in relation to a case study of a youth offending and community safety service. This chapter offers a practitioner perspective on the notion of the distinctiveness of professional ethics first raised as a philosophical question in **Chapter 2**. But whereas Chapter 2 focused largely on the notion of the distinctiveness of professional ethics in general from the ethics of everyday life, this chapter looks at the extent to which each professional group holds its own distinctive set of ethical principles or values and what this means for interprofessional working in practice. Professional ethics or values, however, are only one part of the broader 'ethos' of a profession, an organisation or a service – which also comprises interrelated issues of culture and identity, linked with attitudes, traditions and ways of working. So in this chapter the extent to which members of different professional groups in the service appear to hold different sets of professional values and are concerned about their distinct professional identities and cultures, is explored. The argument in the literature that distinct professional values and ideologies inhibit interprofessional working is considered, and it is suggested that although this seems to have caused initial difficulties in the youth offending and community safety service, many of the distinctive professional values and identities are actually regarded as important within the service and are necessary for the jointly agreed goals to be successfully achieved.

Chapter 6 focuses on the 'new accountability' requirements in the guise of externally imposed assessment proformas, predefined outcomes and targets. Arguably these pose the greatest threat to the traditional notion of professional ethics, presenting a challenge to the autonomy and discretion of both individual professional practitioners and professions in general. The accounts of interviewees suggest that while some value the new accountability requirements as promoting improved outcomes for service users and society, individual consumer rights, equity and fairness, other practitioners find them unhelpful and a challenge to the nature of their relationships with the people with whom they work. These latter practitioners value the importance of context, trust, relationships and a sense of vocation. This links with the discussion of ethical theories in **Chapter 3**, where the distinction between impartial and detached and partial and situated approaches was noted.

Conclusion

The book concludes with some comments about the future of professionalism and the ethical challenge for the social professions to maintain an 'ethic of care', entailing a focus on particularity, context, discretion, compassion and empathy, within a climate where the equally legitimate but dominant paradigm is one of impartial, detached justice, with a focus on individual and societal outcomes, consumer rights, fairness and equity. A brief overview of the variety of practitioner responses to the new demands and challenges of managerialist and modernising approaches to public services is offered, ranging from wholesale acceptance through radical challenging to 'principled quitting' (leaving the job).

The main purpose of this book is not directly to offer practical advice or recommendations to students or practitioners. Nevertheless, it is hoped that this exploration of the contested and constantly changing nature of the social professions, and the implications of this for professional ethics will help in developing our collective understanding and appreciation of the complexity of the issues at stake and the many different perspectives that can be taken on them. In this way our own views and beliefs may be challenged and clarified, and we may be more prepared to take a stand and argue a case for what we think is right. There are noticeable tensions and contradictions in the new agendas for change, particularly between the demands for centralised standardisation alongside calls for more innovation and localised flexibility. Similarly, the popular rhetoric of tackling social exclusion and promoting the participation of service users, residents and communities in policy-making and service delivery leave some space for committed practitioners to hold their ground and re-establish positive aspects of the professional project. Whether this is regarded as a 'new professionalism' or the old professionalism transformed is a matter of perspective. However, it is clear that the stand must be a principled one, in which professional ethics plays a crucial part. The 'calling to care' is an important element in the ethical tradition of the social professions, alongside the more recently articulated principles of social justice. In being 'called to account', it is important that practitioners' accounts of their ideals and their practice do not lose sight of the importance of trusting relationships and compassionate responsiveness in their quest to reach predefined targets and quantifiable outputs for organisational league tables. As one of the social work practitioners interviewed for this book commented:

> You can spend so much time ticking boxes that you can actually forget that there's people that need to be helped.

1

The social professions and the calling to care

Introduction

This book is about ethics in relation to a particular group of related occupations. I have called these occupations the 'social professions', which includes those occupations described in the UK as social work, youth and community work. Already we have introduced two problematic concepts. The first is 'profession' and the second is the 'social professions'. There has been much debate over the meaning of the term 'profession', and, indeed, whether it makes sense to define it at all. For those that have defined it, there is further debate about which occupations can be categorised as professions, with the list I have just given as belonging to the 'social professions' being particularly contested and sometimes referred to as 'emergent', 'new', 'semi' or 'quasi' professions.

Used in a loose sense, the term 'profession' is often used synonymously with 'occupation' to refer to the job someone does, or a recognised type of work. In which case, the social welfare occupations mentioned above, along with others such as bricklayers, farmers, accountants or cleaners, would all quite easily fall into the category of 'profession'. However, used more narrowly, the term has additional connotations, relating to high levels of social status, education, expertise, occupational control over membership, identity as an occupational group and a certain kind of self-consciousness about ethics. Whether the occupations of social work, community work and youth work can legitimately be regarded as professions or not depends on what view is taken of the nature of a profession. In one sense it does not matter

17

what they are called, as our interest is in the nature of these occupations and the ethical challenges they face. On the other hand, there is a body of thinking about 'professional ethics', and if we want to build on and use this, then it would seem to make sense to locate these occupations in relation to 'the professions'. We will now consider the nature of the professions, before moving on to consider the nature of those occupations that I have described as the social professions.

Approaches to the study of professions

'Profession' is a contested concept, in that there is no agreement over its meaning. Some theorists have defined 'profession' as an occupation that possesses certain characteristics or traits. These may include the fact that its members have specialised education and qualifications, a high degree of control over their work, and a code of ethics, and do work that is for the public good. However, there is no agreement over precisely which characteristics are the essential features of a profession. Another approach is to define a profession as an occupation that has successfully gained status or power in relation to other occupational groups. Johnson (1972), for example, regards professionalism as a form of occupational control. However, more recent theorists have noted the unsatisfactory nature of these approaches, and argued that what counts as a 'profession', how professions develop, define themselves and lay claim to status, has changed over time, and is continually shifting (see, for example, Freidson, 1983; Torstendahl, 1990). Moreover, the concept of 'profession' is a peculiarly Anglo-American one, and does not have an exact equivalent in many other European countries. This leads Freidson (1983, p. 22) to comment:

> The problem ... is created by attempting to treat profession as if it were a generic concept rather than a changing historic concept, with particular roots in an industrial nation strongly influenced by Anglo-American institutions.

These different definitions of 'profession' are related to different approaches to the study of the professions, which are in turn based on different sociological and ideological theories. In recent years these different approaches have become a topic of study in themselves (see, for example, Burrage, 1990; Freidson, 1983; Siegrist, 1994). Torstendahl (1990) outlines three approaches to theories of professionalism, which embrace the different definitions given above. These approaches are outlined briefly below as the essentialist, strategic and historical/developmental.

The essentialist approach

This approach is concerned to identify the properties that characterise professionalism and professionals, based on the assumption that professionals have a specific place in society and professionalisation is taking place in a specific way (Parsons, 1939; Wilensky, 1964). This approach is often linked to a functionalist view of society, associated with the work of sociologist Talcott Parsons, and is concerned to identify elements of professionalism that have functional roles for society. Developing from this, what has been called the 'trait theory' of professionalism attempts to produce a comprehensive list of the traits or characteristics essential for an occupation to be regarded as a profession, and hence to determine which occupations are professions. Many different lists of essential characteristics of professions have been produced and they vary as to what they include. Koehn (1994, p. 56), in offering an overview, usefully summarises five frequently cited traits of professionals as:

1. they are licensed by the state to perform a certain act;
2. they belong to an organisation of similarly enfranchised agents who promulgate standards and/or ideals of behaviour and who discipline one another for breaching these standards;
3. they possess so-called 'esoteric' knowledge or skills not shared by other members of the community;
4. they exercise autonomy over their work, which is work that is not well-understood by the wider community;
5. they publicly pledge themselves to render assistance to those in need and as a consequence have special responsibilities or duties not incumbent upon others who have not made this pledge.

The items included in such lists by different theorists vary. For example, Koehn argues that the only defensible trait of professionalism is the public pledge, which, from the description she gives, would seem in many cases to take the form of a written code of ethics. Millerson

(1964, p. 9) on the other hand, argues that the presence or absence of a professional code of ethics does not signify professionalism or non-professionalism, demonstrating how some types of professions have more need for codes than others. He also includes professional education and qualifications in the list of traits, but not licensing by the state. Greenwood (1957) explicitly includes a code of ethics and instead of 'esoteric knowledge', speaks of 'systematic theory'. Whatever traits are included, this approach encourages the categorisation of occupations according to the extent to which they possess, or are in the process of achieving, all or some of these characteristics. So, for example, Carr-Saunders (1955) lists four types of profession: the established professions (such as law, medicine, the clergy); the new professions (such as engineering, chemistry, and the natural and social sciences); the semi-professions (such as nursing, pharmacy and social work); and 'would be' professions (such as hospital managers).

There have been numerous critiques of this approach in recent years, in addition to the fact that no one definitive list of characteristics can be agreed. As Torstendahl himself points out, in order to study the essential characteristics of professions, we first need a definition of 'profession'. So the whole process is rather circular. Indeed, analyses of professionalism commonly start from considering the social relations of doctors and lawyers, and this is because we already know which people are properly categorised by this concept by everyday English speakers. Yet while the term 'profession' is used widely in the English language, it does not always have an equivalent in other European languages. If the same properties are not essential to the corresponding groups in other societies, this approach to professionalism cannot be generalised.

The strategic approach

This approach to the study of professionalism focuses on the types of collective action on which groups of professionals rely, and the identification of the relationships or conflicts between a (professional) occupational group and other groups. Several theorists have developed Weber's concept of 'closure' – the keeping of other people away from the advantages someone has got in society by means of an exclusionary strategy (Collins, 1990; Parkin, 1974, 1979). Collins develops a theory of the professions based on Weberian conflict theory – the idea that we can explain social behaviour and social structure in terms of the interests of individuals in maximising their power, wealth and status. He uses the concept of 'market closure' to describe the process by which occupations attempt to control market conditions, suggesting that those occupational groups that are especially successful are the ones we have come to call 'the professions'. These groups could therefore be described as monopolising certain activities. At the same time, he argues, they also transform their work into 'status honour'. Collins (1990, p. 26) sees these occupational groups as Weberian status groups, that direct attention away from the work they do, towards the 'style, the honour, the moral standards displayed by [their] members'. He suggests that the strong professions are those that have surrounded their work by social rituals, and identifies education as a modern form of ritual and as particularly important in forming the professions (p. 26).

Torstendahl (1990, p. 50) criticises the focus on exclusionary closure as the strategy used by professions, arguing that it is used by other groups, and also that other tactics can be used to enhance collective status and power, including politicisation, cartelisation and maintaining the status quo. Other theorists offer different variations on the strategic approach, but what they have in common is in theorising about how occupational groups gain power and status as part of a professionalizing strategy (see also, Johnson, 1972; Larson, 1977). For example, having initially defined professionalism as a type of occupational control, in his later work Johnson (1984, p. 19) argues that as it has become increasingly difficult for occupational groups to control their own work practices, and professionalism has become more of an occupational ideology than a form of occupational control of work by a collegiate network:

> The term profession has been extended to an increasingly large and diverse group of occupations such that our identification of an occupation as professional has less to do with the reality of a division of labour in which an association of colleagues effectively controls its own work practices, than with a recognition of the strategy of professionalism: a political strategy for occupational advancement.

The historical/developmental approach

This approach looks at how professional groups change over time. According to Torstendahl, the focus is on examining the changes in relationships between occupational groups (taken to be professional) and other groups over a long time period. Here the concern is not with the properties or actions of professionals, but on professionals as forming social groups with patterns that are interesting in themselves. This approach, however, does not assume that all professions go through a series of fixed developmental stages, as, for example, described by Wilensky (1964), based largely on conditions in the USA. Rather, it acknowledges that some societies go through developments that have no real counterparts in other societies (for example, industrialisation in Europe and the USA during the nineteenth century) and this influences the development of the standing of professionals and their activities (Torstendahl and Burrage, 1990).

Siegrist (1994, p. 8) argues that it is important to look at all significant actors influencing the formation and practice of the professions, which may vary according to time and place, and include educational institutions, the state or government, members of professions and their organisations, clients and client organisations, the media and public opinion. He suggests that the issue of state and political intervention has been neglected in research on professions, as this was thought to be more relevant to continental Europe than to the UK and the USA, on which much of the work was based. He identifies three models of professionalisation, differentiated according to the role of the state, government and legislation:

(a) The traditional corporative professions and the weak state – This describes the model in England, whereby the professional corporations established in early modern times by a royal charter (a guild or a college) maintained sole responsibility for the education and entry into the profession of its members. This situation persisted into the nineteenth and twentieth centuries, with the professions themselves playing a key role in their regulation, in cooperation with the government, with little threat to their autonomy.

(b) Professionalisation from above in a bureaucratic authoritarian state in the nineteenth century – While conditions in continental Europe were similar to those in England up to the end of the eighteenth century, the revolutions in government in those countries also transformed the professions, introducing 'top down' unified systems of education, qualifications, state licensing and 'reorienting the "professional sector" towards the goal of common welfare defined by the state' (Siegrist, 1994, p. 11). The old professional corporations were generally disbanded, and in some countries compulsory professional associations were introduced. In the later nineteenth century, the hold of the state relaxed somewhat, and professions were given some more autonomy, particularly in relation to ethical standards, but not over education and examinations. The tradition of state control is still noticeable in these countries.

(c) Professionalisation in the post-revolutionary liberal-democratic societies – This model applies particularly to the USA, but can also be seen in other liberal-democratic societies with weak bureaucracy and few government institutions, such as Switzerland. In the USA, the institutions imported from England were swept away in the 1830s, and professions were allowed to develop and take shape, with the state only introducing legislation when the profession has established itself and won public acceptance. Wilensky's stages of professionalisation chart the process whereby a function of a profession becomes a full-time occupation; the occupational group then lays claims to certain functions; the educational process begins to become regulated; a professional association is established; the association requires examinations and gains monopoly rights over the profession and its services; regulations concerning conduct and ethics are more precisely formulated and supervised by the professional association.

These models are generalisations and during the twentieth century there were some convergences, as elements of formalisation and institutionalisation appeared in the USA and UK, and liberalisation occurred in continental European countries, with voluntary professional organisations emerging in some.

The ideal-typical profession

So what, then, is a 'profession' and does it make sense to continue to use the term? It is clear that a 'profession' is generally regarded as a special category of occupational groups. But precisely how it is defined depends upon what theory of professionalism is adopted, as well as the time period and country. Freidson (1983, p. 32) suggests that:

> the future of profession lies in embracing the concept as an intrinsically ambiguous, multi-faceted folk concept, of which no single definition and no attempt at isolating its essence will ever be generally persuasive.

Different concepts of profession will be advanced by occupations seeking professional status from those advanced by employers or clients seeking to control the jobs they want done, or by government agencies or the general public. Freidson argues (1983, p. 27) that the appropriate research strategy for such a folk concept is 'phenomeno-logical' in character:

> One does not attempt to determine what profession is in an absolute sense, so much as how people in a society determine who is a professional and who is not, how they 'make' or 'accomplish' professions by their activities, and what the consequences are for the way in which they see themselves and their work.

Freidson suggests that the theoretical programme that takes us beyond the folk concept is to look to develop a more general and abstract theory of occupations, according to which the historic professions can be analysed in the same conceptual terms as the other occupations, but without assuming that those professions necessarily represent a single, generic type of occupation. This he does in some of his later work, where he develops, as an intellectual tool, an ideal-typical pro-fessionalism in contrast with the ideal-typical market and bureau-cracy. Although Freidson produces a list of characteristics of his 'ideal-typical' professionalism, his approach is quite different from that of the trait theorists. He is not claiming to describe any real occupation, but rather to develop 'a standard by which to appraise and analyse historic occupations whose characteristics vary in time and place' (Freidson, 2001, pp. 127–8). The interdependent elem-ents of Freidson's (2001, pp. 127, 180) ideal type are enumerated as:

1. a body of knowledge and skill officially recognised as based on abstract concepts and theories and requiring the exercise of considerable discretion;
2. an occupationally controlled division of labour;
3. an occupationally controlled labour market requiring training credentials for entry and career mobility;

4. an occupationally controlled training programme which produces those credentials, schooling that is associated with 'higher learning', segregated from the ordinary labour market and provides an opportunity for the development of new knowledge;
5. an ideology serving some transcendent value and asserting greater devotion to doing good work than to economic reward.

According to Freidson, certain occupations may undergo a process of professionalisation, coming closer to this ideal at some points in time and in some countries, while others in different places and times may move away from the ideal and undergo 'deprofessionalisation'. He identifies key factors influencing the process of professionalisation as: the organisation and policy position of state agencies; the organisation of occupations themselves; and the varying institutional circumstances required for successful practice of different bodies of knowledge and skill. As Freidson points out, many of the classic studies of professions have analysed the process of professionalisation during the nineteenth century and early twentieth (for example, Carr-Saunders and Wilson, 1933; Larson, 1977; Perkin, 1969). Recent work, however, has focused more on the process of deprofessionalisation in the context of the economic and social changes happening in western countries during the later part of the twentieth century (for example, Dominelli, 1996; Harrison and Pollitt, 1994). Freidson's analysis of professionalism will be used later, when examining the nature of the social professions.

The social professions

We have already suggested that this term embraces those occupations in the caring and welfare field, which according to the trait or essentialist theory of professions, have often been regarded as 'semi' or 'quasi' or 'bureau' professions, to denote the fact that these newer occupations (compared with the traditional professions of law, medicine and the clergy) lack some of the 'essential qualities' in relation to autonomy over work, public credibility or status (Etzioni, 1969). However, as has been suggested above, it is less important to establish whether or not these occupations are 'professions' in any essentialist sense of the term, and more useful to look at how they grew and developed over time, what claims to expertise, autonomy and status they have made and how they compare to other occupations at the present time. But we will first discuss the use of the term 'social professions', before outlining the details of the occupations it covers.

The term 'social professions' is little used as yet in English, although its usage has developed as part of the European project to develop transferability of qualifications and greater understandings between those involved in work in the social welfare field, where there is often no exact equivalence in the way the work of different occupational groups is divided up. So we find the term being used by organisations and groups set up at a European-wide level to promote the development of knowledge, mutual understanding and recognition of occupations concerned with the care, control, informal education and empowerment of individuals and groups (see Lorenz and Seibel, 1998, 1999). The term appears in the sub-title of the recently established *European Journal of Social Work* as 'The Forum for the Social Professions'. However, the role of these occupational groups varies from country to country. What is called 'youth work' in the UK may be done by pedagogues in the Scandinavian countries, who also do what we would describe as 'social care work' in the UK. The role of the educator in France somewhat resembles the pedagogue in Scandinavia and Germany, but has many specialisations. Although most countries have an occupational group that translates as social work, the actual configuration of tasks and roles can be different, with social workers in Scandinavian countries, for example, embracing those who take on the role of assessing and distributing welfare benefits, as well as field social workers. Community work may be practised in some countries, such as Holland and Sweden, but it is on a smaller scale than in the UK or USA. Whether these occupations are regulated by the state, have protected titles, prescribed national examinations, professional associations or codes of ethics again varies from country to country and occupation to occupation. In this sense the term 'social' in 'social professions' describes a set of occupations that are diverse in the same way as 'professions' in general.

The development of the social professions

For the purpose of this book, we will focus largely on three occupational groups recognised in the UK as social work, community work and youth work. Descriptions of the history of these groups, their current structures and practices and the ethical issues arising in their work will be located in a UK context. However, many of the features of changing policy and practice that are happening in the UK are also happening elsewhere in Europe, North America and Australasia and impacting on the occupational groups that work in the broad field of social, community and youth work (see Lorenz, 2001).

These occupational groups in the UK have common origins in the philanthropic organisations established in the mid to late nineteenth century. Their histories are often intertwined, and although they developed into separate occupations by the mid to late twentieth century, there have been periods of overlap and certainly even now the boundaries are not always clear. Before we look at the history of these occupations, it may be helpful, therefore, to outline recent definitions of the nature of social work, community work and youth work in order that their changing structure and organisation can be better understood. Of course, there is a plethora of different and changing definitions of these occupations, often at a very general level. Nevertheless, I will simply offer three relatively recent examples of statements of purpose, to highlight the differences and similarities between these occupational groups:

> The purpose of social work is to enable children, adults, families, groups and communities to function, participate and develop in society. (Central Council for Education and Training in Social Work, 1995, p. 16)

> The key purpose of community work is to work with communities experiencing disadvantage, enabling them collectively to identify needs and rights, clarify objectives and take action to meet them within a democratic framework which respects the needs and rights of others. (Harris, 2001, p. 1)

> The purpose of youth work is to facilitate and support young people's growth through dependence to interdependence, by encouraging their personal and social development and enabling them to have a voice, influence and place in their communities and society. (National Youth Agency, 2001, p. 1)

These brief statements describe differences in client groups and the broad focus of the work. Social work focuses on a range of individuals and groups to enable them to 'function' better in society; whereas community work focuses on communities taking action collectively to meet needs; and youth work covers young people's growth and development, encouraging their participation in society. In these particular definitions for social work and youth work, their role in enabling the people they work with *to fit into society* is evident.

The idea of people *developing in society* is mentioned, including enabling them to participate (social work) or have a voice and influence (youth work). The social work definition also refers to people's *functioning in society* and the youth work definition mentions enabling people to have *a place in society*. The community work statement has a different tone, not mentioning 'society', but instead talking of a *democratic framework*, within which to enable people's own collective action. A more emancipatory strand is evident in community work, even in these brief statements.

If we elaborate the differences in actual practice a little further, social work has statutory functions laid down by law (for example, in relation to child protection and mental health), although not all social workers have statutory responsibilities. Social workers tend to work more frequently with individuals and families experiencing difficulties. Community work and youth work have no statutory basis, and usually (but not always) participants engage voluntarily and work is done much more frequently in groups. All three of these occupations could be characterised as having the broad aim of the promotion of social welfare, which includes both individual well-being in a social context, and the notion of a common or communal good. This idea will be further elaborated in the next chapter, so we will now move on to look briefly at the historical development of these occupations.

Nineteenth-century philanthropy

The work that developed into social work, community work and youth work grew up in the mid to late nineteenth century. This came about as the voluntary and charitable bodies with a mission to distribute financial and material resources, encourage self-help and provide moral education to those in poverty became more widespread and organised. Historians of both social work and community work identify the origins of this work particularly in the settlement houses that developed in the late nineteenth century (the first being set up in 1884), and Charity Organisation Society, established in 1869 (see, for example, Baldock, 1974, pp. 3–5; Younghusband, 1981, pp. 11–17). The settlements were established, generally by universities, in the poorer parts of cities, with the aim of providing meeting rooms, space for activities and living accommodation for graduates who would work amongst the poor – the first being Oxford House and Toynbee Hall in the East End of London (Ashworth, 1984; Johnson, 2001;

Picht, 1914). The Charity Organisation Society was set up to coord-inate charitable giving and ensure that resources were well targeted to the 'deserving poor'. Those who worked for these organisations began to keep systematic records, to discuss their experiences, propose ideas about the causes of people's difficulties and how these could be ameliorated and develop methods of working. According to Younghusband (1981, p. 12), the Charity Organisation Society was 'undoubtedly the originator of casework' in so far as it developed systematic processes of assessing individual circumstances, planning action, allocating resources and following up the cases. Yet, as Baldock (1974, p. 4) points out, in its attempts to organise charity and coord-inate the work of many people, it was also reminiscent of community work. The work that went on in the settlements, and in other settings, such as Octavia Hill's pioneering work with tenants or Dr Barnardo's workshops for unemployed boys, involved work with individuals, families, groups and communities. As Younghusband comments, the interweaving of casework, group work and community work was taken for granted.

Furthermore, most of the settlements also involved work with young people (Jeffs, 2001). Indeed the first activity listed as available at the newly opened Oxford House (*The Oxford House*, 1948, p. 10) in 1884 was 'Boys' Club'. However, youth work has its origins inde-pendently of the settlement movement, starting with the Sunday Schools in the mid eighteenth century and developing in earnest with the myriad of clubs and associations set up in the mid to late nine-teenth century, from the YMCA and Boys' Brigade to the Scouts and Guides (Jeffs, 1979; Smith, 1988). A desire to control and educate young people, to instil moral values and prepare them for the respon-sibilities of employment and parenthood were key motivators in the work of many of these organisations and the volunteers who worked in them. Many of these early organisations working in neighbourhoods and with young people had explicitly religious commitments, with an aim to convert their users, or at least to promote character building and 'rescue', alongside the more neutral welfare work (Smith, 1988, pp. 55–7; Younghusband, 1981).

The caseworkers

The linkages and divergences between social work, community work and youth work that developed over time are complex and fascinating.

The 'casework' element, which involved working with individuals and families and eventually became the core of social work, developed more systematic methods and theories. Formal training began in the early twentieth century, with the School of Sociology started in London in 1903, which later amalgamated with the Social Science Department at the London School of Economics (Smith, 1965). In the early twentieth century, social workers were attached to assist people using many of the agencies set up to deal with social problems, including hospitals and courts, but significant growth in the state sector did not develop until the 1940s. However, during the inter-war period, knowledge for social work practice developed, influenced by psychoanalytical theories and approaches from the USA. During the Second World War, the demand for qualified social workers began to develop as problems were experienced with organising and supporting evacuated families. Trained staff was sought, from almoners in hospitals to psychiatric social workers and those working with children and families. By the end of the war, social workers had been appointed in 70 local authorities (Younghusband, 1981, p. 24) and their employment continued to rise after the establishment of the welfare state in 1948. The Children Act, passed in that year, developed out of two reports on child care, which recommended a personal service for children and recruitment of more social workers, who should be graduates (Parrott, 1999, pp. 28–9). The services provided by local authority social workers at this time were specialised and fragmented, overseen by separate committees relating to children, health and welfare.

Early forms of community work

In the meantime, embryonic forms of 'community work' were developing, boosted by the development of community centres and associations following the First World War. In 1928 the New Estates Committee of the National Council of Social Service (which later became the National Federation of Community Associations) was established (Baldock, 1974, p. 6), and workers began to be employed to run the newly-built community centres and encourage community activity and cohesion. The settlements and other neighbourhood-based centres and projects continued to exist, although priorities and structures changed, especially with the pressures of the Second World War (Matthews and Kimmis, 2001, pp. 61–3). Theories and approaches to community work were developed in the 1950s and 1960s, particularly by those workers who had gone abroad to work in what were then British colonies to encourage self-sufficiency and independence – for example Batten's (1967) theories of non-directive work. Baldock (1974, p. 6) comments on the stress in the middle 1960s on what he calls the 'professional consensus approach' to community work, exemplified in texts such as those by Thomason (1969) and Goetschius (1969).

Community work as the third method of social work

Although forms of community work existed independently of social work, the Younghusband report (1959) on local authority social workers identified community work as one of the three methods of social work, alongside casework and group work. These views were reinforced by powerful thinking from the USA, and despite moves by Batten and others to see community work as having a strong educational focus, the social work interests dominated (Thomas, 1983, p. 30). The Gulbenkian report (Gulbenkian Study Group, 1968), recommending the expansion and development of community work, came out in the same year as the report of the Seebohm Committee (Seebohm Report, 1968), set up to review the fragmented state of social work. This latter report reflected some of the developments in community work, and the unified social services departments set up in local authorities following this report in the early 1970s often comprised community development officers or community workers. Many social work education programmes in universities included community work within the curriculum and for a brief period there were several specialist community work programmes on offer.

The emergence of youth and community work

At the same time, youth work, which had grown in local authority education departments following the 1944 Education Act, also began to link more closely with community work. Following the Milson-Fairbairn Report (1969), local authority youth services became 'youth and community services' and embraced work with adults and communities, often with a focus on community centres, but also developing more broadly. Training courses had been set up for youth workers at several universities and colleges, with the National College for the Training of Youth Leaders opening in Leicester in 1961, and in the 1970s further programmes developed with a focus on youth and community work (Davies, 1999a, pp. 179–94). The identity of community work hence remained somewhat divided between social work, youth work, and an occupational group in its own right. Certainly in terms of values, theories and methods, community work developed its own literature and a radical and political strand, exemplified by the publications stemming from the action research projects of the late 1960s and early 1970s associated with the large area-based national Community Development Programme sponsored by the Home Office (Green and Chapman, 1992).

The ambivalence towards professionalisation

Thomas (1983, p. 47) sees this period as the point where community work, which could have developed as a professional occupation with an identifiable set of skills, lost its way and chose instead the path of political action. It did develop its own association, the Association of Community Workers, in 1968, but this has never been strong, with a low membership, no code of ethics or any of the other trappings of a traditional professional association. Social work and youth and community work have also demonstrated an identifiable strand of reluctance towards moves to professionalise, seeing the development of exclusive professional bodies and requirements for training and expertise as creating a distance between the workers and those with whom they work. Yet at the same time there has been a strong voice within these occupations arguing for the importance of a coherent occupational identity and status, in order to maintain credibility with the public and other more powerful professions, and recently to resist deprofessionalising tendencies.

Although social work also had a 'radical phase', with groups of academics and practitioners advocating Marxist approaches to social work through alliances with welfare claimants, clients' rights groups and trade unions (Bailey and Brake, 1975; Corrigan and Leonard, 1978), this was perhaps less influential in the occupation as a whole. In spite of the arguments against professionalisation put forward in the manifesto of the radical social workers' organisation, 'Case Con' (reprinted in Bailey and Brake, 1975, pp. 144–7), which criticised the main method of social work (casework) for blaming the individual for poverty and diverting attention from the real social and economic causes, social work nevertheless set out on a slow course towards attempted professionalisation. National regulation of professional education programmes came in 1971 with the founding of the Central Council for Education and Training in Social Work. The British Association of Social Workers, founded in 1970, from the previously separate social work associations, developed a code of ethics in 1975.

Youth and community work was a much smaller and more disparate occupational group with a strong anti-professional element within it too. In 1971 the Community and Youth Service Association was formed from the merger of the Youth Service and Community Service Associations. Despite several attempts to develop codes of ethics for youth and community work in the 1970s and 1980s, these were unsuccessful (see Banks, 1996, pp. 15–16). In 1983, the Community and Youth Service Association became the Community and Youth Workers' Union, which represented a conscious decision to opt for trade unionism as opposed to professionalisation (Davies, 1988, 1999b). In 1982 the Council for Education and Training in Youth and Community Work was established to provide nationally recognised endorsement for education and training programmes. No such nationally recognised educational body existed for community work, which again found itself split between attempting to promote community work education within both social work and youth and community work programmes.

Threats to the professions: the mixed economy of welfare and increasing state control

In the early 1970s the social professions looked set to expand in the public sector, with the development of the new unified social services departments employing both social workers and community workers, and youth and community workers largely based in education departments working in youth and community centres and beginning to develop forms of outreach and detached youth work. However, the promised expansion in the local authorities slowed down from the mid-1970s, with the monetary crisis in Britain. From 1979, with the Conservative government of Margaret Thatcher in power, there came a whole series of changes impacting on the professions associated with the welfare state. These included the growth of private and voluntary sector provision, attempts to control and undermine the power and status of all professional groups, the introduction of market principles and a growing concern with economy and efficiency, resulting in a focus on outputs and outcomes, targeting of resources and specialisation of work. Moves were made to encompass professional education and training within the remit of competency-based vocational qualifications, with a stress on work-based learning (see Banks, 1996; Dominelli, 1996). These moves were successful in relation to the social professions, all of which have now developed national occupational standards, which specify the competencies required for qualified workers in relatively specific and mechanistic terms.

Dissatisfaction with the lack of priority given to community work by social work and youth and community work education programmes, finally led to a group of community workers in the 1990s taking advantage of the government resources available to map occupational groups and develop standards for vocational training. This has resulted in a separate set of occupational standards for community work (Federation of Community Work Training Groups, 2002), and the promotion of workplace training, although as yet this has not resulted in the development of more than a handful of separate education programmes in higher education. The National Youth Agency, which took over the endorsement and validation functions from the Council for Education and Training in Youth and Community Work in 1991, has re-emphasised the importance of youth work, and published a statement of ethical principles for youth work (National Youth Agency, 2001). At the same time as attempts are being made to affirm the occupational identity of youth work, local authority youth services are also being required to work in partnership with careers services and other agencies in an interprofessional Connexions Service for young people (Department for Education and Employment, 2000; 2001). This requires training (for a personal adviser role) over and above youth and community work qualifications, leading in some cases to an interchangeability of roles with careers advisers. Social work is similarly engaged in health and social care partnerships, with multi-disciplinary teams often developing interchangeable roles (for example between nurses and social workers in the community mental health field). Furthermore, after many years of argument, central government has established General Councils (regulatory bodies) covering the social care occupations in the countries of the UK, which are now developing codes of conduct, disciplinary and regulatory systems (see General Social Care Council, http://www. gscc.org.uk).

On the one hand these moves towards standardising practice can be seen as advancing the 'professional project,' insofar as they have resulted in clear definitions of the purpose and nature of the work of the occupations and, in the case of the General Councils in the social care field, regulation of entry and standards of conduct. This could be seen to advance the credibility, status and public trust in the occupational groups. On the other hand, the standards and controls have been initiated by the state, and although practitioners have had a role in their development, their room for manoeuvre has been somewhat limited (see Smith, 2003, for a discussion of the narrowness of vision of the 'transforming youth work' agenda).

Key themes in the development and work of the social professions

The brief account of aspects of the history of social work, youth work and community work given above can do no more than hint at the complexity of the relationships between these groups, and at the social, political, economic and ideological influences on their development. However, for the purposes of this book, it is sufficient to enable some of the key features of the social professions to be drawn out as follows:

(1) *The calling to care*. The origins of the social professions lie in the philanthropic and charitable work initiated and carried out by volunteers in the nineteenth century, often within explicitly religious organisations. Some of those who led the work have become well-known figures, such as the Barnetts who founded Toynbee Hall, Octavia Hill who developed housing associations, Dr Barnardo who established children's homes. Their motivations are described as stemming from a profound sense of outrage at levels of poverty, poor housing and lack of education seen in inner-city areas. They, and the numerous other pioneers whose stories are not told in the history books, along with the volunteers who carried out the work, are portrayed as having a commitment to improve individual lives and social conditions, moved perhaps by a 'calling' or 'vocation' to devote their lives to working for change. According to Younghusband (1981, p. 13):

These pioneers all believed in treating people as individuals; the Barnetts' motto was 'one by one', Octavia Hill thought 'knowledge of the passions, hopes and history of people' was crucial. They all spoke of treating people as equals, of friendship and the power of love.

Some of the early writings explicitly describe the role of the volunteer workers as to act as 'friends' to the people they were working with. The settlers in the settlement houses were regarded as serving as role models, but the importance of personal relationships was also stressed. According to Picht (1914, p. 2), writing of Toynbee Hall:

> He [the settler] mistrusts dead organisations, and would replace them by personal relationships. *Not as an official but as a friend does he approach the poor*, and he knows that he is thereby not only the giver but the receiver. (my emphasis)

(2) *The cooption to welfare and control.* Whilst for many of the early volunteers the motivation to care for individuals and serve as a friend may have been dominant, the agenda for some of the organisations was also one of 'control'. The fear that the poor would get out of hand, that young people would be corrupted, that moral standards were declining was also present in some of the early religious organisations. As the welfare state emerged, the work of the volunteers and voluntary organisations began to be subsumed within it, and became part of a welfare bureaucracy – a system for delivering redistributive measures to those in need, as well as controlling unruly or anti-social behaviour (from child abusers to child criminals).

(3) *The commitment to change.* Whether from a position of reform-ist or radical, alongside the 'do-gooding' philanthropists working with individuals and families in need, there has also existed a vocal group within the social professions who have advocated the need for changes in policies, structures and attitudes. This approach was perhaps most noticeable in the late in 1960s and early 1970s with the emergence of 'radical' work and a rather nihilistic view of the role of the social professions as agents of a repressive state – part of the system of maintaining the status quo of fundamental inequalities in society. This developed in the 1980s and 1990s into a concern with anti-oppressive practice, and a commitment on the part of social professionals to challenge racism, sexism, disablism, and so on.

(4) *An ambivalence towards professionalisation.* Partly because of their origins in voluntary organisations and volunteer work, with the

desire to work close to those in need or poverty, as well as the radical aim to form alliances with the poor and working class, the social professions have had an uneasy relationship with the idea of professionalisation. Professionals have been characterised as elitist, self-serving and distant from the people with whom they work. Hence there have always been arguments within the occupational groups about the need for codes of ethics, registration of practitioners or the value of university-level education. These debates, coupled with societal ambivalence towards the role of these occupational groups (how necessary are they? what expertise do they have? are they supporting the feckless and idle? are they interfering excessively in family life?) has resulted in a slow and often agonising move towards some of the trappings of the ideal-typical profession.

(5) *The effects of 'deprofessionalising' trends*. Just as the social professions were expanding and becoming established, there came a questioning and restructuring of the welfare state, within which they had become embedded. Although moves have been made in recent years to clarify roles, purposes and standards of work for all professional groups, this has also resulted in greater specification and prescription, which appears to challenge the scope of professional discretion and 'autonomy', often thought to be at the heart of professional work and professional ethics. This may be viewed as a process of 'deprofessionalisation', although it can also be seen as contributing to an emerging 'new professionalism' or simply a reflection of the constantly changing state of professions. Before proceeding to consider the 'deprofessionalisation' debate, it is important to place it in the context of the broader changes in the welfare state alluded to earlier in this chapter, and in particular the challenge to professionalism from managerialism.

Managerialism and professionalism in public services

Since the late 1970s, the welfare state has undergone a profound restructuring process based on economic demands to cut costs, ideological antipathy towards its bureaucratic and paternalistic structures and processes, and an imperative to improve the quality of the services provided. A restructuring of welfare services has taken place in many countries, albeit in different ways, at different paces and often for different types of reasons (see Flynn, 2000). In the UK, the attack on the welfare state, and the professionals and administrators who worked within it, gathered momentum after the election of the Conservative government under Margaret Thatcher in 1979. During the 1980s and 1990s the 'New Right' government introduced a whole series of reforms based around the theme of 'markets' and 'managers' as 'guarantors of efficiency, choice, dynamism and responsiveness' (Clarke, 1998, p. 238). The idea of the state as provider of services was challenged, with the introduction of competition, voluntary and private sector provision and contracting out, as well as internal markets and purchaser–provider splits within the public sector. The dominance of bureaucrats and professionals within the public services was challenged and what has been called 'the new managerialism' or 'new public management' (NPM) developed, based on the view, according to Clark (1998, p. 238) that managers 'inhabited the world of market action, and were thus the natural bearers of its entrepreneurialism, its dynamism and the full gamut of "good business practices" from which organisations in the public sector needed to learn'.

There are many accounts of the development and characteristics of the new public management. As Clarke *et al.* (2000, p. 7) point out, there is no one model and it is a mistake to regard NPM as a unified form of managerial coordination of public services. However, they do offer a list of features (adapted from Dunleavy and Hood, 1994) typically ascribed to the NPM, as follows (Clarke *et al.*, 2000, p. 6):

- attention to outputs and performance rather than inputs;
- organisations being viewed as chains of low-trust relationships, linked by contracts or contractual type processes;
- the separation of purchaser and provider or client and contractor roles within formerly integrated processes or organisations;
- breaking down large-scale organisations and using competition to enable 'exit' or 'choice' by service users;
- decentralisation of budgetary and personal authority to line managers.

Clarke (1998, p. 239), in his analysis of managerialism as a new mode of coordination for social welfare organisations, suggests that it has three dimensions: an ideology focused on extending the right to manage in pursuit of greater efficiency; a calculative framework which orders knowledge, typically around efficiency and competitive positioning; and a series of overlapping discourses articulating conceptions of how and what to manage. He sees managerialisation as a process of establishing managerial authority over resources and decisions; establishing calculative frameworks defining the terms of decision-making; and creating forms of managing and types of managers (including hybrid professional-managers and a general managerial consciousness within organisations). A central issue in the managerialisation of public services has been the 'concerted effort to displace or subordinate the claims of professionalism' (Clarke *et al.*, 2000, p. 9).

The election of the New Labour government in the UK in 1997 brought with it a new discourse of 'modernising' public services, which sought to use the language and methods of the NPM in pursuit of its own political agenda (with a particular focus on reforms in the fields of social services, health, crime and local government). There are many continuities between the NPM of the New Right and New Labour's 'modern management' agenda – most notably the continuing emphasis on efficiency and performance. Indeed, Clarke *et al.* (2000, p. 23) note the enhanced role of practices designed to 'monitor, assess and regulate' the performance of organisations delivering public services. Measures to impose centrally defined performance standards on organisations have been strengthened, along with rewards and threats for 'beacon' or failing organisations. The focus on accountability to service users and other stakeholders has also been sharpened, along with a continued attack on monopoly provision of services and a search for business solutions to social problems (Newman, 2000).

However, as Newman (2000, p. 47) points out, the discourse of modern public management involves subtle shifts from the NPM. It can be seen as a fundamentally political project, linking New Labour's elusive 'Third Way' in politics with a process of public sector reform. She identifies several features of modern management, which distinguish it from the 'cut and thrust' and 'lean and mean' discourses of business turnaround and downsizing of the 1980s, as follows:

- it is presented as a set of tools to achieve policy outcomes on improved education, social exclusion and welfare reform;
- it claims to have a focus not just on short-term efficiency, but also on longer-term effectiveness;
- it places more emphasis on collaboration (rather than competition) and stresses the need for 'joined up' government and managerial techniques of building partnerships.

Newman draws out several emergent themes in the modernising agenda, which provide useful insights into the climate in which the social professions are currently operating. These are:

1.   *Innovation.* Many policy documents stress the need for change and innovation – in order to break free from old traditions and vested interests and to achieve better outcomes for citizens and the nation in a changing and competitive global economy (see, for example, Department of Trade and Industry, 1998). This is linked with an entrepreneurial business spirit that needs to be applied to transform the role and shape of the public sector. In the field of youth work, for example, the National Youth Agency has hosted a specific project to research and promote innovation in youth work (see Merton, 2001).

2.   *Performance.* Newman (2000) also notes the move away from compulsory competition and the rigid boundaries between purchasers and providers in public services, towards a more pragmatic approach to the use of the market. More scope is being offered to managers to make decentralised purchasing and contracting decisions. Yet at the same time, as already mentioned, there has been a strengthening of central government controls over the setting of targets and standards of performance for particular services or organisations (for example, local authority social services departments, health trusts, schools or youth services) and powers to intervene if standards are not achieved. In the case of social services, new regional Commissions for Care Standards have been established to regulate residential and home care services, along with the national General Councils previously mentioned to regulate professional training and standards of work (Department of Health, 1998a; Hudson, 2000). These moves can be seen as part of a trend to control and standardise activities previously within the sphere of professional judgement. This focus on centrally defined performance contrasts with the language of decentralisation, flexibility and innovation.

3.   *'Joined-up' government.* The need for reform at the level of policy (not just management) to make it more strategic at both central and local government level is another key theme of the modernising agenda. The tendency of the NPM to result in fragmentation, with organisations judged in terms of their individual achievements, has been recognised, and the collaboration between

different government departments, local authorities, private, voluntary and community sector organisations in tackling issues of health, crime, education, social exclusion and regeneration is encouraged. There is an increased emphasis on partnership working in most fields, with a particularly notable example being policies for neighbourhood renewal (see Mayo and Taylor, 2001; Social Exclusion Unit, 2001).

4. *Participation.* Central to many of the New Labour policies is the theme of public participation in decision-making and service delivery. This forms part of its drive to renew social democracy, revive community spirit and ensure that the decisions made and services delivered are meeting the needs of service users and citizens (Department of the Environment, Transport and the Regions, 1998; Rao, 2000). Whereas the NPM focused attention on the consumers of services, the modernising agenda has a focus on active citizens and communities. In many areas of public services there is a requirement for local people or services users to be members of boards or decision-making bodies. This not only challenges the supremacy of professionals, but also managers and politicians.

The extent to which the modernising agenda can actually be realised is debatable. Newman (2000, p. 58) refers to 'modernisation' as a 'discourse', suggesting it provides a vocabulary within which politicians, managers and professionals can legitimate their actions:

> the paraphernalia of participation, the ritual of efficiency plans, the celebration of partnership and so on can all be adopted as ceremonial forms of action which remain loosely coupled to the realities of organisational action and the delivery of services.

There are also inevitable contradictions within this agenda for change. There are tensions between the requirements for annual efficiency gains and longer-term effectiveness; between centralised control and decentralised decision-making, flexibility and innovation; between systems of regulation and audit that focus on individual organisations and the demand for contributions to cross-cutting strategic partnership working; between citizen control and managerial control. Aspects of the new discourse of modernisation may be more acceptable to staff working in public services than the New Right focus on privatisation and the strong antipathy to the public sector. But the continued focus on efficiency and performance, with strong central control and a tendency towards standardisation of work practices, continues to exert pressure on the public service organisations and the staff who work in them, including the professionals. As one youth worker was reported as commenting, in response to a recent national policy document on 'transforming youth work' which stresses targets, outcomes and curriculum: 'The government has given us what we wanted [extra resources] but also completely taken away what we are and what we do' (quoted in Smith, 2003, p. 15). Later chapters will explore these themes further in practice-based contexts.

Deprofessionalisation, the 'new professionalism' and the evolving social professions

In assessing the impact of the growth of managerialism on the social professions, it may be useful to refer back to Freidson's (2001) ideal type of professionalism as summarised below:

1. *A body of knowledge and skill officially recognised as based on abstract concepts and theories and requiring the exercise of considerable discretion.* Although bodies of knowledge and skill have been defined for social work, youth and community work, it is arguable as to whether these are recognised as based on abstract concepts and theories. Discretion of practitioners appears to have been curtailed, as more and more tasks and procedures are prescribed, targets set and general standards applied. However, in the day-to-day encounters with service users, there is still a great deal of unpredictability and a need for discretion in how people are treated and how rules or procedures are applied.

2. *An occupationally controlled division of labour.* The division of labour between occupational groups is blurring, as interprofessional working is increasingly required. Occupational control of the division of labour appears to be declining, as the state or the 'market' appears to be more influential.

3. *An occupationally controlled labour market requiring training credentials for entry and career mobility.* The labour markets are increasingly requiring educational credentials for entry and career progression, although this is less so in community work. But the

extent to which the labour market is occupationally controlled is limited.

4. *An occupationally controlled training programme associated with 'higher learning', providing an opportunity for the development of new knowledge*. Training programmes for the social professions are both in higher education and the workplace. Insofar as there is a research agenda in higher education, then 'new knowledge' is being created and this has grown rapidly, particularly in the social work field, in recent decades. The extent to which the occupation controls the training programmes is, however, debatable.

5. *An ideology serving some transcendent value*. There is no doubt that the occupations themselves claim to some extent a 'transcendent value' and a greater devotion to doing good work than to economic reward, as can be seen in all their statements of values and principles (or codes of ethics, in the case of social work and youth work). But the extent to which this ideology has widespread public or government credibility is questionable.

Many commentators have regarded the trends mentioned above as signalling a process of 'deprofessionalisation' in relation to professions in general. In respect of the social professions, there has been most discussion in the literature in relation to social work, both because social work has developed further with and perhaps is more committed to the so-called 'professional project' and because there is much less literature on youth work and community work generally. Commentators have noted as part of this trend: the increasing control over professional work by managers (managerialism); the introduction of competency-based training, with a focus on discrete technical skills, driven by employer needs (a technicist and reductionist approach to professional work); and the development of markets in the field of social care, including the contracting relationship between purchasers and providers (a market- and contract-based approach). The introduction of community care in the social work field is seen as particularly significant in this respect (see Hadley and Clough, 1997; Lymbery, 2000). Deprofessionalisation is variously associated with: decline in the status of an occupation; increasing external controls (from managers, employing agencies, government) along with declining professional autonomy and discretion; a threat to the core values of the work (in particular, anti-oppressive and anti-discriminatory values); and a diminishing of the importance of relationships and processes in the work, with greater weight being placed on outputs, outcomes and value for money (see, for example: Dominelli, 1996; Hugman, 1998a, b; Langan, 2000; Payne, 1996).

Some of the commentators who highlight the deprofessionalising trends nevertheless suggest that there may be scope to move towards what Lymbery (2000, p. 133), following Larson (1977), calls a 'repro-fessionalisation' process. In the social work field the term 'new professionalism' was introduced as long ago as the 1980s to encapsulate the potential for rising to the challenge of the radical critique of the professions as elitist, distant and parentalist, signifying a move towards a more equal and empowering relationship with users of services. The term is still being used, although with slightly differently nuanced meanings, to refer to a form of professionalism that works with collectivities, is participatory and acknowledges a primary responsibility to users (Hadley and Clough, 1997, p. 210; Hugman, 1998a, pp. 194–7). Bottery (1998, p. 173), in concluding his research on professionals and policy, calls for a redefinition of the role of the professional, suggesting that this should involve being 'more prepared to communicate with, educate and learn from the client', in order to secure a firmer foundation for professional practice and public trust. However, although professional education and training, revised codes of ethics, and academic and practice-based literature reflect anti-discriminatory and participatory approaches to the work of the social professions, the realities of everyday practice make such approaches hard to implement. Lymbery (2000, p. 133) suggests that whilst this may be the preferred paradigm for professional practice (compared with traditional professionalism and deprofessionalisation), it does not have 'significant purchase' at the present time, since a range of factors mediate the professional–service user relationship, restricting the capacity of workers to make creative responses to need. However, the increased emphasis in the modernising management agenda on active citizen and community participation, suggests this could be an area for professional practitioners to hold on to, build on and promote. Indeed, according to some commentators, they have a moral duty to do so. According to Tronto (2001, pp. 189, 195), professionals now face a 'fateful choice in thinking about their status in society' and she is in no doubt that they need to become 'more democratic, less elitist, and more relational'.

If we view the development of occupations and the professional-isation process over the long term (in the light of our earlier discussions in this chapter), whilst the trends mentioned above represent major shifts in policy and practice, they could also be seen as demonstrating how what counts as being a 'profession' shifts over time. We have already presented the argument that there are no essential features of professionalism, but rather a set of variables, the content and balance of which changes over time. On this view, it would not necessarily be impossible to regard an occupation that exercises limited autonomy over its work and performs largely technical tasks as a 'profession'. The notion of professionalism as constantly evolving takes account of the shifts towards technical competencies, increasing market influence and managerial control (often characterised as deprofessionalising trends), as well as more equal and participatory relationships with service users (sometimes characterised as part of a move towards a new professionalism), but does not necessarily see them as signifying a radical break with the past.

Concluding comments

In reviewing various approaches to the study of professionalism, the historical/developmental approach seems to be the most useful. It allows the occupations comprising the social professions to be viewed in relation to other occupations, and sees the process of professionalisation as relative to time, place and other social, economic and political circumstances. Consideration of the historical development of the occupations of social, youth and community work in the UK suggests that the notion of 'vocation' is an important aspect of the tradition of the social professions, as is a concern for social welfare (with overtones of social control) and a strong strand of anti-professionalism (in the sense of anti-elitism). A move towards a 'new professionalism' (with a focus on participatory relationships with service users) may not save them from the 'de-professionalising' trends affecting all occupations. However, these trends may also be viewed as part of the ever-changing concept of professionalism, rather than signifying the end of the professions, or, more specifically, the 'end of social work', or the 'end of youth work' as some commentators have predicted (Clarke, 1995; Payne, 1995; Smith, 2003).

This discussion of the nature of professions and professionalism is important in that it sheds light on the nature of the social professions (the main area of focus of this book), and paves the way for the more specific discussion of the ethics of professional groups. The rest of this book will explore the theme of professional ethics in relation to the ever-changing social professions, with the next chapter debating the extent to which the idea of professional ethics, as distinct from the ethics of ordinary life, makes sense at all.

2

Philosophical perspectives I: professional ethics and ordinary ethics

Introduction

In this chapter we will explore the nature of 'professional ethics' (as a set of professional norms) and the extent to which professional ethics can legitimately be regarded as special, or indeed separate from the ethics of ordinary life. The fact that we talk of 'professional ethics' implies that these ethics are not only important and legitimate, but also in some way different from what we might call 'ordinary ethics' (that is, the norms we follow in 'non-professional' or 'everyday' life). The existence of categories such as 'social work ethics', 'medical ethics' or 'legal ethics', and the fact that occupational groups have their own codes of ethics, could be taken to suggest that it is important, or even necessary, that each professional group has a distinctive set of ethics, and that these are different from each other and from 'ordinary ethics'. But how important is this, and how distinctive are they, or should they be?

In this chapter we will first consider the variety of meanings of the term 'ethics', before proceeding to explore various uses of the term 'professional ethics'. We will then outline arguments relating to whether the professions can legitimately and credibly lay claim to special sets of ethics that justify their trustworthiness, before moving on to discuss the extent to which it makes sense to regard professionals' ethics as distinctive in relation to the ethics of ordinary or everyday life. In addition to the themes of professional and ordinary ethics, the discussion in this chapter raises again the professionalisation/deprofessionalisation debate and introduces the notion of trust versus contract as the basis of the professional relationship.

'Ethics'

The term 'ethics' can be used in two broadly different ways:

1.   'Ethics' can be used to refer to the *actual norms* people follow concerning what is right or wrong, good or bad (sometimes also called 'morals'). For example, we might say of a young person who revealed the source of some stolen goods to the police: 'John's ethics forbade him to lie'. This suggests that John holds a set of ethical principles or rules or has certain qualities of character, which dispose him towards truthfulness. The question of how we come by such principles or qualities, and make decisions about when to lie, leads us to the second usage of the term.

2.   'Ethics' can also refer to the *study of moral norms*. Here the term is often used synonymously with 'moral philosophy', which involves the analysis of ethical concepts and the development and evaluation of theories of ethics (often known as 'meta-ethics' and 'normative ethics' respectively). For example, we might say: 'Joanne is taking a course in ethics at university'. This may involve studying different theories about the nature of right action, how we make moral judgements, or the meanings of concepts like 'good', 'right', 'duty', 'conscience' or 'care', for example. Studies of moral norms may also be carried out in other disciplines, such as anthropology or sociology, with more of an empirical focus on finding out what people actually believe or do (often called 'descriptive ethics').

In the first sense of ethics (as norms), the terms 'morals' and 'ethics' are often used interchangeably, as are the adjectives 'moral' and 'ethical'. Although the terms come from two different roots, the one Latin ('mores'), and the other Greek ('ethos'), they have the same meaning of habits, customs or norms. Some theorists, however, particularly in the non-UK European literature, do make a distinction between the two terms. Confusingly, not all theorists make the same distinction. The distinction most commonly made in some of the European literature is between morals as externally imposed universalisable values or duties, and ethics as 'constructed norms of internal consistency' (Osborne, 1998, p. 222) or 'the set of principles which are at the foundation of each person's conduct' (Bouquet, 1999, p. 27). However, it is important to mention that Bauman, whose socio-logical account of postmodern ethics is beginning to be referred to and utilised in the literature of the social professions (for example, Clifford, 2002; Husband, 1995; Parton and O'Byrne, 2000), uses the terms in almost the opposite way. He regards 'ethics' as an externally imposed set of universal standards (as in 'code of ethics') and 'morality' as more of an impulse of responsibility generated by the face-to-face encounter with another person (Bauman, 1993, 1994, 1995). However, already in making this distinction, we are entering the disputed territory of 'ethics' in the second sense (moral philoso-phy), because the very distinction presupposes certain theories about the origins of norms pertaining to the right and the good and the nature of human agency. Since we are concerned here with distinguishing broad usages of the terms, rather than advocating any particular ethical theory, we will follow the common usage in English of employing the terms 'ethics' and 'morals' interchangeably.

The fact that there are two terms ('ethics' and 'morals') sometimes used interchangeably and sometimes not, and that 'ethics' can be used to refer both to a certain category of norms and to the study of these norms, leads to some confusion. This is compounded by the fact that the sphere of ethics – that is, what counts as an ethical issue or ques-tion – is highly contestable, and how it is constituted depends on what ethical theory is held. For example, does the domain of the 'ethical' include or exclude emotions? Are ethical judgements prescriptions for action or descriptions of feelings? Is ethics centrally about princi-ples of action or qualities of character? Does it make sense to distin-guish ethical issues from personal issues and political issues? We will look at these debates in Chapter 3 when we consider ethical theories.

'Professional ethics'

Building on the two broad meanings of 'ethics' introduced at the beginning of the last section, there are several ways in which we can construe 'professional ethics':

1. *Professional ethics as special norms*, that is, the principles/ standards/rules of behaviour or qualities of character of people in

a defined occupational group (as a specialised version of the first sense of 'ethics'). For example, we might say: 'A doctor's professional ethics would prohibit the giving of information to the police about a patient gained in the course of the professional relationship.' In this sense, 'professional ethics' means the code or norms accepted by the members of that professional group – a group of agents who develop their own principles and standards, who have expertise, who count themselves as serving the public/clients and pledge themselves to do so. The term 'professional ethics' is often epitomised by 'codes of ethics', which generally comprise general ethical principles and rules of professional conduct. But the term can also be used to refer to the unwritten norms and standards actually operating in a professional group. This leads to a possible distinction, which we will make here and elaborate upon later, between what I will call:

(a) *espoused professional ethics* – the ideals, principles, rules and statements of purpose found in public documents such as professional codes of ethics; and

(b) *enacted professional ethics* – the standards and norms of behaviour actually accepted and followed by members of a professional group.

2.   *Professional ethics as the study of the special norms of defined occupational groups*. This can be divided into two categories:

(a) *the study of the principles of right action or qualities of a good professional*. This is commonly done by moral philosophers, as normative ethics or meta-ethics, which may involve applying ethical theories, developing prescriptions for action or analysing the meanings of ethical terms in a professional context.

(b) *the study of the ethical issues that arise in professional practice*. Such studies involve looking at what moral beliefs people hold and how they act in relation to the tensions and dilemmas that arise in everyday practice ('descriptive ethics'). This might also involve looking at the new issues that are arising and how they are or should be handled, and linking them to ethical theories. This may be carried out by philosophers, but more likely by social scientists or professionals themselves. This may seem little different from (a), and indeed many ethical studies (including the work in this book) cover both areas. But the difference between (a) and (b) lies in the starting point and main focus of the study: whether it is general ethical principles and qualities of character, or attitudes, actions and dilemmas in practice.

The legitimacy of professional ethics

The fact that we talk of professional ethics in the first sense defined above (as norms) implies that there is a distinct set of ethical principles or qualities that apply to people in professional roles that are different from, or at least a specific sub-set of, the ethical principles and qualities of ordinary life. Whilst the extent of the distinctiveness of professional ethics and the nature of their link with 'ordinary morality' has been debated, what is clear is that the professions do make strong claims for their own unique sets of ethical standards. The codes of ethics or professional conduct that have been developed for different professional groups over the years are testimony to these claims. However, the extent to which commentators on the professions and professional ethics view such claims as legitimate or logical depends on their view of both the nature of professionalism and the nature of ethics. Two possible positions can be identified at the opposite ends of a spectrum of views:

1. *The essentialist (traditional) view.* As outlined in Chapter 1, the traditional view of the nature of the professions, particularly as put forward by those theorists that were described as following the 'essentialist' approach' to professionalism, asserts the legitimacy of the claims of professions to a special set of ethics. Adherence to a special set of ethics (often formalised as a code of ethics) is often regarded as one of the key characteristics of a profession. Such a position may be justified using a number of arguments, often deriving from the fact that professions have a service ideal or a commitment to a particular good (for example, health in the case of medicine, justice in the case of law, or welfare in the case of social work), which they exercise in relation to clients who may be vulnerable or lack expertise, hence requiring the professional to be particularly trustworthy. They therefore have a special set of professional ethics, which entails duties over and above those required of the ordinary citizen, and

a commitment to producing certain social goods. According to Wilensky (1964, p. 140): 'the norm of selflessness is more than lip service. It is probably acted out in the established professions at a somewhat higher rate than in other occupations.'

2. *The strategic (cynical) view.* However, those holding a strategic view of the nature of professionalism are often more cynical about professionals' claims to a special set of ethics, arguing that the basis of these claims is ideological, as part of the professions' strategy for gaining status and power. For example, Collins (1990, pp. 35–6) comments:

> [Professions] surround their work with an ideological covering. It is a 'calling', not merely a job. It is carried out from high motives of altruism, of glory, or of moral, spiritual or aesthetic commitment, rather than for mundane gain.

This suggests that the idea of the 'service ethic' can be viewed merely as part of the move towards professionalisation, as 'a powerful justification of power and privilege' (Wilding, 1982, p. 77). Codes of ethics can best be seen as largely rhetorical devices designed to persuade the public that the professions merit their higher status, economic rewards and protected labour market. Such codes are often not taken seriously by members of a profession.

This kind of 'cynical' view of professional ethics is vigorously opposed by Koehn (1994), an American philosopher, who offers a carefully argued defence of a modified version of the traditional view of professionalism. Koehn offers one of the most sustained recent defences of the moral legitimacy of the professions, arguing for a pledge-based ethics, which grounds the moral legitimacy of the professions in their pledge to serve others. Whilst rejecting the trait theory of professionalism, and particularly the idea that the possession of special kinds of expertise is a legitimate grounding for professionalism, she is basically developing an essentialist theory. For she argues that the professional pledge made by members of an occupation to serve particular goods is the very essence of professionalism and the basis of the trust that clients place in professionals. Without this service ideal, the professions are diminished and narrowed – or even condemned to decay. Koehn (1994, p. 7) argues that each professional practice has its own special set of ethics which derives its distinctive character from the profession's end of 'engendering and preserving the trust of clients who lack a specific genuine good such as health or legal justice'. In this case, she is referring to the professions of medicine and law. Koehn argues that the three professions on which she focuses (medicine, law and the ministry) can be construed as ethical practices in themselves, structured to merit the trust of their clients, rather than mere ideologies based on a striving for financial and status rewards. Her arguments hinge on the identification of particular goods or ends served by these professions ('service ideals'), namely, health, legal justice and salvation, to which the members of the respective professions pledge their commitment.

The question of whether Koehn's largely philosophical arguments in defence of a form of essentialism can stand up against the sociological critique of the professions will not be the subject of extended discussion here. Stated briefly, as above, both the modified essentialist and the strategic approaches to professionalism may seem respectively excessively idealistic and excessively cynical. They also seem to represent a fossilised picture of the professional world, rather than seeing the importance of different occupational groups having different purposes and characteristics, and moving through different phases over time. Are the two positions necessarily mutually exclusive? It seems more realistic to view the claims of professions to special sets of ethics, as exemplified in their codes of ethics, as serving both a genuinely expressed and legitimate function of guiding practitioners by outlining specific responsibilities and duties, as well as a rhetorical or credibility-enhancing function. If we take an historical/developmental outlook on the nature of professionalism (as described in Chapter 1), then it might be suggested that the balance between these two functions may be different for different professions at different times, depending on the stage of development of the profession, what type of work its members do and how strongly it is supported by the state or the general public. This will be further explored in Chapter 4 when we look at professional codes of ethics.

The social professions and their service ideal

But what of the social professions, which are different in many respects (whatever theory of professionalism one holds) from law, medicine and the ministry – the three professions that are the subject matter of Koehn's study? For even if her defence of the moral legitimacy of these 'traditional' professions can be sustained, what of the many other 'professions'? Koehn (1994, p. 179) does claim that her analysis can be extended to other occupational groups, although she does not explore this further, except briefly in relation to nursing. Her comments about nursing are, however, significant for us in relation to the social professions. She claims that nurses possess moral legitimacy, insofar as they, like doctors, promote the patient's good of health – that is, health is the service ideal of nursing. However, if nurses were to conceive of themselves as 'generalised caregivers', this legitimacy would be called into question. She claims that care, unlike health, legal justice and salvation, is not a good in itself: 'Care can have and sometimes does have a dark side, and to say that a relation is caring is not to say that it is necessarily moral' (Koehn, 1994, p. 179). Koehn does not elaborate upon what she means by 'care' here, but we assume that by 'dark side' she is referring to the fact that care can be controlling, parentalist or overwhelming. But we need to ask whether the 'dark side' is part of the essence of care, or arises in the way it is practised. If it is the latter, then surely this is no different from health, in that the pursuit of a patient's health can be achieved in a manner that is parentalist or disrespectful. In her book on professional ethics she does not produce any arguments to demonstrate that care is not necessarily moral in the same way as she thinks health is, although in her later work (Koehn, 1998), she does develop an extended critique of 'the ethic of care'.

However, if we assume that Koehn's arguments are successful, this then raises questions for the social professions, the core purpose of which, along with nursing, has sometimes been construed as caring. For if it is not possible to identify a 'good in itself' as the end of a 'profession', then according to Koehn it is not a morally legitimate profession. Abbott and Meerabeau (1998, p. 13), in common with many other theorists, speak of nursing and social work as 'the caring professions'. However, they comment that:

> there is a contradiction in the nature of these professions. 'Care' is their core activity and justification, but it has been argued from a variety of perspectives that their expert knowledge is not used primarily to meet the needs of clients but to 'police' and monitor them. The caring professions are exercising social control over their clients.

It is not clear whether this comment is acknowledging the 'dark side' of caring (either as a form of control, or a practice that can be used to control) or the fact that caring is not the sole purpose of nursing and social work. Either way, it might lead us to question whether the characterisation of social work as a 'caring' profession should be taken literally to mean that its core purpose is 'care', and indeed whether it has enough similarities with nursing to share a core purpose. Social work has also been characterised as a 'welfare profession'. For example, according to Clark (2000, p. 128), 'social work aims to promote welfare'. And our category of the 'social professions' links social work with community and youth work (rather than nursing) – occupations that have common origins and some overlaps in their formation in the context of the 'welfare state'. 'Welfare' can perhaps more easily be construed as a goal or end in itself than care. Indeed, Airaksinen (1994), who argues that engineering is not a profession on the grounds that it does not have a good that is internal to it, implies, in contrast, that social work is. He only mentions social work in passing, but it is interesting that he identifies the good or internal value of social work as welfare (alongside health for medicine; justice for law; and learning for education).

The ideal of welfare

So, in relation to the social professions, this leaves us with the question of whether we think 'welfare' is an adequate characterisation of their core purpose, and if so, whether it can be regarded as an internal good in the same way as health. An internal good, in this context, is a good that constitutes the professional practice as its core purpose – without which the practice would not be, say, law, medicine or social work. So, for example, according to Koehn's view, a doctor whose primary purpose in her job is to maximise income, could not be said to be practising medicine, or at the very least she would be practising a deficient form of medicine. This is not to say that earning a living is not a valid part of being a doctor, but that this is an external good, not an internal one. Similarly with the social professions, welfare could be construed as their internal good, even though there are other externally generated purposes associated with their work, one of which might be social control. Alternatively it might be the case that the concept of 'welfare', as an internal good as it applies to the social professions, actually embraces 'social control', in some sense. We need to examine 'welfare' in a little more depth, although this is not an easy task, as it is an all-embracing concept with numerous interpretations and meanings.

As Brandt (1976, p. 68) comments in his essay on the concept of welfare:

> It may seem that the job of picking a useful and relevant meaning for 'welfare' is a wholly amorphous one, too indefinite to qualify as a job at which one could either succeed or fail.

He and others examining this concept (for example, Marshall, 1976) resort to dictionary definitions in a search for enlightenment, but to no real avail. Here we find welfare defined as: 'Happiness, well-being, good health or fortune (of a person, community, etc.)' (*The New Shorter Oxford English Dictionary*, 1993, p. 3,653). This is surely too vague to serve as the core purpose of the social professions. As the definition above suggests, the term 'welfare' embraces both individual welfare (the well-being of individual people) and social welfare (which may be regarded as the sum total of all individuals' welfare, or as some form of communal or collective well-being, not necessarily reducible to the sum of individuals' welfare). What is regarded as comprising welfare or well-being will vary between individuals and societies over time, but in this respect it is probably no more problematic as a concept than is 'health'.

In our use of the term 'welfare' in relation to the social professions, it immediately has connotations of 'welfare state', given that many of the professionals work within or are at least mandated and controlled through the social and community services of the local and central state. So those aspects of well-being that are the business of the social professions tend to be linked to mitigating the ill-effects of poverty, social exclusion, abusive behaviour and individual psychological and physical challenges, and to promoting community cohesion and democratic participation. This includes a concern with both individual and social welfare. While the individuals of day-to-day concern to most professionals are current service users or participants, professionals also have a significant concern for potential service users, ordinary citizens and taxpayers. Hence 'welfare' includes an element of 'social control', both indirectly in its attempts to mitigate certain social problems at individual level, and more overtly in its work to prevent and challenge child abuse or youth offending, to create cohesive neighbourhoods or to prevent people from harming themselves and others in cases of mental ill health, for example.

So, we may ask, is 'welfare' as a core professional purpose any different in this respect from health? The core purpose of medicine is often assumed to be to promote the health of individuals. But medical practitioners also have a public health role. They have a duty to notify certain infectious diseases, for example. Some medical practitioners actually practise in the field of 'public health'. The difference for the social professions may be one of degree. The 'social welfare' aspect of their core purpose is more dominant than the 'public health' aspect of the medical role.

Social welfare

However, is 'welfare' specific enough to fulfil the function of the core purpose of the social professions? Clark (2000), in exploring the core purpose of social work, suggests that welfare is too broad and is shared with other parts of the welfare state. He suggests a more specific purpose as 'to promote the realisation of ordinary life' (p. 129). Social workers intervene when there is a discrepancy between the normative standards generally understood in a particular community and the actual conditions of ordinary life. This is still rather general, but as Clark points out, social work is committed to the indivisibility of welfare – that is, individual well-being encompasses safety, health, housing, financial security and so on. His characterisation of the core purpose is more specific than our dictionary definition of 'welfare'. For it locates well-being in a social context of commonly accepted standards of what counts as ordinary living, which may be disputed and will change over time. That is, it suggests a focus on *social* welfare.

If we accept this slightly more specific characterisation of purpose for social work, this then raises the question of whether we should also identify more specific purposes for youth work and community work. Can we assume that all the occupations comprising what I have called the 'social professions' share the same core purpose? At a very general level, I think we can. Firstly, the core purpose of 'promoting the realisation of ordinary life' is hardly sufficient to distinguish social work from many other professions, including youth work and community work. Secondly, the kinds of 'goods' required to serve as legitimating ideals or core purposes for the professions are necessarily very general. If they are made more specific, then either they begin to include 'external goods' (such as profit or agency reputation) and/or they begin to exclude certain specialisms or specific settings of professional practice, of which there are often many. For example, medicine includes people who work as general practitioners in neighbourhoods, specialist consultants in hospitals, and community-based specialists in psychiatric health, some of whom also undertake research, teaching and advisory roles. Social work includes practitioners who specialise in child protection, mental health, and disability, and who may work in local authority neighbourhood offices, hospitals, clinics and specialist voluntary agencies, for example. The core purposes, the sense of service ideals or internal goods, identified in the literature on professional ethics are so general that they are inevitably shared between different professions. For example, Koehn indicates that the intrinsic good of nursing is also 'health'. It could be suggested that health as an intrinsic good might be shared by physiotherapy, osteopathy or other related occupations. Airaksinen (1994) identifies learning as the core purpose of education. This will be shared by different professions, including school teachers and university lecturers.

Thus, we may conclude that if we had to identify a general all-embracing core purpose or service ideal for the social professions comparable to those identified in much of the literature on professional ethics for medicine and law, then 'welfare' would fulfil this role. More specifically, this could be construed as 'social welfare', if we want to encapsulate the notion of the promotion of individual well-being in a social context as well as communal or collective well-being. However, although we have shown it is possible to identify a service ideal for the social professions, how necessary and helpful is this?

Trust and the legitimacy of professional ethics

Even if it is necessary, as Koehn argues, for a profession to have a service ideal or core purpose to ground its professional ethics, why is it necessary to ground, or legitimate, professional ethics? Do we really need a *special* ethics for professions? According to Koehn, grounded professional ethics is the foundation of public trust in the professions. If this trust breaks down, then professionalism breaks down. And professionalism is a good way of organising the distribution of certain goods and services to people in society. She comments (Koehn, 1994, p. 5):

It is indeed hard to see why clients should trust the medical and legal professions with their lives and liberty if the latter are no more than ideo-logically driven institutional arrangements designed to gratify doctors' and lawyers' lust for status and wealth.

She therefore defends professionalism against its critics, and con-cludes that 'when true to their covenants, professionals do merit the trust they proclaim themselves worthy of receiving' (p. 181). She ends her book with a plea that we should not desert them. As she comments (p. 5):

We must not forget that the professions represent the only mechanism we have for collectively providing ourselves with the goods of health, legal justice, and spiritual peace. If professionals are not trustworthy, whom should we trust?

Yet as she notes, trust in the professions is breaking down, or at least being questioned to some extent (although perhaps not as seriously as popular belief might suggest – a point made by O'Neill (2002b) in the BBC Reith Lectures). The professional pledge or covenant is not the only way of attempting to ensure that professionals' drive for status and wealth, or an individual's sheer evil, do not get in the way of delivering fair and good services. Contracts, regulation and audit are alternatives. These may indicate a loss of trust, and indeed may exacerbate further the breakdown of trust (O'Neill, 2002a, pp. 129–34), but they are nevertheless alternatives. They embody a different version of 'professionalism' from that proposed by Koehn. This alternative is based on the model of the professional as technician, with some expertise, but whose work needs to be guided, conduct regulated and outputs checked in order to guard against poor prac-tice, mistakes, self-interest or criminal behaviour. Chadwick and Levitt (1997, p. 57) speak of this response as an 'ethics of distrust'.

Writing this chapter at the time of the publication of the first part of the report on the case of Shipman, the British doctor who killed over 200 of his patients, leaves one in no doubt about the further regulation of medical practice that will happen to ensure that such cases of 'exceptional evil' will 'never happen again' (see Carter and Ward, 2002, for details of this report). Yet we know that no matter how many safeguards are put in place, there can be no *guarantee* that a doctor will not murder patients. We know it is highly unlikely, but this is the case even without increased safeguards. If there were such a guarantee, then trust would not be necessary. As O'Neill (2002a, p. 13) comments: 'trust is needed precisely when we lack certainty about others' future action: it is redundant when action or outcomes are guaranteed'. Because of the complexity and uncertainty of professionals' roles, there will always be a need to trust in them, even if their work is as highly regulated as it can be. We are, in fact, living with several models of professionalism. The traditional, essentialist view of the professions as specially worthy of trust, whether 'genuine' or simply a myth or construction, is still prevalent – which is why the Shipman case was hailed above all as a betrayal of 'professional trust'. Yet reaction to this case and other similar ones is not to seek to reground trust in the professions and to strengthen the trustworthiness of professionalism through rethinking professional education, for example, but rather to resort to an 'ethics of distrust'. This is based on the model of the professional as potentially self-seeking and liable to do harm, as a special kind of technical expert who should be required to work within fairly tight guidelines, closely monitored, towards predefined goals. It has been argued that this has been exacerbated by the fact that the professions have placed too much emphasis on their expertise (Koehn, 1994) and that this is not an adequate basis for grounding professional trust as it divorces the professional knowledge and skills from a particular purpose or end and from serving clients. Furthermore, the stress on positivistic conceptions of professional expertise, underpinned by 'scientific' or technical knowledge, excludes the most important components of competent practice. As Schön (1992, p. 54) comments:

> By defining rigour in terms of technical rationality, we exclude as non-rigorous much of what competent practitioners actually do, including the skilful performance of problem-setting and judgement on which technical problem-solving depends.

'Professional ethics' and 'ordinary ethics'

Regardless of whether we believe professionals' claims to special sets of ethics are justified or not, there is a further question which relates to whether it even makes sense to think there could or should be special sets of ethics applying to particular professions which are different from each other and from those applying in ordinary life. Following on from the essentialist view of the nature of professionalism, some philosophers suggest that professionals, as loyal advocates of their clients' welfare, are governed by norms that are different from those of ordinary morality, whereas others have argued that professionals do not need – indeed, should not have – a separate set of ethics but should be governed by those prevailing in society. A middle position can be adopted which suggests that professional ethics are an intensification of ordinary ethics – in particular, according to Koehn (1994), in relation to interpersonal trust.

Before we go on to consider substantive questions about the relationship between 'professional ethics' and 'ordinary ethics', it is important to clarify further our use of these terms. We are concerned here with the use of the term 'ethics' in its first sense as defined at the beginning of the chapter, that is, moral norms, rather than the study of moral norms. We suggested a distinction between espoused professional ethics and enacted professional ethics. There are also at least two ways of looking at what I have called 'ordinary ethics'. These four distinctions can be summarised as follows:

Professional ethics as:
1. The espoused and publicly stated principles, rules or character traits that ought to be followed by members of a profession. These are often written down in the form of codes of ethics, statements of principle or conduct. In order to distinguish this sense of professional ethics from the second sense, I will call these *'espoused professional ethics'*;
2. The generally acceptable standards of behaviour that are actually manifested in a professional group. This is what Oakley and Cocking (2001, p. 96) are referring to when they speak of 'the traditional medical ethic' of doctors regarding themselves as having special authority to withhold diagnoses if they think this is in the best interests of the patient. I will call these standards *'enacted professional ethics'*.

Ordinary ethics as:
1. The normative principles, character traits and so on put forward by ethical theories covering how we ought to act in everyday life. This is what is meant when Oakley and Cocking (2001, p. 95 ff), for example, talk of *'broad-based ethical theory'*. This term is quite a useful way of distinguishing this sense of ordinary ethics from the second sense below;

2.   The commonly accepted standards of behaviour manifested in a society or community. This is what Koehn (1994, pp. 150–3) means when she talks of 'ordinary morality' or *'prevailing public morality'*. The latter term is, perhaps, more useful in distinguishing this sense of ethics from the first sense, so I will adopt this here.

It would be expected in the cases of both professional ethics and ordinary ethics that (1) and (2) should be connected. For example, it has been argued that espoused professional ethics are to some extent derived from, based on or justified with reference to, enacted professional ethics. For example, Harris (1994, p. 109) suggests that the principles in codes of ethics are a codification of existing good practice. On the other hand, it has also been claimed that enacted professional ethics are derived from or justified with reference to espoused professional ethics. For example, most codes of ethics assume that professionals will be guided in their practice, or at least conform to, the standards articulated in the code. Both of these claims have some plausibility, which suggests that the relationship between espoused and enacted professional ethics is a dynamic and circular one, rather than linear and one-way. We might expect a similar relationship between broad-based ethical theory and prevailing public morality – although some commentators are quite cynical about the relationship of ethical theory to everyday life (see, for example, Williams, 1985). However, despite the obvious relationship between (1) and (2) in the cases of both professional and ordinary ethics (see Figure 2.1), it is important to maintain the distinction, which reflects the age-old gap that still appears, despite our best efforts, between people's espoused values and their actual behaviour, and between theory and practice.

Our concern, however, is less about the relationship between espoused and enacted professional ethics or broad-based moral theory and prevailing public morality, but more with that between professional ethics and ordinary ethics. However, because professional ethics and ordinary ethics can be understood in several different ways, some of the discussions in the literature on this topic can be confusing, as it is not always clear which senses of 'professional ethics' and 'ordinary ethics' are being used. For example, Oakley and Cocking (2001) in their philosophical study of professional ethics in medicine and the law, seem to slide between comparing enacted

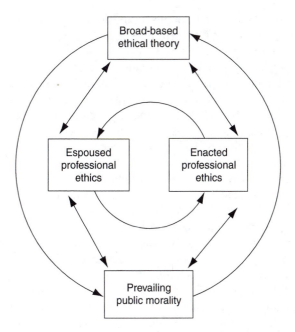

Figure 2.1 Interrelationships between aspects of ordinary and professional ethics

professional ethics with both broad-based ethical theory and prevailing public morality.

Professional ethics are the same as ordinary ethics

Some commentators have questioned the need for professions to have a special set of ethics. Ronnby (1993), in considering social work, argues that social workers' ethics 'do not differ from those that characterise others' humanistic ideals' and suggests that many of the principles contained in codes of ethics, such as 'respect every human being's worth and integrity', are not peculiar to social work. He appears to be arguing that the espoused professional ethics (particularly in the form of codes of ethics) of social work are no different from the ethics we ought to adopt in everyday life (for him, ordinary ethics appears to be the prevailing morality, based on humanistic ethical theory). This kind of view entails a questioning of the necessity for espoused professional ethics (in the form of written codes), as they simply state the obvious. On this view, a good social worker should act how a good person would. It could be argued that there are no special principles and rules that distinguish morally acceptable attitudes and actions in social work from attitudes and actions in ordinary life. Ronnby himself goes further by arguing not only that it is unnecessary for professionals to espouse special sets of ethics, but that it can be positively deleterious for them to do so, as it encourages them to act in ways that are ethically unacceptable according to prevailing morality. According to Ronnby (1993, pp. 5–6): 'the social worker must be capable of being herself with open senses, feelings and empathy' (as opposed to being a detached professional acting according to an externally defined code).

Koehn (1994, pp. 147–50) considers the arguments of several other proponents of the view that professional ethics are identical with prevailing morality, including the philosopher Goldman (1980), who argues that professional ethics, like ordinary ethics, must consist in honouring the rights of all autonomous persons. That is, he adopts a view of prevailing public morality based on a universalist theory of rights. He claims that professionals have no special loyalty to their clients and therefore no special sets of espoused or enacted professional ethics. This would entail, for example, that the lawyer would not be required callously and ruthlessly to undermine a witness statement for the sake of their client, nor would a doctor be required to keep the HIV status of a patient confidential from their employer on the request of the patient. For all individuals have rights that should be respected equally by professionals. This does not just apply to their clients or potential clients. But according to Koehn (1994, p. 148), this kind of position misrepresents prevailing public morality (or what Goldman calls 'ordinary morality'). For clearly in ordinary life we do have specific obligations owed to certain individuals and categories of people (such as our family or friends), which are not owed to others. These arise from our past actions, promises and other commitments to these people. Similarly, professionals who have made a commitment to undertake a certain role (which on Koehn's view involves promoting the good of those who qualify as clients) could justifiably be placed in a special moral relationship to their actual or potential clients. Koehn (1994, p. 148) also makes the point that 'patients go to the doctor to be healed, not to have their autonomy respected'. That is, medicine, and other professions, are set up with particular goods, such as health, at their core. If this is not acknowledged through some form of special professional ethics, then the whole basis of professionalism would disintegrate.

In the context of medicine, Oakley and Cocking (2001, p. 97) discuss the views of Veatch (1981, p. 106), who also argues that 'it makes no sense in theory or in practice' to use professionally generated ethical standards, as opposed to 'those rooted in some more universally accessible source of morality'. What he is advocating is an appeal to broad-based ethical theories (such as Kantianism or utilitarianism, as described in Chapter 3) to offer a more plausible account of doctors' relationships with their patients. Oakley and Cocking (2001, p. 97) argue, however, that universalist ethical theories are too 'thin' to do justice to the nuances and sensitivities of the professional role. This applies not just to Kantian and utilitarian ethical theories as might be expected, but also to broad-based virtue ethics. The general virtues applicable in ordinary life are not good exemplars in a professional context (p. 116), where it could be argued, for example, that some 'ordinary vices' such as ruthlessness, might be regarded as virtues.

Professional ethics are special ethics

Some theorists have therefore argued that the norms governing professional roles (this may include espoused or enacted professional ethics) are different from those of ordinary life (prevailing public morality, which may or may not be based on broad-based ethical theories such as Kantianism, utilitarianism or virtue ethics). There are several variations of the arguments used.

(1) *Professionals are special advocates of clients' welfare.* Some commentators point to the fact that inherent in the professional role is a commitment staunchly to advocate the interests and welfare of clients. This may entail acting in a way that would be regarded as ethically unacceptable in a non-professional context. For example, Freedman (1975) argues that the professional duty of a lawyer defending an accused rapist might entail questioning the alleged victim in ways that make her appear promiscuous, even when the

lawyer believes that she is not and that the client is guilty. If we acted similarly in ordinary life, it would be regarded as ethically unacceptable. Oakley and Cocking (2001, p. 118) give the example of counsellors, which would equally apply to social workers, required by their role 'to ask clients searching and intimate questions that would often seem inappropriate outside this professional context'.

(2) *Professionals have special roles/duties, but they must be justified with reference to broad-based ethical theory*. The staunch advocacy of clients' rights does not mean, however, that professional ethics is completely divorced from 'ordinary ethics'. Even Freedman, who holds quite an extreme view, acknowledges that lawyers' roles must be properly set up within a justifiable legal system before we can regard their role requirements as decisive when they conflict with broader moral requirements. That is, the existence of the role of lawyer, following certain specified norms, must be regarded as beneficial or serving a good purpose in society, for its peculiar set of professional ethics to be regarded as legitimate. Indeed Freedman argues that certain behaviour and tactics are required on the part of lawyers in order for their clients' autonomy to be respected – which, as Oakley and Cocking point out, links the lawyer's role to values (such as respect for autonomy) that would be endorsed by broad-based ethical theory (in this case, perhaps, Kantian principle-based theory).

(3) *Professionals have special duties to clients, but these must be balanced with duties to other stakeholders and with reference to the profession's service ideal*. Oakley and Cocking (2001, p. 118) themselves concur that professional roles 'may have some degree of independence from what broad-based morality would ordinarily permit or require people to do in a non-professional context'. However, they believe this can be justified not with reference to general principle-based ethical theory, but rather in relation to a specific version of virtue-based theory (see Chapter 3 for an outline of virtue ethics). They go one step further than Freedman in allowing that it may be appropriate in some circumstances for ordinary morality to override what appears to be the requirements of the professional role. On their view a good profession is one that is established on the basis that it contributes to human flourishing. That is, it has a core purpose (what we have called a 'service ideal' and they variously call a 'founding value' or 'guiding goal') – such as justice, in the case of the legal profession, or health in the case of medicine. Oakley and

Cocking (2001, p. 127) argue that if the demand to advocate as fully as possible for the client's rights or welfare would entail undermining justice itself, then the professional should modify or abandon certain role obligations. They also point out, as does Koehn (1994, p. 147), that exclusive loyalty to particular current clients is not the overriding duty of the professional, who also has duties to the court, to potential clients and the public. This links to the point made earlier about the concern of medical practitioners with public health and of social professionals with social welfare. Oakley and Cocking (2001, p. 131) conclude that:

> While it is 'naïve' to use ordinary morality as the sole arbiter of people's behaviour in professional roles, it is another thing to say that individuals can legitimately violate the founding value of their profession, in circumstances where their role seems to require such an action of them.

This makes the professional's ethics less free-floating, whilst acknowledging that they are distinctive.

(4) *Professionals have special duties to clients which are an intensification of the relationship of trust in ordinary life*. Koehn (1994, pp. 153 ff) offers a slightly different picture of the relationship between professional ethics and ordinary morality. She also wishes to acknowledge the distinctiveness of professional ethics, whilst linking them to prevailing public morality. She argues that they are an intensification of the relationship of trust. For Koehn (1994, p. 153), professional ethics are grounded in the publicly made pledges professionals make which commit them to pursuing a genuinely good end according to publicly understood limits 'acceptable to reasonable men and women'. Therefore professional roles and professional ethics do not arise in a vacuum, nor are they invented by the professions themselves. They are, in fact, extensions of ordinary morality. She claims that professional ethics can be understood as an intensification of the value of trust in interpersonal relations. She justifies this by claiming that trust is inevitably at a premium in relationships between strangers and vulnerable people, and therefore trust features more in professional ethics than it does in other relations governed by contracts. She adds that professionals have spent a long time working out the conditions for trust – through refining, developing and debating their purposes and codes of ethics. In addition, the structure of professions enables

trust to grow. At the first meeting between a professional and client, the client's trust may have a large element of hope in it. But over time, as the professional adheres to their pledge, the trust is 'intensified'.

Concluding comments

The argument made by Koehn as outlined above that professional ethics are an extension of ordinary ethics seems plausible. We may therefore conclude that professional ethics are different from, yet derived from, the ethics of everyday life.

However, it is important to note that this argument rests on a particular vision of the nature of the professional relationship: that it is essentially one based on a pledge to be trustworthy, rather than, for example, a contract or binding agreement specifying exactly the terms and conditions and penalties for default. Koehn argues strongly against contracts as the basis of professional ethics, noting, as we have already observed, that they engender loss of trust. Yet she also acknowledges that 'Decades of attacks on professional legitimacy are bound to take their toll' (Koehn, 1994, p. 181). Indeed, the attacks on professionalism have had an impact. It could be argued that we live in societies in the western world today where we desire *both* trusting relationships *and* guarantees of good outcomes (based on a contract-type relationship) from our professionals and service providers; where we operate within the traditional model of professionalism, whilst at the same time deriding and undermining it. As O'Neill (2002b) points out, in spite of our protestations of distrust we still do place trust in experts and professionals.

Professionalism may appear to be in a state of flux – moving from the preponderance of relationships based on trust, to the dominance of contract-based relationships; from the notion of there being a special professional ethics, to the subsuming of professional ethics completely within ordinary ethics. In which case, 'professions' may be about to disappear (as part of the 'deprofessionalisation' process). Alternatively, we may be working towards a new definition of professionalism, which, as Freidson (2001) and other commentators have pointed out, has always changed and developed over time. Later chapters will explore these themes further. In the meantime, the key themes emerging so far can be summarised in Figure 2.2, which suggests a state of flux along the various axes shown.

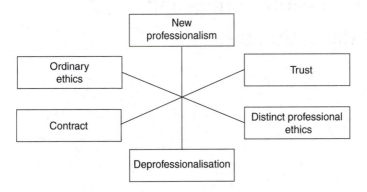

Figure 2.2   Key themes in professional ethics

3

Philosophical perspectives II: professional ethics and ethical theory

Introduction

This chapter considers professional ethics in the second of the senses identified in Chapter 2, namely as the study of the moral norms of occupational groups. It explores the relationship between professional ethics and moral philosophy (as ethical theory). We will discuss the view that professional ethics can be regarded as 'living a life of its own', quite apart from moral philosophy, and should not be seen simply as comprising the application of ethical theories to professional life. Whilst this position makes some sense, it is also argued that the ethical theories and theoretical approaches of moral philosophy can offer useful insights for professional ethics. A brief overview of different theoretical approaches and how they might be of relevance to professional ethics is outlined, divided into two broad sections: impartial and detached approaches (covering ethical theories based on principles, rights, discourse and cases), and partial and situated approaches (covering ethical theories based on virtue, care, community and the relationship with the 'other'). Some discussion of whether the idea of an 'ethical theory' makes sense in the light of postmodern critiques is offered, with the suggestion that in the context of professional ethics it is hard to sustain a 'postmodern' viewpoint on ethics.

Professional ethics as part of moral philosophy or social science?

Häyry and Häyry (1998), in charting the growth in applied philosophy during the latter half of the twentieth century, note the particular attention paid to 'ethico-political' problems. These may range from the morality of euthanasia or terrorism to the distribution of scarce health care resources or corporate responsibility for pollution. They also suggest that professional ethics, along with bioethics and business ethics, are activities 'which are now beginning to live their own lives quite apart from any truly philosophical concerns' (Häyry and Häyry, 1998, p. 93). They do not elaborate upon precisely what they mean by this, but the implication is that the issues studied in, say, professional ethics may be those of topicality and importance in the professional field, studied for their own sake, rather than as illustrations of philosophical problems. For example, the issue of trust in the professional relationship may be studied in the context of an apparent diminution of trust in the new regimes of accountability and audit at the beginning of the twenty-first century, rather than merely as an example of a particular type of trusting relationship in the context of the larger philosophical issue of the nature of trust. Häyry and Häyry may also be referring to the fact that it is becoming more common for academics and practitioners in professional fields (such as law, medicine, accountancy or social work) to study ethical issues relevant to the professions. Their studies may be less about developing and applying ethical theories or even meta-ethical analyses, and more in the area of 'descriptive ethics' – studying professional practitioners' accounts of what they believe and do, and what ethical issues arise in their practice.

However, while it may be true to some extent that professional ethics has a life of its own, many non-philosophers who write in the field of professional ethics nevertheless draw on philosophical analysis and ethical theories. But it is more common for such literature to draw on normative ethical theories (about what is good and right) than it is to utilise philosophical analysis or engage in meta-ethical discussion. For example, in textbooks on professional ethics, whether this be for medicine, engineering, or social work, it is very common to find chapters giving an overview of a variety of ethical theories developed by moral philosophers (for example, Banks, 2001, pp. 23–55; Beauchamp and Childress, 1994, pp. 44–111; Rhodes, 1986, pp. 24–43; Wilmot, 1997, pp. 8–23). Yet, as Winkler (1996, p. 59) points out in relation to bioethics, they often seem curiously dissociated from the problems they are meant to illuminate. The kinds of principles put forward in the field of professional ethics, he claims, while having some association with the main traditions of normative theory, are not clearly derived from these traditions. For example, we may talk of the 'Kantian principle of respect for the autonomy of service users or clients'. Yet, strictly speaking, according to Kant's ethical theory, the principle would be 'respect for the autonomy of all persons' (not just those in a specific category, in this case 'clients'). For Kantian theory is a universalist theory, applying to all people, not just a subset. This leads Harris (1994) to describe the principles articulated in codes of professional ethics as 'flawed Kantian principles'. It also raises the question of how useful it is to refer to ethical theories at all in the field of professional ethics. Harris assumes that for principles in professional codes to have genuine moral content, they must be seen as applied principles of some general ethical theory. Kantianism is the best fit, although admittedly it is imperfect. Harris concludes that we should try to ensure that codes fit the Kantian model better by rectifying some of their shortcomings. However, an alternative conclusion might be just to acknowledge that professional codes of ethics have their own form and purpose, in relation to the work and ideologies of the professions for which they are designed. To try to fit such codes into a theory of philosophical ethics is inappropriate as well as impossible, as will be further elaborated in Chapter 4. Indeed, Winkler (1996, p. 50) argues that 'most traditional forms of normative theory face severe difficulty in accommodating the kind of domain specificity in moral reasoning common in applied ethics'. This may not be surprising, given, as Walker (2001, p. 3) comments:

> Most philosophers today continue to make theory about morality as if it were effectively ideal, even if they do not literally believe that – that is, they treat it as a subject matter largely independent of empirical information about the real histories and contingencies of human relations in society.

So, does this mean we should try to coax moral philosophers gently out of this field and abandon all attempts to relate ethical theory to the subject matter of professional ethics? This is not necessarily the case. Rather, we need to pay attention to the different purposes and norms of different academic disciplines and to the nature of the 'ethical theories' being applied. For not only do academics and practitioners from non-philosophical disciplines make use of philosophical theories they only partially understand, but many moral philosophers present arguments based on empirical claims that are unsupported or poorly supported by evidence (see Zussman, 2000). Philosophers often make use of odd anecdotes, or accounts from individual professionals readily available in newspapers or autobiographies, apparently to back up, or at least illustrate, their arguments about the nature of professional roles and relationships. For example, Oakley and Cocking (2001) in developing a virtue theory of professional ethics, make reference to accounts from Albert Schweitzer and several other outstanding individual medical practitioners who worked tirelessly in parts of the developing world. Social scientists wanting an account of how medical practitioners see their role would regard extracts from autobiographies of 'great men' of the late nineteenth century and early twentieth as highly inadequate. They would prefer to seek evidence, perhaps, by interviewing or observing a sample of current practitioners, located in place, time and culture, and differentiated by gender, ethnicity and other relevant characteristics.

There is, however, an interesting trend in the field of applied ethics for some philosophers to engage in empirical studies. For example, Jonathan Glover, a London-based moral philosopher, has been conducting interviews with people with antisocial behaviour disorder (ASBD) as part of a research study looking at the cognitive, emotional and moral capacities of people with ASBD. He reports that this is the first piece of empirical research he has done (*Wellcome News*, 2000, p. 20). There is also a growing trend for social scientists to turn their attention specifically to ethics, and even to describe themselves as doing 'descriptive ethics' (which is usually a category used by philosophers to refer what philosophers do not do). Often such studies take the form of interviewing or surveying people about their attitudes towards controversial issues or moral dilemmas, or analysing the kinds of moral issues that come up for them in their lives or professional practice. Haimes (2002), for example, lists several pieces of social scientific empirical research from the field of assisted reproduction, which themselves raise further theoretical and ethical questions about the nature of choice, professional power, and so on, through engaging with people's 'detailed contextualised dilemmas'. Indeed, it was from empirical studies of people's responses to ethical dilemmas (especially young people's) that Gilligan presented the notion of the different moral voice – the 'ethic of care' – which has been developed as a very influential challenge to impartialist and principle-based ethical theory (see Gilligan, 1982; Gilligan, Lyons and Hamner, 1990; Gilligan, Ward, Taylor and Bardridge, 1988).

So, to end this section we may conclude that while many of the issues and approaches covered in professional ethics draw on moral philosophy when useful in terms of ethical theories, analysis of relevant concepts and arguments, they do belong to a specific domain which focuses on the roles, relationships and actions of professionals. Professional themselves, sociologists, historians and anthropologists also have a lot to contribute on these topics. Nevertheless, this does not undermine the value of looking at some of the main traditions of thought in philosophical ethics. Indeed, it is important to be able to locate professional ethics in the broader field of philosophical ethics and use the insights and arguments of philosophy to illuminate and develop our thinking. As Sorell (2000, p. 31), defending ethical theory in relation to applied ethics, comments, it 'wakes us from our dogmatic slumbers'. Therefore I will briefly list some of the main types of philosophical theories of ethics and theoretical approaches, indicating how these have been used in the field of professional ethics, with particular reference to the social professions. However, since the literature on professional ethics for the social professions is much less well-developed than that in other areas (especially medicine), examples will be given from other fields to illustrate the application of these theories to the professions.

Ethical theories and theoretical approaches to ethics

It is hard to present a brief overview of ethical theories in a way that both does justice to their complexities and makes sense to a general reader. If one studies the various introductory texts on ethics, or the sections in the professional ethics textbooks on ethical theories, they vary noticeably both in terms of which theories they include and in how they classify and compare them. Most ethical theories have been developed over time (some over many centuries) and have been modified and built upon in many different ways. Insofar as ethical theories generally attempt to offer a comprehensive all-embracing account of our moral life and moral thinking, they are often criticised by their rivals for leaving out or minimising important aspects of morality. The theorists in each tradition have then attempted to take on board critiques offered by their rivals and sometimes even to show how their theories can subsume others. So, for example, those who claim that morality is based upon universal and impartial principles for moral action try to show how the character traits of moral agents, a feature that has been claimed as central by rival theorists, can be accounted for in terms of principles for action. So what is usually at stake is a question of the emphasis and starting point of a moral theory.

Looking at these theories at a time when the search for grand, all-embracing and universally applicable theories is in question, when the awareness of difference, diversity and pluralism is growing, the desire to develop or to adhere to a single systematic theory that can account for all aspects of morality is less pressing than it was in the past. Indeed, in addition to the critique of particular theories for leaving out important aspects of our moral life, there has also been a strong critique of the whole idea of ethical theories *per se*, especially if ethical theories are regarded as necessarily universally applicable and foundationalist (that is, they seek to ground ethics in one core principle or value from which all others can be derived or against which actions or motives can be judged). Such theories, it is claimed, are unable to capture the 'messiness' of life – the particularities and complexities of each situation, relationship or conflict (see, for example, Hekman, 1995; Williams, 1985). Indeed, moral theory has been described as 'one of the last bastions of modernist thought' (Hekman, 1995, p. 159) and has been subject to recent attack from a variety of quarters, particularly those writing from certain types of postmodernist and feminist viewpoints. This has led some philosophers to propose different kinds of theory (non-foundational, relativist or pluralist) and others to eschew ethical theory altogether. I will use the term 'theoretical approach' rather than 'theory' to cover the last category, since the approaches offered are nevertheless attempts to characterise 'ethical' aspects of life.

In this section, therefore, I will briefly look at some of the traditional and alternative ethical theories and 'theoretical approaches' to ethics to help us identify which have been used, or may be useful, in the context of the social professions. My selection is necessarily partial and simplified. For there are many ways of differentiating ethical theories and approaches according to the presuppositions upon which they rest or the stance they take on certain issues. Are they foundational or non-foundational (as described above)? Are they universalist (applying globally to all people in all similar circumstances), relativist (assuming different cultures or communities have different systems of moral evaluation), pluralist (assuming that there are several different, but interwoven and co-existing moral voices or systems of moral evaluation) or particularist (focusing on the details of specific situations and contexts)? Do they focus on action as the entry point for moral theory, or characteristics of the moral agent, or relationships between people or the practices undertaken in communities? Do they give primacy to reasoned argument, to dispositions of character or to emotional faculties in moral evaluation? Do they assume the 'moral point of view' as defined by the position taken by an impartial observer, an isolated individual self, abstracted from particular circumstances, or a relational or situated self, embedded in a web of socially constructed roles, relationships and responsibilities? Are they offering a traditional theory (foundationalist and universalist), an alternative theory (non-foundationalist, but perhaps still universalist), a theoretical approach or 'anti-theory' position (perhaps claiming we cannot move beyond particularity or diversity)?

Not surprisingly, different people may categorise the same theory in different ways. Different theorists may develop differently nuanced versions of the same theory (say, virtue ethics), some of which may aim, for example, to be foundationalist and universalist ethical theories while others do not. For the purpose of this book, I have divided ethical theories/theoretical approaches into two kinds: those that stress morality as being about acting as a rational detached moral agent as any person would act in similar circumstances (unclouded by personal feelings, concern for particular relationships), and those that place more emphasis on the cultivation of character traits or virtues and/or stress the importance of communal practices, personal relationships, attitudes, emotions and motives. Table 3.1 outlines some broad distinctions between these two types of approach. It should be noted that many of the latter approaches, but not all, are explicitly 'anti-theory' in its modernist sense. In contemporary professional ethics there has tended to be an emphasis on the former approach, which is reflected particularly in a concern to articulate principles and rules for professional decision-making and conduct. However, some commentators suggest that an ethics stressing the importance of personal relationships and the cultivation of certain

Table 3.1 Approaches to ethics – some generalisations

Impartial, detached approaches	*Partial, situated approaches*
Ethics as universal.	Ethics as particular, relative to context, time, place.
Ethics involves generalisations.	Ethics is specific.
Ethics involves abstraction.	Ethics is concrete, contextual.
Ethics requires impartiality.	Ethics is about partiality.
Ethics is based on principles.	Ethics is based on relationships, roles or virtues, traditions, stories.
The core focus of ethics is justice; duty.	The core focus of ethics is care; or responsibility/dispositions, character.
Focus on action: what should I do?	Focus on response: 'How should I respond?', or focus on character: 'How should I live?'
Ethics involves principled decision-making, moving deductively from general principles to what to do in particular cases.	Ethics involves an attitude of care, attentiveness, concern towards a particular other, or a character trait or disposition to act for the good and the ability to make good judgements (phronesis).
Ethical decisions should be justified through a process of reasoning with reference to universal/general principles.	Ethics is not about justification, but about genuinely caring/developing and acting upon a disposition to live well and act in accordance with what makes for the good.
Moral agent as rational.	Moral agent as having emotions as well.
Moral agent as isolated individual; an 'unencumbered self'.	Moral agent as person with a history, responsibilities, particular commitments, part of a community; an 'embedded self'.
Separation of the right and the good. Focus on the right.	Focus on the good; and/or inseparability of the right and the good.

character traits is particularly appropriate for the professions (Oakley and Cocking, 2001; Rhodes, 1986, p. 42) and this is an area that is beginning to be explored further in recent literature. We will now look briefly at the nature of a selection of theories and theoretical approaches that are relevant to professional ethics particularly in the social welfare field.

Impartial and detached approaches

Principle-based ethics

I am calling 'principle-based' those ethical theories holding that what is morally right and wrong is determined according to one or more core ethical principles. According to Beauchamp (1996, pp. 80–1), a principle is 'an essential norm in a system of thought or belief, forming a basis of moral reasoning in that system'. Some theorists have postulated one fundamental principle from which all other principles and rules can be derived or actions measured – for example, Kant's principle of 'respect for persons' or utilitarianism's 'promotion of the greatest good of the greatest number of people'. Kant's ethical theory, developed in eighteenth-century Germany and refined by neo-Kantians such as O'Neill (1996) and Baron (1995), emphasises our duty to treat people as free and self-determining agents and would regard certain actions as wrong in themselves – such as lying, deception, breaking promises, theft or murder (Kant, 1964). Utilitarian theories, on the other hand (stemming from Bentham and Mill in nineteenth-century Britain), see the rightness and wrongness of actions as being determined by their consequences and would regard the right action as that which produces the greatest balance of good over evil (Mill, 1972; Shaw, 1999). Both these theories are 'foundationalist' in that they seek to ground morality in one single principle. Other theorists have suggested that there are several key principles which may include variations on both those mentioned above, that these will inevitably conflict and that the moral agent will have to balance concerns for respect for individual self-determination, for example, against the greater good of society (for example, Beauchamp and Childress's (1994) 'common morality' approach in bioethics, or Downie and Telfer's (1980) Kantian-utilitarian approach for medicine and social work).

Many textbooks include contractarianism in their lists of ethical theories, but as often presented it is not an ethical theory as such, but an account of how we are to arrive at correct moral principles. Such approaches have frequently been developed in opposition to utilitarianism, which allows the individual to be sacrificed for the common good. The basic idea of contractarian theories is that 'rationally acceptable moral principles are those which everyone could agree to as principles to govern their dealings with one another, and that if everyone could agree to them, then no one's interests are being sacrificed' (Norman, 1998, p. 189). The work of Rawls (1973, 1993) is perhaps the most well-known, and he develops a theory of justice (not a complete ethical theory). He imagines individuals making their choice of principles behind a 'veil of ignorance' (not knowing what particular skills they will have nor what position they will occupy in society) and argues that they would choose two basic principles: that everyone should have an equal right to the most extensive liberty compatible with a similar liberty for others; and that inequalities should be arranged so that they benefit the least advantaged and are attached to offices open to all under conditions of fair equality of opportunity (Rawls, 1973, pp. 60–1). One of the criticisms of his 'original position' has been that it already assumes a certain kind of moral agent (a person who holds liberal individualist values). Rawls (1993) later acknowledged that his theory must be regarded as reflecting the culture-bound judgements of liberal democracy. It is important to note Rawls's articulation of 'political liberalism' as it has been influential in the refinement of the principle-based approach, particularly in relation to bioethics where his notion of 'wide reflect-ive equilibrium' (the process of mutual adjustment of principles and considered judgements) has been employed (see Daniels, 1996).

In the field of professional ethics, principle-based approaches tend to be dominant, with the emphasis on the professional as an impartial moral agent, acting rationally by applying principles, weigh-ing up the consequences of various courses of action and prioritising the various principles in particular cases. This is apparent not just in the codes of ethics or conduct produced by many professional bodies, but also in the literature on professional ethics. In the social professions as a whole, a lot of attention has been paid to the 'values' underpinning the work, where 'values' usually take the form of general ethical principles relating to how professionals should treat the people they work with and what sorts of actions are regarded as right or wrong. So, for example, one of the standard texts in medical ethics is entitled 'Principles of Biomedical Ethics' which identifies and then discusses in some depth the four principles of autonomy, beneficence, non-maleficence and justice (Beauchamp and Childress, 1994). These principles are also taken up by Bond (2000) in the standard British text on counselling ethics. In social work, various different sets of values have been identified in texts called *Social Work Values* (Timms, 1983), *Values in Social Work* (Horne, 1999),

Social Work Values and Ethics (Reamer, 1999), *Social Work Ethics* (Clark, 2000) or *Ethics and Values in Social Work* (Banks, 2001). In my own text I identified: respect for and promotion of individuals' rights to self-determination; promotion of welfare or well-being; equality; and distributive justice (Banks, 2001, pp. 38–40). A concern with identifying and discussing values and principles also features in the sparser literature on youth work and community work (Banks, 1996, 1999a; Harris, 2001; Popple, 1995). For example, in youth work core values have been identified as: treating young people with respect; respecting and promoting their rights to make choices; promoting and ensuring welfare; and promoting social justice (National Youth Agency, 2001). However, as mentioned earlier, whilst the principles may have some connections with the traditions of Kantian and utilitarian theories, they are generally used as 'middle level' principles divorced from any foundational theory. Some have characterised this approach to professional ethics, based on Beauchamp and Childress's 'common morality approach', as 'the paradigm theory' (Winkler, 1996).

Rights-based ethics

This type of ethical theory is based on the notion that individuals have moral rights which should not be violated – for example, the right to life and liberty (Nozick, 1974) or particular rights to liberties such as free speech (Dworkin, 1977). Those adopting this approach are not seeking a foundationalist theory about what makes for the good society, recognising that people may have different conceptions of this (Rhodes, 1986, p. 33), but instead concentrate on protecting an individual's freedom from encroachment by others. Again such approaches can be seen as a defence against utilitarianism, which would permit the interests of individuals or minorities to be sacrificed for the greater good. However, the big question to be answered is how we know what rights human beings have. Some have argued that this is self-evident, or that rights are 'natural' or god-given. However, as Norman (1998, p. 133) argues, these hardly seem more than 'untenable fictions'. He suggests that the concept of rights is derivative rather than foundational, and that in order to determine what rights people have, 'we have to refer to some more basic account of what needs and interests human beings have' (p. 134).

Beauchamp and Childress in their review of such theories argue that rights-based accounts are not comprehensive or complete theories, but rather accounts of the 'minimal and enforceable rules that communities and individuals must observe in their treatment of all persons' (Beauchamp and Childress, 1994, p. 76). Indeed, many rights-based theorists seem to underpin their accounts with the Kantian notion of respect for persons (see Nozick, 1974). This kind of approach has sometimes been regarded as relevant for the social professions (especially social work), where it is difficult to apply a full-blown Kantian theory, but conceptions of universal human rights can be used to provide the ethical legitimacy for the work. For example, several codes of ethics make reference to various United Nations declarations and protocols on human rights (for example, International Federation of Social Workers, 1994) and Reamer (1990) adopts a rights-based approach for social work.

Discourse-based ethics

Discourse ethics, of which Habermas (1984, 1987, 1990), a contemporary German philosopher and social theorist, is the leading exponent, can be viewed in one sense as another development of Kantian ethical theory – although it is also a development of many other social theories, including those of Marx and Mead (see May, 1996, pp. 139–57). As Habermas (1988, p. 241) comments: 'only theories of morality and justice developed in the Kantian tradition hold out the promise of an *impartial* procedure for the justification and assessment of principles'. Habermas's theory is, therefore, about the form of moral judgement not the content. However, he moves on from the Kantian notion of the moral agent as an individual working out what is his/her duty in isolation, to a recognition of the intersubjective nature of morality – seeing universal moral principles as those that are validated in an ideal system of rational discourse. He argues that communicative interaction presupposes the nucleus of morality, in that it is oriented towards mutual understanding. These presuppositions are (Habermas, 1990, p. 89, quoted in Vetlesen, 1994, p. 295):

1. Every subject with the competence to speak and act is allowed to take part in a discourse.
2. a. Everyone is allowed to question any assertion whatsoever.

      b. Everyone is allowed to introduce any assertion whatever into the discourse.
      c. Everyone is allowed to express his attitudes, desires and needs.
   3. No speaker may be prevented, by internal or external coercion, from exercising his rights as laid down in (1) and (2).

The basic principle of ethical validity is, according to Vetlesen (1994, p. 296): 'formulated in terms of *rational, universal* and *uncoerced* consensus'. Accordingly, only those norms that could be agreed to by all concerned participants in a practical discourse may claim validity (Habermas, 1990, p. 93). Like Rawls's 'original position', Habermas's speech situation is an ideal one, but, he argues, in accomplishing a speech act we act as if it were real.

Given that a key feature of discourse ethics is inter-subjective communication, based on structures that promote rational consensus (such as, allowing everyone concerned a 'fair' hearing and removing the distorting domination of wealth and power), it is not surprising that it has been suggested that it may have promise for the social professions (see Blaug, 1995; also Blindenbacher, 1999, although the latter focuses more on aspects of Habermas's social theory). This is especially true given the other aspects of Habermas's social theory, which charts the growth of instrumental rationalism, including technical and bureaucratic procedures ('system') and its incursion into the communicative practices essential to moral thinking ('lifeworld').

Case-based ethics

Recently there has been a revival of 'casuistry' in ethics (see Jonsen and Toulmin, 1988) which argues that moral judgements are based on a detailed understanding of particular situations and the historical record of particular cases rather than simply the application of general principles. While the role of principles is not denied, their centrality and their use as a starting point in moral judgements *is*. As Kuczewski (1997, p. 5) comments in relation to bioethics, rather than starting from a framework of principles and applying it to cases, 'concepts from our cultural dialogue suggest themselves as the relevant categories to be employed in the discussion'. Jonsen (1996) talks of the importance of the 'morally appreciated circumstances' of each case, which might include considering questions such as who is involved, their histories, ages, the likelihood of certain risks occur-ring. According to Jonsen (1996, p. 46):

> Principles and maxims 'come into focus' against a background of circum-stances. Change the background either by the addition or removal of some fact or by heightening or shading of the circumstances, and one or another maxim will appear more vividly and centrally. Seeing these patterns constitutes an essential feature of moral judgement.

With its focus on individual cases, there has been some interest in casuistry in the field of applied ethics, particularly medicine and bioethics (see Arras, 1991). Casuistry draws our attention to areas often neglected by principle-based approaches, including the use of paradigm cases and the nature of practical reasoning, reminding us that 'moral judgement is a patterned whole into which principles, values, circumstances and consequences must be fitted' (Jonsen, 1996, p. 45). On this account, the differences between casuistry and principle-based ethics may be more one of emphasis than anything else, since we also find the leading exponents of a principle-based approach in bioethics claiming that 'sensitivity to context and indi-vidual differences is essential for the discerning use of principles' (Beauchamp and Childress, 1994, p. 100). Indeed, some casuists talk of 'middle level principles' which are not fundamental because they are derived from several different theories (Kuczewski, 1997, p. 5) and are principles that 'reasonable people know', which is very remi-niscent of Beauchamp and Childress's (1994) 'common morality' approach mentioned earlier.

However, this stress on context and particularity is an important trend in ethics, which can also be found in other types of approaches to ethics which focus less on detached moral reasoning about action and more on the nature of moral agents and their relationships with particular others, with which we shall concern ourselves in the next section of this chapter. Casuistry may seem out of place in this section, particularly given its ancestry in Aristotelian ethics (covered in the next section) and the fact that it seems to be advocating some-thing more like a methodology than a theory of what is to count as right action. However, the problem with attempting to categorise theories and approaches is where to place those that do not fit neatly. The categories can be changed, a new one created or an 'outlier' allowed. All these theories and approaches have overlapping family resemblances, reflected in the fact that they are developed and built upon aspects of each other. So the decision to place case-based ethics here, is partly because of the way it is currently being used in *reasoning* systematically about public policy matters, including developing 'guiding principles' in the context of national commissions on issues such as reproductive technologies or human experimentation (see, for example, Kymlicka, 1996; Toulmin, 1987).

Partial and situated approaches

Recently within the field of philosophical ethics there has been a range of challenges to the 'impartialist' theories of ethics outlined in the last section, in particular to the abstract principlism of what some have called 'enlightenment ethics', which has tended to leave out important aspects not only of the situational context of particular decisions, but also of the character, dispositions, motives, emotional faculties, particular relationships and commitments of the moral agents and the others in relation to whom they act. By 'enlightenment ethics' is meant the ethical theories and systems espoused by Kant in the eighteenth century, by Mill and Bentham in the nineteenth century and refined and developed by people like Rawls and Hare in the latter part of the twentieth century. These critiques have come from a broad range of directions and have been accompanied by an equally broad range of alternative theories or approaches to ethics, not all of which are necessarily 'new'. Nussbaum comments on the critiques as follows:

> Anglo-American moral philosophy is turning from an ethics based on enlightenment ideals of universality to an ethics based on tradition and particularity; from an ethics based on principles to an ethics based on virtue; from an ethics dedicated to the elaboration of systematic theoretical justification to an ethics suspicious of theory and respectful of local wisdom; from an ethics based on the isolated individual to an ethics based on affiliation and care; from an ahistorical detached ethics to an ethics rooted in concreteness and history.(Nussbaum 1992, quoted in Hekman, 1995, pp. 37–8)

If these critiques are taken seriously, then there are a number of options, in addition to abandoning ethical theory, as suggested by some 'pessimistic' postmodernist theorists, such as Lyotard (1984).

Existing ethical theories can be slightly modified to take more account of particularity, context, and so on, as Hare (1981) does with utilitarianism, or O'Neill (1996) with Kantianism. Another option is to develop a different type of ethical theory, which gives equal weight to both universal and particularist concerns, as attempted by Nussbaum (1986, 2002) or Slote (2001) in different ways for virtue ethics. Alternatively it is possible to develop what I will call a 'theoretical approach', which explicitly rejects traditional ethical theory, and has no pretension to universality or foundationalism, but which is nevertheless expressing a view about the nature of ethics. For example, Walker develops an 'expressive-collaborative' model which is explicitly not a moral theory, but a 'template and interpretive grid for moral inquiry' (Walker 1998, p. 9). Hekman's (1995) 'discursive ethics' is another such approach, which she develops from a particular reading of Gilligan's influential work on the ethic of care. Those who could be characterised as 'optimistic' postmodernists might also fall into this category. Other philosophers propounding feminist or communitarian approaches (Baier, 1985; Blum, 1994) also explicitly eschew ethical theories, although several critics question how successful they are in actually achieving this (see Hekman, 1995, pp. 42–3).

Agent-focused ethics

Virtue ethics is one of the commonest forms of what we might call 'agent-focused' ethics, which stresses the character of the person making the moral decision or taking the action, as opposed to the action itself. This kind of approach was common in ancient philosophy, with Aristotle (1954), living in fourth-century BC Greece, as one of its most well-known exponents. It has recently undergone a revival in contemporary moral philosophy, given impetus by the work of Foot (1978), MacIntyre (1985) and many others (see Crisp, 1996; Crisp and Slote, 1997). Although there are many different forms of virtue ethics, according to Slote (2000, 2001) they share two characteristics: they all specify what is moral in relation to inner factors like character and motives; and they treat 'aretaic' notions (relating to excellences of character) like 'admirable' or 'excellent' as fundamental to the enterprise of ethics. The revival of virtue ethics is in part a reaction against the principle-based approaches of Kant and utilitarianism, which focus on the rightness and wrongness of actions (as opposed to the character or motives of the people who carry out the actions), and see ethics as a matter of articulating and applying very abstract, universal principles. As Statman (1997, p. 7) comments, 'under the tyranny of principles, the person seems to disappear'.

As already noted, there are several different versions of virtue ethics. According to Hursthouse (1999, pp. 28–9), who develops a neo-Aristotelian view of virtue ethics, an action is right if and only if it is what a virtuous agent (that is, someone who has, and exercises the virtues) would characteristically do in the circumstances. And a virtue is a character trait a human being needs in order to flourish or live well. Hence evaluations of agents and actions are grounded in the concept of human flourishing ('eudaimonia'). Slote (2001), on the other hand, argues that we derive our evaluation of actions from their relation to people's motives, which can be admirable independent of whether they lead to human happiness. He gives the examples of strength of purpose or benevolence. He characterises his view as '*agent-based*', in that he regards evaluation of moral agents as basic and in no need of justification in terms of human flourishing, as distinct from Hursthouse, who offers merely an '*agent-focused*' view. He also claims to have developed virtue ethics as a moral theory, based on the virtues of universal benevolence and balanced caring, unlike many other exponents of virtue ethics approaches who are explicitly anti-theoretical, some of whom locate the virtues required for human flourishing within historically situated communities and hence can be accused of relativism, or at least espouse some form of communitarian view.

MacIntyre's (1985) version of virtue ethics, for example, sees the virtues as relative to culture and role, and defines them as qualities 'the possession and exercise of which tends to enable us to achieve those goods which are internal to practices' (p. 191). MacIntyre bases his notion of a 'practice' on something like the craft or guild organisations, which would include occupations such as farmer or doctor, which have a good internal to them, learnt and lived by those practising the occupation. MacIntyre also develops the concept of the narrative unity of a life, emphasising the importance of tradition in shaping people's identities, enabling them to tell the story of who they are and to decide what sort of person they want to be and become. This particular aspect of MacIntyre's thinking can be linked to narrative approaches to ethics, but these also have other origins, such as postmodernist and feminist approaches, which may also include narratives of resistance (rather than conformity to tradition) (see Nelson, 1997).

This focus on the virtues in relation to a social role in the context of a community of practitioners, has been seen as particularly pertinent for the professions, where one of the important questions to be considered, as Rhodes (1986, p. 42) points out in relation to social work, is: 'What sort of person ought a "professional" social worker to be?' Although Rhodes considers some of the questions that virtue ethics would raise for social work, she does not apply a virtue ethical theory in the sense of identifying the virtues or qualities of a good social worker. However, she does mention compassion, detached caring, warmth, honesty, a certain kind of moral courage, hopefulness and humility as qualities that might be appropriate (Rhodes 1986, pp. 42–3). In the field of medical ethics, however, much more explicit attempts have been made by philosophers to develop or apply a virtue ethical theory to medicine. Oakley and Cocking (2001), for example, offer a well-developed application of virtue ethics to medical and legal practice. They suggest that the character traits that would count as virtues in the role of a doctor include: beneficence; truthfulness; trustworthiness; courage; humility; and justice (pp. 92–3).

Community-based ethics

Recently there has been a resurgence of communitarian ethics, which focuses on the primacy of communal goods, and, like virtue ethics (with which it is sometimes linked) has its roots in ancient (particularly Aristotelian) and medieval philosophies, which ground ethical evaluations in a shared understanding of the good life (that is, what counts as human flourishing) within a particular community or society. There are many variations of communitarianism, some of which are more conservative than others, some of which are descriptive, and some prescriptive (relating to the need to restore a shared vision of the good life). Many versions of communitarianism are also developed more explicitly as a political philosophy than an ethical theory.

One of the main features of recent communitarian thinking is the critique of political liberalism of the kind developed, for example, by Rawls, which was briefly outlined earlier (see Mulhall and Swift, 1992; Sandel, 1998; Tam, 1998; Taylor, 1989; Walzer, 1983). Sandel

(1998, p. xii) gives a good example of the difference between liberal and communitarian thinking using the case of religious liberty. 'Why should this be protected?' he asks. He suggests that liberals invoke respect for the individuals who hold the religious views, rather than the religion itself, seeing this as a particular instance of the more general right to individual autonomy. But, argues Sandel, this 'misses the role religion plays in the lives of those for whom observance of religious duties is a constitutive end, essential to their good and indispensable to their identity', which is recognised by the communitarian viewpoint. Liberalism is seen to put the 'right' (action) before the 'good' (life). It also depends on the Kantian notion of the self, as an individual rational agent acting in accordance with a self-legislated moral law in abstraction from any community or society. This 'unencumbered' view of the self sees it as prior to its socially given roles and responsibilities, whereas, according to communitarian theorists, such practices and roles are partially constitutive of the self. As MacIntyre comments: 'we all approach our own circumstances as bearers of a particular identity...Hence what is good for me has to be the good for those that inhabit those roles' (MacIntyre, 1981, pp. 204–5, quoted in Kymlicka, 1996, p. 208). Liberalism, on the other hand, as Kymlicka (1996, p. 199) points out, gives priority to the self-determination of the individual, and the importance of people being free to make choices in relation to what they regard as their own good (except, of course, in cases where people are not competent to do so, or others may be significantly harmed). Although liberals have a conception of the 'common good', it is adjusted to fit the preferences and conceptions of the good held by individuals (sometimes this form of 'common good' is called 'public good'). Communitarians, on the other hand, conceive of the 'common good' (we might call this 'communal good' to distinguish it clearly from 'public good') as a substantive conception of the good life, which defines the community's way of life and should be used as the standard by which individual preferences are evaluated. The weight given to people's preferences depends on the extent to which they conform or contribute to the common good.

There have, of course, been many critiques of communitarianism, not just from its liberal rivals, but also from feminists, and many others who see the embedding of moral value within communities and the apparent loss of the ability of the moral agent to transcend what may be the oppressive and narrow values of their given community or role as regressive. Nevertheless, such an approach as a practical political philosophy gained support in the latter part of the twentieth century as a way of 'remoralising' society, establishing reciprocal rights and responsibilities at neighbourhood and societal level and encouraging active citizenship and participation in shared goals and projects (Etzioni, 1995a, b; Giddens, 1998). Tam (1998, p. vii) claims to formulate a unified communitarian theory with clear implications for practical reforms, centred on the notion of 'building inclusive communities'. He identifies what he calls three 'communitarian principles': co-operative inquiry as a way of validating what is to be accepted as true; mutual responsibilities determined on the basis of common values (such as love, wisdom, justice and fulfilment) validated by the communities of cooperative inquirers; citizen participation based on reforming power relations at every level of society so that all those affected can participate as equal citizens in determining how the power in question is to be exercised (Tam, 1998, pp. 12–18). Needless to say, some of the 'liberal' values of equality and fairness are evident in Tam's sets of principles, as might be expected in the context of the liberal democratic tradition within which he is situated. The conditions for 'cooperative inquiry' have some resonances with Habermas's presuppositions of communicative interaction, although inevitably Tam's theory has substantive content in his characterisation of the 'common values', which is what distinguishes it as 'communitarian'.

In Britain, elements of the 'new communitarian' thinking are evident in many of the policies and projects of the New Labour government, with a focus on social inclusion and neighbourhood regeneration (see, for example, Social Exclusion Unit, 1998, 2001). Insofar as many of these programmes and projects are carried out by the social professions, in particular community workers, such ideas are inevitably permeating their work and are being taken account of in recent literature (see Henderson and Salmon, 1998; Sites, 1998).

Relationship-based ethics

What I call 'relationship-based ethics' encompasses a range of approaches to ethics, which are perhaps almost too diverse to be placed under one heading, yet to deal with each separately would involve an endless proliferation of distinctions. Many of the approaches of feminist ethicists focus attention, broadly speaking, on the moral significance of aspects of people's relationships with each other. Although sharing some features with virtue ethics and communitarian ethics in their concern with people's attitudes, motives and their 'situated' selves constituted in relationships with others, there is more of a focus on relationships of vulnerability and dependency and the kinds of qualities, attitudes or practices appropriate to such situations – such as care, compassion, trust or empathy (see, for example, Addelson, 1994; Baier, 1986; Held, 1993; Kittay, 1999; Manning, 1992; Meyers, 1994; Walker, 1998). One of the most influential approaches in feminist ethics has been the 'ethic of care' developed almost simultaneously by Gilligan (1982) in her empirical, psychological studies of 'the different voice' in which women tend to speak of their ethical choices, and by Noddings (1984) in her philosophical account of 'the caring relationship as ethically basic'.

In her researches, Gilligan noticed two different ways of thinking about the nature of moral problems and how they should be resolved, which she termed the 'ethic of justice' and the 'ethic of care'. She distinguishes these as follows:

> From the perspective of someone seeking or loving justice, relationships are organised in terms of equality, symbolised by the balancing of scales. Moral concerns focus on the problems of oppression, problems stemming from inequality, and the moral ideal is one of reciprocity or equal respect. From the perspective of someone seeking or valuing care, relationship connotes responsiveness or engagement, a resiliency of connection that is symbolised by a network or web. Moral concerns focus on problems of detachment, on disconnection or abandonment or indifference, and the moral ideal is one of attention and response. (Gilligan, 1988, pp. xvii–xviii)

She argues that the two perspectives are complementary, in that they focus attention on different types of concern, and neither is superior to the other. This is a direct challenge to the moral development theory of the psychologist Kohlberg (1981), whose research had been based only on the responses of boys, which placed 'justice' type concerns at the highest stage of moral development. Gilligan associates the ethic of justice with the responses of men and boys, and the ethic of care with the responses of women and girls. Although she is at pains to stress that this is not a necessary connection, some feminists have been wary of her work, as it could easily be interpreted as either biologically essentialist, or as reinforcing the culturally stereotypical role of women as care-givers. Tronto (1993, p. 84) argues that the ethic of care is not exclusively the province of women, and suggests that Afro-American people, for example, adopt a view of the self which focuses on cooperation, interdependence and collective responsibility. Others have criticised Gilligan for implying that women have only one voice. Moody-Adams (1991) points out that in Gilligan's early studies she gave a lot of credence to a study of women's decisions concerning abortion. Yet if she had asked them about sexual harassment in the workplace, rape or pornography, or had she interviewed women who had experienced poverty, racial or ethnic exclusion, she might have heard different types of responses (to do with duties of non-interference and separation). That is, different types of problem might tend to generate different types of responses, and Gilligan's work, while important in identifying an alternative moral voice to that of justice, neglects 'the plurality of women's voices' (Moody-Adams, 1991, p. 209), and, therefore by implication, people's voices. This is a point taken up by Hekman (1995) who goes on to articulate a 'discursive moral theory', positing a number of different voices, as a development of Gilligan's work.

Not surprisingly, given the focus on the caring relationship, attempts have been made to relate the ethic of care to several of the 'caring professions', particularly nursing (see, for example, Allmark, 1995; Bowden, 1997; Bradshaw, 1996; Hanford, 1994). Kittay (1999), in her essays on the theme of women, equality and dependency, relates an ethic of care to the practice of what she calls 'dependency workers' (those who care for vulnerable people), where there are ties between concrete others that may not have been voluntarily assigned. Her text, as with several other feminist authors, is context-ualised with examples from her own life, including caring for a child with cerebral palsy. Sevenhuisen (1998) locates her discussion of a political concept of an ethic of care in the public debates in the Netherlands on child custody and health care policies. Rauner (2000) offers a particularly pertinent study of the role of caring in youth development programmes in the USA, where she incorporates the idea of an ethic of care as a practice in her study of the relationships between youth workers and young people in a series of different projects. Rauner (2000, p. 7) utilises three of Tronto's (1993, pp. 127–36) elements of an ethic of care (although she does not actually acknow-ledge Tronto), to which I have added Tronto's fourth element as follows:

- Attentiveness – actively seeking awareness of others and their needs and points of view;
- Responsiveness – the motivation to extend oneself on behalf of others;
- Competence – one's ability to do something about another's needs;
- Responsibility – taking care of, assuming responsibility for care – with responsibility being embedded in a set of implicit cultural practices (rather than a set of formal rules or series of promises).

'Other'-based ethics

'The meeting of the Other face to face defies reduction. How can this irreducibile quality be conveyed into an ethics?' This is how Vetlesen (1997, p. 1) introduces 'an ethics of proximity'. In common with the ethic of care and virtue ethics, this approach to ethics shares a dissatisfaction with the abstraction from context required by the impartialist and reason-based ethical theories. It may seem to have some similarities with the ethic of care, insofar as it emphasises the face-to-face relationship with the other, but the approaches of thinkers who develop an ethics of proximity originate in a different tradition, and lack the contextuality and situatedness of the feminist accounts of moral agency described above. This tradition includes the existentialists and phenomenologists of continental Europe: Kierkegaard, Sartre, Buber, Husserl, Heidegger, and the later developments and critiques offered by Løgstrup and Levinas. According to these philosophers, ethics arises from an experiential basis – not from abstract and universalising theorising. As Vetlesen (1997, p. 5) comments, the 'human dyad' (the I–thou relationship between two people) is regarded as the basic seat of concern and responsibility. Therefore the cognitive and emotional abilities needed for adopting a moral point of view are 'fostered in a setting of proximity, in interaction with close and, as one might say, irreplaceable others'.

Bauman (1993, 1995), in his work on postmodern ethics, has been particularly influenced by the thinking of Levinas. Bauman describes the demise of ethics (as externally imposed principles and rules by which we can live our lives) in postmodern society, and suggests that what we are left with is 'the moral impulse', the demand of the Other for our response. This refers to Levinas's description of the face of 'the Other' (the other human being) which summons my responsibility.

Hand (1989, p. v) describes Levinas, a Lithuanian-born Jewish French philosopher, as 'one of the most profound, exacting and original philosophers of twentieth-century Europe'. It is not easy, therefore, to summarise his thought, which places ethics as the first philosophy, prior to ontology (the study of being) and incorporates some of his religious thinking. Levinas takes as his starting point not the Kantian abstract knowing subject, nor the intentional consciousness of Husserl, but 'pre-reflective self-consciousness', which cannot be controlled by will and exists without attributes or aims, as 'a pure passivity' with no name, no situation, no status (Levinas, 1989, pp. 80–1). He says that one has to respond to one's right to be, 'not by referring to some abstract and anonymous law, or judicial entity, but because of one's fear for the Other' (p. 82). He speaks of the 'irruption' of the face of the Other, in its nakedness, vulnerability, 'like a shot "at point blank range"' (p. 83):

> The Other becomes my neighbour precisely through the way the face summons me, calls for me, begs for me, and in so doing recalls my responsibility, and calls me into question.

He speaks of a 'guiltless responsibility' that goes beyond what I may or may not have done to the Other, 'as if I were devoted to the other man before being devoted to myself'. To be oneself, therefore, is to be *for the Other*. In the face of the Other, Levinas claims, I am inescapably responsible and consequently 'the unique and chosen one' (p. 84). He speaks of the 'uniqueness of the non-interchangeable'. For Levinas, unlike Buber, the relationship with the Other is not a reciprocal one, concerned with what each may give and take (see Levinas, 1997). Rather it is a readiness to give unconditionally and is non-negotiable. As Vetlesen (1997, p. 10) comments: 'morality is not an option but a predicament, part and parcel of human existence. The Other commits me to being-for-him by his sheer co-existence.'

So, here we have responsibility as the core of 'being-for' – a response to the call from the Other, received prevoluntarily. But we may well ask, as Vetlesen does (1997, p. 9), what about justice, goodness, happiness – the subject-matter that usually defines ethics? These all matter, Vetlesen says, but they come later. Morality, as Levinas understands it, is not for the sake of anything. It defines us. And this is why he characterises ethics as first philosophy. Llewelyn (1995, p. 4), in his study of Levinas's work, notes that the term 'ethics' is used by Levinas in a different way from that classically employed by Aristotle or Kant, for example. He suggests that it might be less misleading to call it 'proto-ethics'. He points out that Levinas is concerned with the 'genealogy of ethics'. We may conclude, therefore, that what Levinas calls 'ethics' is, perhaps, best seen as a starting point for ethics, an exploration in metaphysics, certainly not an ethical theory.

Not surprisingly, I do not know of any Levinasian account of professional ethics *per se*. But there are accounts that draw on existentialist thought (for example, Thompson (1992) in relation to social work) and on the I–Thou relationship (explored by Downie and Jodalen (1997) in relation to the doctor–patient relationship). And, as mentioned earlier, the work of Bauman has been used by some in social work, both his description of the current state of professional life (the obsession with prescriptive rules, the ambivalence and uncertainty about what is right or good) and his suggestion that this leaves the way open to a return to the more basic state of individual moral responsibility. But even Husband (1995, p. 9), who toys with this approach, has to acknowledge that 'the pure individuality of the moral impulse would render it an anarchic basis for organised systems of care in contemporary society'. Indeed, it is hard to see how the rather contextless meeting with the singular other, despite Bauman's (1997) attempts, can be developed to go beyond 'the moral party of two' to take account of the 'third'; how it can move to an ethics (or 'morality', to use Bauman's preferred term) of practice as opposed to an ethics of relationship. This critique is well expressed by Lash (1996).

The end of ethics or postmodern ethics?

What are we to make of this multitude of different theories and approaches, many of which claim to capture the whole 'truth' of the nature of ethical life, while some are more modest and particular? MacIntyre's response to this 'Babel' is to return to the security of the pre-modern tradition of virtue and communitarian ethics. Other thinkers argue that this state of affairs in philosophy, which is mirrored in Western thought generally, reflects the 'postmodern condition'; that we are living in a world where 'incredulity towards metanarratives' (Lyotard, 1984, p. xxiv) predominates, where 'experts' differ about what is right and good and there are multiple truths valid for different purposes. As Bauman (1993, p. 20) comments:

> there are too many rules for comfort: they speak in different voices, one praising what the other condemns. They clash and contradict each other, each claiming the authority the others deny.

With this pluralism of rules, he continues, the moral choices we make, therefore, appear 'intrinsically and irreparably *ambivalent*. Ours are the times of *strongly felt moral ambiguity*' (p. 21).

When people talk of 'the end of ethics', this can refer to various interrelated positions. For example, it can mean the end of moral philosophy as a totalising discourse, of universalising ethical theories (Caputo, 2000, pp. 111–12); the rejection of commonly accepted principles and rules as a guide to action in a context of radical particularity and diversity (Bauman, 1994); or the removal of the boundaries between the ethical, aesthetic and technical (McBeath and Webb, 1991). What implications these views have for modernist institutions and practices such as the professions and the notions of 'professional ethics' that permeate them, depends to some extent on whether a 'sceptical' or 'affirmative' postmodernist viewpoint is adopted, to use the distinction made by Rosenau (1992, p. 15). Sceptical postmodernists, she suggests, inspired by continental European philosophers such as Nietzsche and Heidegger, offer a 'pessimistic, negative, gloomy assessment', characterising the postmodern age as one of fragmentation, malaise, meaninglessness, absence of moral parameters and societal chaos (see Lyotard, 1984). She describes affirmative postmodernists as more in line with Anglo-North American culture; while agreeing with the diagnosis of the ills of modernity, they have a more optimistic view of the postmodern age. They are either content with the recognition of personal non-dogmatic projects (New Age religion or lifestyles) and a situational ethics of personal responsibility (see Bauman, 1993; Caputo, 2000), or are open to positive political action, and may actually argue that certain value choices are superior to others (see, for example, Leonard, 1995; Weeks, 1993; Young, 1993).

Some of these ideas have been influential in relation to the social professions. A postmodernist viewpoint can be used to describe the kind of society in which the social professions are practised. McBeath and Webb (1991, p. 759), for example, argue that:

> Postmodern social work rejects ethical ambitions and rationalises its functions to be able to provide consumer responsive services, criteria of efficiency and tighter budgetary controls.

They suggest that it is characterised by consumer responsiveness and decentralised care packages, attempting to satisfy specific needs as and when they occur, aiming for efficiency and 'performativity' – a term used by Lyotard (1984, p. 46) as 'the best possible input/output equation', which suggests a stress on usefulness, value for money and technology (as opposed to the promotion of the common good through the welfare state). They note the 'theoretical heterogeneity' of social work and suggest that it might do well to give up its pretensions to 'an ethical teleology of personhood and helpful interventions', unified as a discipline, and become 'a set of irreducible sub-disciplines emerging in response to the self-evident needs of the community' (McBeath and Webb, 1991, p. 755).

Another more affirmative approach is to accept a kind of radical pluralism, involving an acknowledgement of the multiplicity of different moral voices (building on some of the feminist theorising and Foucault's discourse theory), but to see this as a practical opportunity to reconstruct social work as a moral (as opposed to technical) activity. In social work, for example, Milner (2001) articulates practical ways of using narrative in social work which are basically about listening to and working with people's own constructions of their lives through their stories, at an individual level. Parton and O'Byrne (2000) have developed what they call 'constructive social work', a practical approach to working with social work service users using aspects of solution-focused therapy and narrative approaches, which they link with social theories associated with postmodernism and social constructionism. They note the tendency for organisational frameworks to operate as if issues are determinate and resolvable in a scientific sense (p. 44), adopting a 'rational-technical approach', and argue that social work is better characterised as a 'practical moral activity' (p. 3). They argue for the rehabilitation of the idea of uncertainty, suggesting that social work needs to 'rediscover its traditional strengths in working with ambiguity, uncertainty and complexity' (pp. 44–5). They quote Howe's (1995) comment that: 'uncertainty is the domain of the educated professional' –

although a professional in Parton and O'Byrne's sense would in no way be an 'expert', but rather a co-constructor of meaning with the service user.

Those who might be characterised as 'political postmodernists' take this further, often building on a Marxist tradition, seeing the questioning and critique of the notion of power and knowledge in the professions as a positive move, in that it 'opens up space for aligning professions with a radical democratic project' (Rossiter, Prilleltensky and Walsh-Bowers, 2000, pp. 83–4). In their exploration of 'postmodern professional ethics' in the context of social work, Rossiter *et al.* deconstruct the professional norms of the ethical codes as based on the 'autonomous, independent, masculine ideal of the Enlightenment', in place of which they advocate an open, fair Habermasian-type dialogue. Whilst acknowledging that Habermas's views are universalist, and that his approach has been critiqued by feminists for its gender-blindness, they see its potential for liberatory action through the formulation of just norms by means of a dialogical process which recognises the legitimacy of different voices (see Dean, 1995 for a useful discussion of these issues). Similarly Briskman and Noble (1999), noting the universalist assumptions of codes of ethics, argue not for their abandonment, but reformulation to take account of diversity and difference. They offer the example of the New Zealand code of ethics for social work, which incorporates a separate bicultural code of practice, affirming the rights of Maori people to independence and calling on social workers to challenge monocultural power over resources (New Zealand Association of Social Workers, 1993). They suggest that different 'agency-based and/or constituency-based codes would give acknowledgement and voice to different actors and a positive validation to difference' (Briskman and Noble, 1999, p. 67). This is a move against the assimilation of different cultures and groups, but as Young (1993) points out in her discussion of New Zealand biculturalism, it needs to go beyond mere separation to a relational view of difference and diversity. This is reminiscent of the 'radical humanism' of Weeks (1995), which 'values individual freedom and celebrates the rich diversity of human goals, whilst affirming the importance of human solidarity', or what Soper (1993, pp. 28–9) describes as 'post-post structuralism':

> It would involve giving up on the grand idea of a single truth, without giving up on the idea of truth as a regulative ideal, something we should

be working to attain in all our behaviours and critical responses...It would acknowledge the constructed nature of subjectivity without supposing this makes all humanist questions of ethics and agency redundant.

Leonard (1997, p. xv) speaks of an 'ethics of reconstruction', drawing upon both the postmodern emphasis on the Other and the feminist and Marxist concern with interdependence, advocating an alliance of different social movements, each pursuing its own vision and interests, but with potential for solidarity. In applying this to professional practice, he argues, we will need to counteract the homogenising impulse of professional expertise, and instead think of co-authorship of a joint narrative about problems, needs and claims. He suggests the recognition of diversity should be central to the practice of professionals, and 'their claims to exclusive and invariably superior knowledge reduced to the status of a narrative alongside other narratives' which means that there must be spaces in the organisation of welfare for the expression of difference (p. 164).

Impartialist and partialist approaches to professional ethics

The reader may expect, or indeed hope, that this chapter will end with a recommendation for a particular theory, or approach, as better or more useful or relevant for life in general as well as professional ethics. But the situation is not quite as simple as that, as our discussions above may have indicated.

The impartial 'view from nowhere'

Most of the theories or approaches, insofar as they are about something called 'ethics', either implicitly or explicitly involve demarcating the sphere of the ethical. For the 'impartialists' (to use a shorthand term for the approaches placed together in the first group we looked at), ethics is about making reasoned judgements in particular situations by being as 'objective' as possible. That is, what I should do in this situation is what any other reasonable person should also do in this situation. Whilst we do have to take into account features of the situation that might make it different for someone else, in principle the right decision and the right action should be universalisable. I should not be 'partial' in the sense of, say, giving a job to my friend, for no other reason than that she is my friend. A moral judgement is not one that is based on emotions or feelings; it involves standing back and assessing a situation in a broader context, and asking, what would happen if everyone did this?

So, according to the impartialist view, the domain of ethics is the domain of reason and universalisability. In making an ethical judgement, I am in fact making a prescription for action – both for myself and others. If I say 'killing is wrong', that entails the prescription 'do not kill'. It is not merely an expression of a feeling or preference of the form 'I don't like the idea of killing', which might entail 'I'd prefer it if you did not kill'. However, for a utilitarian (but not for a Kantian) that does not mean that it might not on occasion be right to kill; for we may be faced with a choice between killing one person and saving the lives of several others. But that choice must be made through a process of rational deliberation, which can be justified, and which we would expect someone else, in a similar situation, to make. In this sense, the moral agent, the person making the decision, is replaceable. Someone else in the same situation should make the same decision. We know, in reality, that someone else (a real living person, rather than an abstract moral agent) may actually make a different decision, or act for a different reason, because they are weaker-willed, they feel too afraid, or they are swayed by a personal relationship. But although these factors do actually come into play, they are *not morally relevant* factors in making a decision. The moral agent must have, in Nagel's (1986) words, 'the view from nowhere', rather like Rawls's (1973) idea of the 'veil of ignorance'. Those who hold this view of the nature of ethics and ethical decision-making are not so naïve as to think we ever can have a 'view from nowhere', but this is the ideal position of the moral agent. We must abstract ourselves from our personal and particular concerns and contexts and put ourselves in the position of an impartial observer.

The partial, situated moral agent

Those theorists that might be termed 'partialist' state the obvious fact that every moral agent is situated or embedded in a web of relationships, commitments, roles and practices. The impartialists do not disagree about this; they may even acknowledge that they have traditionally paid less attention to this feature of our lives, and, of course, every situation is different, and we need to pay attention to this in order to decide what is right in these circumstances. But impartialists would hold that these are contextual details surrounding a rational and impartial decision that anyone else in this context would make. Those of a 'partialist' persuasion, however, suggest that people's embeddedness and 'encumbrances' are an important part of the sphere of the ethical. For they constitute the moral agent. They are not merely part of the background, detachable, but rather they are constitutive of the person who is making a moral decision. The moral agent is irreplaceable. My concerns, my relationships, my commitments, my emotions play a large and important part in making an ethical decision, and to reduce ethics to abstract reasoning is to narrow the sphere of the ethical too greatly. Different types of partialist approach stress different aspects of the encumbered moral agents – whether the focus is on their character or motives, the practices or communities in which they engage and through which they are formed, or the particular relationships with others. But they all have in common the centrality of a 'situated self', as some have called it (Benhabib, 1992).

The inherent replaceability and irreplaceability of professional judgements and relationships

In professional life, 'impartiality' is regarded as especially important, both in how professionals do their business, and in grounding the legitimacy of the professions' role in society. Most professionals have multiple clients, and it is regarded as important that they do not offer differential services or treatment on unjustifiable grounds (on the basis of personal prejudice or favouritism, or to make a large personal profit). Therefore to be able to show that the professions are grounded in universal principles of justice and welfare, for example, gives them their legitimacy. Principle-based approaches to professional ethics enable professionals to use a language to justify their decisions (and perhaps even offer some guidance about how to make decisions) that stresses the objectivity and fairness of their practice. The professional may be expected to have a special commitment to her or his clients over and above anyone else. For example, in certain sorts of situations it will be the lawyer's job to win this person's case, not impartially to consider what might be in the best interests of all concerned; it may be the job of a child care social worker to consider the best interests of the child, not the family as a whole. But this is part of the professional's role, and in that sense it may be done 'impartially' – out of a sense of duty or on the basis of a contract, rather than any special commitment to this particular person other than in the relationship of being a client.

Yet, equally, for some professions more than others (and this includes the social professions), the relationship with a client (who may be an individual, family, group or organisation) has been regarded as requiring a certain kind of trust, based not just on a formal contract (drawn up in a standard format with individual variations), but on a personal relationship. In residential social care work, in certain types of youth and community work and social work, part of the role of the worker is to care for and care about the people with whom they work. This may involve empathy and compassion and the development of a particular relationship. In this sense the worker is irreplaceable. Yet professional practitioners *are* replaced, of course, and in another sense the very nature of their role is that they are replaceable. They change jobs, go on holiday or get transferred to new cases. The definitions of the role and organisational structures have to ensure that, for example, a social worker who leaves can be replaced and the same basic service offered to the clients. This suggests that we cannot regard them as irreplaceable in the same sense that, say, a child's mother is irreplaceable. If the mother leaves and her role is taken over by a stepmother, many of the motherly tasks may be performed and a relationship developed, but it does not replace the unique relationship with the child's mother. We know that the professional care worker who undertakes some motherly tasks and has a motherly relationship with the young women in a children's home leaves at 5.30 pm; she may change jobs or retire. But nevertheless, for many of the young people she is also irreplaceable. The relationship with her is unique, and this ability to make such relationships may be part of the role of the social care worker, and of her identity in that role. As Rauner (2000, p. 12) comments, in relation to her study of youth development workers, 'no two care relationships are alike'. So the care worker is both replaceable and irreplaceable, as are the young people with whom she works.

The importance of impartial principles and particular relationships

As a young man using a drop-in centre studied by Rauner (2000, p. 34) said: 'They let anyone in here, but you are not nobody when you come in.' This neatly encapsulates the impartiality of the non-discriminatory principles of open access applied by the project and the workers in it, alongside the personal relationship developed with each individual. It might be said to epitomise the 'justice' and 'care' distinction made by Gilligan (1982). It might be regarded as too simplistic to identify just two broad types of moral voice, as Gilligan does, but it is nevertheless useful for the time being. Members of the social professions may base their decisions on how to be and act, and explain and justify their actions, in relation to both justice and care perspectives. Some jobs require a more impartialist approach than others. Some situations call for more care, empathy and attentive-ness to personal relationships than others. Some professionals may see their work and their roles more in terms of one perspective than another. It seems generally accepted that the two perspectives are complementary, and both are needed, in life generally, and in professional life. The early workers in the embryonic social professi-ons were often volunteers, and made much less distinction between their 'personal' and 'professional' roles and lives than is the case in the professions today. They spoke in terms of 'care' (which has both parentalist and controlling dimensions, as well as its benevolent ones), and were concerned with the nature of the relationship, even acting as a 'friend'. As the professions became more organised and regulated, then so too developed the concern with professional distance, with 'controlled' emotional involvement, and with the kind of universal principles and impartialist language we now recognise in the codes of ethics. Yet the tradition of care and empathy still remains, not just as a remnant of a world we have lost, but as an inescapable part of what it means to be human.

Poole (1991) in considering ethical approaches based on virtues and care, concludes that these are no longer available in the modern public realm; that they belong to personal life, the realm of the family and personal projects, but not to the modern world of work. At first this seems convincing; as one looks at the world of work, pol-itics and policy, then the principles of justice and social welfare seem to hold sway; our decisions must be justified with reference to reason and in the context of certain types of bureaucratic rules, regulations and laws. The voice of care, therefore, may be partly the voice of a left-over tradition in the social professions; a tradition associated with philanthropy, class, superiority and paternalism, from which we have been liberated through the universal principles of fairness, anti-discrimination and equality. It may particularly be a voice that women bring, finding it hard to separate out their personal roles from their professional ones. Yet this is precisely the kind of distinction, between personal and professional, private and public, that feminists wish to challenge. It is also why some feminists have been very wary of Gilligan's 'different voice' being associated with women. For although she claims the voice of care is of equal value to the voice of justice, there is a constant danger that it will be relegated to the personal, private world; an inferior women's world of emotion, irrationality and a commitment to pre-defined roles of giving, caring and self-sacrifice. For feminists it is important, therefore, to see the distinction between the personal and professional, public and private, as a false one. It may also be important to see the voices of justice and care not as separate, but somehow intertwined. They are irreducible to each other, but at the same time related. That is, we must not allow the impartialists to subsume the care voice within a justice approach (as Hekman (1995) suggests Kohlberg persists in doing even after apparently accepting Gilligan's arguments).

Hekman (1995, p. 10) points out Gilligan's use in her recent work of the musical metaphor to describe the relationship between justice and care. She likens this relationship to a 'double fugue', where there are two distinct melodies which complement each other and both are essential to make up the whole (Gilligan, Rogers and Brown, 1990, p. 321 ff.). Hekman (1995, p. 18) also invokes Kuhn's (1970) concept of 'paradigms'. Put simply, a paradigm (a term used by Kuhn in his characterisation of the nature of changes in scientific knowledge) is a distinct way of seeing the world, theorising and making sense of it, which is internally coherent and consistent and does the job we require of it. But there may be several different paradigms, with completely different assumptions about the nature of the world and how things work operating at the same time, and people function within them perfectly happily until certain internal contradictions occur. These paradigms (such as Newtonian and Einsteinian physics) are incommensurable, that is, they cannot be compared, because there are no common criteria for comparing them. A shift may occur from one to the other, but this is usually a sudden 'revolutionary' break with the previous tradition and an almost irrational step into a different way of viewing the world. A person cannot operate within both paradigms simultaneously.

Figure 3.1   The 'duck-rabbit'
Source: Wittgenstein (1972, p. 194).

Gilligan herself makes reference to what is known as the 'duck-rabbit' figure to illustrate the point that people can see moral conflict in terms of either justice or care, but not both simultaneously (Bernstein and Gilligan, 1990). Wittgenstein (1972, p. 194) discussed this figure in the *Philosophical Investigations*. The drawing (depicted in Figure 3.1) can be viewed either as a duck, or as a rabbit, but not simultaneously as both. Both perspectives are present in the drawing and constitute its whole. Hekman (1995, p. 9), following Gilligan, also suggests that this is a good way of characterising the relationship between justice and care, arguing that moral conflicts are not resolved by balancing justice and care, but by taking one perspective rather than the other. However, she further suggests that a paradigm shift is taking place in thinking about ethics (something not claimed by Gilligan), arguing that we are moving from a justice world to one inhabited by multiple moral voices.

Concluding comments

In this chapter we have reviewed and discussed various theories and theoretical approaches to ethics in the light of their relevance to professional life. We may conclude that no one approach can encapsulate the whole of what we think is important in the sphere of the 'ethical'. Unless we wish to propound a very narrow view of 'ethics', then these approaches (broadly divided into two: the 'impartialist'/ 'justice' and the 'partialist'/'care' approaches) are not necessarily mutually exclusive. However, they may be incommensurable – that is, we can look at the ethical issues in professional life from a number of theoretical perspectives, or speak about them in several different moral voices, all of which have something to offer (depending on the situation), but they cannot be ranked in importance, with some regarded as inherently more valid than others. Some of these issues will be further explored, especially in Chapter 6, in relation to professional practitioners' perspectives on the changes in their work.

4

From philosophical principles to professional practice: the form and function of codes of ethics

Introduction

This chapter examines certain features of professional codes of ethics and some of the critiques that have been directed at them. Three recent codes of ethics for the social professions are examined to show how they vary greatly in their form, content and in the purposes they are intended to serve, and how criticism of codes *per se* may often miss the mark. Just like the professions they relate to, the form, content and functions of codes of ethics will vary over time, place and according to the social, economic and political conditions in which the professions exist. Codes exemplify the coexistence of several apparently contradictory or incompatible models of professionalism and professional ethics.

The rationale for exploring ethical codes

Codes of ethics are one manifestation of what we called 'espoused professional ethics' in Chapter 2. They are not the only example – other sources would include the statements of values and principles articulated in the academic literature (especially textbooks) and in professional literature, such as that produced by bodies responsible for professional education. However, codes of ethics are particularly interesting for at least three reasons:

1. Codes of ethics commonly encompass the 'professional pledge' identified by Koehn (1994) as the ground of professional ethics – expressing professionals' commitment to a particular service ideal or core purpose and hence meriting public trust.

2. The form and content of codes of ethics tends to change over time. They have shifted from taking the form of a short oath (for example: 'I pledge to serve my clients without self-interest and to be trustworthy') to encompassing principles of action (such as: 'promote client self-determination') and often also more detailed sets of rules (such as: 'social workers should not discuss confidential information relating to their clients in elevators or hallways . . . '). Some of these documents then begin to take on the appearance of rather a strange hybrid, reflecting the traditional model of professional ethics as distinctive based on the pledge to be trustworthy, whilst also expressing professional values framed in terms of ethical principles loosely related to universal ethical theories such as Kantianism and utilitarianism (to ensure the distinctiveness of professional ethics does not allow for paternalism or inequities) and incorporating some more detailed rules of conduct to ensure good practice can be guaranteed through regulatory and disciplinary procedures. In this respect they form a bridge between the philosophical part of the book and the practice-based part (with a focus on the changing experience of practitioners).

3. Codes of ethics have been subject to a lot of criticism, from both philosophers and social scientists. For since codes contain statements that appear to take the form of general ethical principles, philosophers criticise them for lack of consistency or the fact that the principles are not directly related to an ethical theory. Since some of the codes contain rules of conduct, they are also criticised for the 'unethical' nature of their purpose (that is, they encourage unreflective following of rules, rather than independent ethical reflection). Since codes of ethics usually contain a written version of the equivalent of the professional pledge, those theorists who are cynical about the disinterested and altruistic nature of the professions tend to regard codes as designed to claim or enhance status, rather than as genuine expressions of commitments.

What is a code of ethics?

A code of ethics is usually a written document produced by a professional association, occupational regulatory body or other professional body with the stated aim of guiding the practitioners who are members, protecting service users and safeguarding the reputation of the profession. I say 'usually', because strictly speaking a code does not have to be written down, and sometimes other bodies, for example employing agencies, may produce documents called 'codes of ethics'. However, in this chapter my concern will be with written documents produced by professional bodies.

In English we tend to talk of 'ethical codes' rather than 'deontological codes' as is the case in several other southern European countries (for example, France, Italy or Spain). This distinction may not seem particularly significant, as we all know that the kind of document called 'code de déontologie' in French, is the same kind of item as a document called in English, 'code of ethics'. But the meanings of the terms 'ethics' and 'deontology' are slightly different, with ethics usually regarded as a more general term covering issues relating to right and wrong, good and bad, and deontology referring particularly to duties. In a professional context, these are usually 'professional duties' – that is, duties that relate specifically to a person doing a professional job. It is important to note this distinction in relation to some of the criticisms of codes of ethics in the English-speaking literature. For some of the criticisms may rest on a misunderstanding of what a code of ethics is and what it is for. Such misunderstandings might be increased because of the use of the term 'ethics', which has several meanings, as we have already noted, ranging from the study of moral norms ('moral philosophy') to the actual moral norms themselves ('morals').

Through studying codes of ethics for a range of different professions, including codes for architects, engineers, various health-related professions (Banks, 1998a) and for social work from 20 different countries (Banks, 2001, pp. 91–102), it appears that contemporary codes generally contain all or some of the following:

- *Statements about the core purpose or service ideal of the profession –* for example: 'the primary mission of the social work profession is to enhance human well-being'.

- *Statements about the character/attributes of the professional* – for example: 'professional practitioners should be honest, trustworthy and reliable'.
- *Ethical principles* – general statements of ethical principles underpinning the work; for example: 'respect for the autonomy of service users'; 'promotion of human welfare'.
- *Ethical rules* – some general 'do's and don'ts', for example: 'do not permit knowledge to be used for discriminatory policies'; 'protect all confidential information'.
- *Principles of professional practice* – general statements about how to achieve what is intended for the good of the service user, for example: 'collaboration with colleagues'.
- *Rules of professional practice* – very specific guidance relating to professional practice, for example: 'declare a bequest in a client's will'; 'advertising should not claim superiority'.

I have distinguished here between principles and rules; and between content that is primarily ethical in nature and that which relates to professional practice. Principles have a much broader scope than rules, tending to apply to all people in all circumstances (although in the case of the social professions, principles often refer to 'all service users'). So, for example, 'social workers should respect the inherent dignity and worth of the person' is an ethical principle; whereas, 'social workers should not disclose confidential information to third-party payers unless clients have authorised such disclosure' might be regarded as an ethical rule. 'Ethical' content relates to attitudes, rights and duties about human welfare, such as respecting human dignity, promoting social justice, whereas 'professional practice' matters have less direct ethical content, and may even include issues of 'professional etiquette', such as how to dress and how to advertise. Whilst codes vary greatly in their wording, and the types of rules they include, the ethical principles are often variations on the following: respect for persons; respect for and promotion of the autonomy of service users; promotion of human welfare; social justice and professional integrity (Banks, 1998b). Current codes of ethics for the social professions rarely contain statements about the character (or virtues) of practitioners. Such statements were more common in the past, and can still be found in the codes of several other occupational groups, although the virtue terms often appear in the form of an adjective describing behaviour or action (see, for example, Royal Institute of British Architects, 1997; Royal Town Planning Institute, 1997). Many codes, but not all, have some kind of preamble, which may state the core purpose and broad aims of the profession.

The form and content of the codes is linked to the functions they are intended to perform. There are a number of different functions that can be identified for codes of ethics (developed from Banks, 2001, pp. 106–10):

- *Protection of clients or service users* through the public pledge to be trustworthy and by explicitly stating what can be expected of a professional practitioner.
- *Guidance to practitioners* about how to act and how to make ethical decisions, either through encouraging ethical awareness and reflection or through explicit rules.
- *Enhancement of professional status*, through the mere existence of a code of ethics, since this is supposed to be one of the hallmarks of a profession.
- *Creating and maintaining professional identity* through the explicit statement of the service ideal, key ethical principles, the kinds of qualities expected of people who belong to this profession and the kinds of conduct required.
- *Professional regulation* through requiring members of a professional group to adhere to the code and using it for disciplinary purposes in cases of misconduct.

Examples of codes of ethics

I will now examine three codes of ethics in more detail, one of which is a relatively new code for youth workers in England, with the development of which I have been involved. They have been chosen because they demonstrate interesting differences in style, length, format and function. These are the *Code of Ethics* of the South African Black Social Workers' Association (SABSWA, no date, received 1999); the *Statement of principles of ethical conduct for youth work* of the English National Youth Agency (NYA, 2001); and the *Code of Ethics* of the National Association of Social Workers, USA (NASW, 1996). Table 4.1 summarises the differences between the three codes.

Table 4.1   Three contrasting codes of ethics

Code	Length (pages)	Form	Balance of principles and rules	Disciplinary function?
S. Africa (black social workers)	1	Oath	Ethical principles in the form of statements of beliefs and about the character of the professional	No
England (youth workers)	4.5	Statement of principles	Ethical and practice principles	No
USA (social workers)	28	Statements of principles and standards	Ethical and practice principles and rules	Yes

(1) *The South African social work code* produced by SABSWA, a professional association with a voluntary membership for black social workers, takes the form of a one-page oath or professional pledge. It begins with a statement of beliefs: 'I believe I am a member of a profession which strives to promote the social well-being of all people.' It ends with a declaration:

> I do solemnly therefore undertake to serve with dignity, honour, diligence and faith in this profession which I am making my own, to endeavour to promote and advance it; to be conscientious, sincere and unselfish in my work.

This is a very traditional format, reminiscent of the Hippocratic Oath (c. 420 BC), the first code of ethics developed for doctors, which begins: 'I swear by Apollo....'. It is the only contemporary code of ethics for the social professions that I have seen in this format. It is also distinctive in that it includes many references to the qualities or character traits of social workers (such as conscientiousness, sincerity and integrity). It contains no rules of conduct and even the statements we might regard as ethical principles are framed as beliefs, rather than principles of action. No reference is made to any disciplinary action against social workers failing to act in accordance with the code. Surprisingly, given the code was developed by a group for black social workers, this code makes no reference to anything specific about being a black (as opposed to white) social worker. It has a rather timeless and context-less quality.

(2) *The English statement of ethical principles for youth work* was published in 2001 by the National Youth Agency, a government-funded independent body, which promotes and supports youth work, but does not have individual members and is not a professional association. The document does not have the title of 'code', although it fulfils the functions of a code and when consultation was undertaken to assess the need for such a statement it was referred to as a 'code of ethics'. This code is four and a half pages and comprises four ethical principles and four professional principles. Under each there are several 'practice principles', which, it is claimed, are not meant to be exhaustive. For example, the first ethical principle states that youth workers have a commitment to: 'Treat young people with respect'. Practice principles under this heading include:

- valuing each young person and acting in a way that does not exploit or negatively discriminate against certain young people on irrelevant grounds such as 'race', religion, gender, ability or sexual orientation; and
- explaining the nature and limits of confidentiality and recognising that confidential information clearly entrusted for one purpose should not be used for another purpose without the agreement of the young person – except where there is clear evidence of danger to the young person, worker, other persons or the community. (National Youth Agency, 2001, p. 5)

No mention is made of the term 'rules', although some of the practice principles in this code are akin to what I have termed 'ethical rules' above. But a conscious decision was made by the drafters of the code not to use the term 'rule' or 'standard', in order not to prescribe youth workers' actions. This statement makes no reference to any disciplinary action, and indeed there is no overall professional or regulatory body for youth work that could perform such a function at the present time.

(3) *The code of ethics for American social work* is a new code produced in 1996 (revised 1999), developed from the first code created in 1960 by NASW, a professional association with voluntary membership for social workers in the USA. It is the longest of all the codes I have consulted, comprising 28 pages, accompanied by

a two-page index. The code consists of two pages outlining six ethical principles, followed by a 21-page section entitled 'ethical standards', which contains a mixture of principles and more detailed ethical and practice rules. It clearly divides the standards into responsibilities to clients, colleagues, to the social work profession, to broader society, responsibilities in practice settings and responsibilities as professionals. Some of the standards are quite detailed: for example, the section on 'informed consent' comprises six paragraphs and begins as follows:

> Social workers should provide services to clients only in the context of a professional relationship based, when appropriate, on valid informed consent. Social workers should use clear and understandable language to inform clients of the purpose of the services, risks related to the services, limits to the services because of the requirements of a third-party payer, relevant costs, reasonable alternatives, clients' right to refuse or withdraw consent, and the time frame covered by the consent. Social workers should provide clients with an opportunity to ask questions. (National Association of Social Workers, 1996, pp. 7–8)

This kind of detailed rule of professional practice (relating to costs and time frames) is not found in the other two codes, nor indeed in many of the European social work codes I have studied (although such practice issues are more common in the codes for Canada, New Zealand, Australia and Singapore). It is on the basis of such rules or 'standards' that the American code states at the beginning that it has a procedure for taking disciplinary proceedings in cases where members are alleged to have engaged in unethical conduct.

Codes of ethics as a mistaken enterprise

We will now explore some of the criticisms of codes of ethics, particularly those stemming from moral philosophers.

Codes of ethics as codes of moral philosophy: a contradiction in terms?

Ladd, an American philosopher, criticises the entire concept of codes of ethics as nonsense, because:

> ethics is basically an open-ended, reflective and critical intellectual activity...
> Ethical principles can be established only as a result of deliberation and

argumentation. These principles are not the kind of thing that can be settled by fiat, by agreement or by authority. To assume that they can be is to confuse ethics with law-making, rule-making, policy-making and other kinds of decision-making. It follows that, ethical principles, as such, cannot be established by associations, organisations, or by consensus of their members. (Ladd, 1998, p. 211)

So, does this mean that all the thousands of codes of ethics that have been created by so many different professions are an elaborate mistake? Or is Ladd's understanding of 'ethics' different from that of the many worthy people and professional associations who have created such codes? What if we called the codes 'deontological' rather than 'ethical'? That is, what if we explained to Ladd that what we have in a code of ethics is a statement articulating a set of professional duties? We could argue that in the context of professional codes of ethics, the term 'ethics' is used in a special way, not to mean moral philosophy ('a reflective critical activity') but to refer to a set of ethical principles and rules of professional conduct. The aims and language of professional associations in producing codes are not the same as those of the moral philosophers who examine them. This is not to say that critical comments from moral philosophers are not important. They are particularly useful in encouraging the committees that draft such documents to think more clearly and avoid some of the unnecessary and confusing contradictions and ambiguities. For there is no doubt that codes of ethics are rather strange documents, comprising a mixture of statements taking the form of ideals, general ethical principles, rules of conduct, rules of professional etiquette, guidance, advice and threats of disciplinary action, which are sometimes ambiguous and contradictory. If espoused professional ethics are regarded as to some extent distinctive (whether because they express a service ideal or a special kind of trustworthiness, as discussed in Chapter 2), their relationship both to the prevailing public morality and to broad-based theories of ethics articulated by moral philosophers is not a clear one.

Codes of ethics as flawed statements of Kantian ethical principles?

Harris (1994) is prepared to acknowledge that codes of ethics contain clauses (or statements) that purport to be ethical principles. However, he argues that if they are to have genuine ethical content, then they need to be seen as applied principles of some general moral theory. In looking at many examples of codes of ethics,

he concludes that most clauses take the form of 'categorical imperatives' (that is, a command that must be obeyed, such as 'respect the
self-determination of service users') and that they therefore fit most
easily into a Kantian moral theory of the deontological kind. By this
is meant the kind of theory that asserts that certain actions are right
or wrong in themselves, regardless of the consequences, and that the
right action is that done from the motive of duty. However, Harris
recognises that there are some problems with fitting the clauses in
codes into a Kantian theory. For a Kantian it is important for
individuals to take responsibility themselves for deciding where their
duty lies, rather than have this decided by an external body (such as
a professional association). Secondly, in Kantian ethics, the categorical imperative applies to every human agent, not just to a sub-set of
people, as is the case with professional codes of ethics, which only
apply to members of that profession. Harris concludes, therefore,
that the clauses in codes of ethics should be seen as 'flawed' Kantian
principles. He comes to this conclusion because although the clauses
in codes of ethics are hard to reconcile with Kantian moral theory, it
is even less plausible to base them on any other moral theory
(because they generally take the form of imperatives). This does not
mean that they cannot be given any moral justification at all, but just
that as Kantian principles they are flawed. He suggests that we should
'try to ensure that codes fit the Kantian model better by seeking to
rectify their current shortcomings' (Harris, 1994, p. 114).

We could make at least two responses to Harris. Firstly we could
argue that the types of clauses contained in ethical codes by no means
all have a 'Kantian' form or content. There are some clauses that
contain statements about the qualities or virtues of professionals that
could be linked to theories of virtue ethics (as in the SABSWA code),
and others that focus on the consequences of action, stressing the
promotion of the greatest good in society, that could be linked to
utilitarian ethics. Far from trying to ensure that codes of ethics
consistently reflect Kantian moral theory, perhaps we could accept
that they are in fact based on several types of moral theory, which
reflect the ethical norms and traditions that we use in ordinary
everyday life (see Chapter 3 of this book, and Beauchamp and
Childress, 1994, pp. 100–2, for a discussion of 'common morality'
ethics). Alternatively, we could argue that codes of ethics are not
the kinds of documents that aim to be, or should be regarded as,
applications of moral theory. They serve many other roles in addition
to providing philosophically consistent guides to action.

Codes of ethics as unethical?

Another critique of codes of ethics coming from a philosopher is based on the argument that if professionals are given their codes of ethics by professional bodies (rather than thinking the ethical issues through themselves) they may unthinkingly follow rules rather than engage in genuine ethical reflection and debate. This is the view of Dawson, who suggests that it could be argued that codes are unethical because:

> they minimise the responsibility of the professional for his or her actions... The professional is liable to follow pre-established rules rather than respond to the individual case and the individual client, and thereby become desensitised to the morally relevant factors in the particular circumstances. (Dawson, 1994, p. 133)

We may make two responses to Dawson. Firstly, even if we accept the argument that pre-established rules encourage moral insensitivity, this criticism only applies to codes which contain many detailed rules. As our discussion of the South African social work code and the English youth work code show, many codes do not contain 'rules'. Even those like the American social work code that contain some ethical and practice rules, also comprise ethical principles and ideals. So Dawson's criticism does not thereby condemn all codes – only those of a certain type. Secondly, Dawson's criticism rests on the premise that the main purpose of a code of ethics is to encourage, or indeed to ensure, ethical conduct. His argument is that, if the result of there being a code is actually to inhibit practitioners from acting ethically, then it is failing in its core purpose and the whole enterprise of developing a code would appear to be a contradictory one. However, is this the main or only purpose of a code of ethics? Several other purposes were identified earlier in this chapter and will now be discussed in more detail.

Codes of ethics as more than they seem

All the criticisms of codes detailed above result from taking them literally. The critiques assume that if a code purports to be about ethics, then it must be a version of ethics as understood by moral philosophers; that if codes purport to contain ethical principles, then these must be coherently underpinned by an ethical theory; and if codes claim to be about guiding practitioners and promoting ethical conduct, this guidance must come from literally following the principles or rules. If we invited a social scientist to look at the codes of ethics, we might find a different critique.

Codes of ethics as rhetorical devices

If we adopt a strategic or developmental approach to the study of the professions (as outlined in Chapter 1), this might lead us to ask why codes are produced by particular occupational groups at particular times, what function they serve in wider society and how they link with professional power and elitism. One response to these questions would be to argue that they serve to legitimate the privileges and autonomy of the professions. As Wilding comments:

> Codes of ethics are political counters constructed as much to serve as public evidence of professional intentions and ideals as to provide actual behavioural guidelines for practitioners. (Wilding, 1982, p. 77)

Edgar (1994b) gives the example of the code of ethics of the American Police Force, pointing out the tension between the ideals seemingly espoused in the code and the actual practice of police officers. He argues that the code conforms to the expectations of public morality, but it is not generally followed in the police force:

> New recruits must therefore learn to subordinate their lay understanding and implementation of the code to its actual professional abuse. (In effect, the professional life world recognises an important caveat for interpreting the code: these rules are not to be taken seriously.). (Edgar, 1994b, pp. 151–2)

This is an extreme version of the cynical (or 'ironical' as Edgar calls it) use of a professional code. But even professional groups that have good intentions in developing a code may still value it as a means of establishing and maintaining professional status and credibility as much as guiding practitioners or protecting service users. In the consultations leading to the statement of ethical principles for youth workers in England, some of the reasons given for regarding ethics and ethical behaviour as a priority issue in youth work included: 'it is part of professionalising the service'; 'raising the profile of the service'; and it would 'raise the status of youth workers' (Banks, 2000).

Codes of ethics as aspirational

Many codes of ethics contain universal statements about the nature of the good society, followed by more specific statements about the service ideal of the profession and the role of the professional worker. These statements may take the form of ethical principles, although it may not be possible for them to be implemented fully. They can be regarded as ideals or aspirations. Some codes contain more statements of this form than others. For example, the 1991 version of the code of ethics of the Swedish Union of Social Workers states the following: 'Wheresoever [in the world] social and other injustice occurs, the social worker has a responsibility to fight them' (SSR, 1991, p. viii).

Social workers must know that they cannot achieve these ideals, so we might ask why they are included? It is debatable whether such statements serve any purpose, though those who would defend them might argue that they could be regarded as akin to the Universal Declarations of Human Rights, or the Rights of the Child, which are equally impossible to implement in many parts of the world at the present time, but serve a role as a 'permanent possibility of human rights' which should be regarded as an ideal to strive towards. Ladd criticises what he calls the 'inspirational' function of codes of ethics, suggesting that this may contribute to the fact that 'many respectable members of a profession regard its code as a joke and not to be taken seriously' (Ladd, 1998, p. 215). He may have a point, particularly in a twenty-first century society where the emphasis in professional practice is on setting realistic targets and achieving measurable outcomes. The language of such codes sounds plain old-fashioned. This is true particularly of those codes that take the form of an oath, where we find statements such as this at the start of the SABSWA code: 'I believe it is my sacred duty to serve all people.' Such codes seem like relics of a past time, no longer relevant in the fragmented, postmodern world where the public trust in experts and professionals has seriously diminished. Yet it is important to see codes and their content as part of an evolving and developing tradition, linked to the past of a profession as well as looking to its future. We would expect to find 'relics of the past' in codes of ethics, as they are part of a 'living tradition' within a professional group. The danger comes if they get completely fossilised and divorced from the world of current professional practice (Edgar, 1994a).

Codes of ethics as educational

When the British Association of Social Workers first introduced its code of ethics, Rice (1975, p. 381) stressed that the code should not be expected to give detailed guidance about how to act in every possible situation a social worker might encounter; rather: 'A code of ethics creates the spirit and standard of ethical reflection in that community [of social workers].'

This was very much the motivation behind the recently drafted statement of principles for youth work in England:

> Its aim is primarily to develop ethical awareness and to encourage reflection as the basis for ethical conduct rather than to tell youth workers exactly how to act in particular cases. (National Youth Agency, 2001, p. i)

In outlining some general principles of conduct, a code can highlight areas of potential conflict in the work, and provide a framework and a vocabulary for thinking about and debating the ethics of certain attitudes, policies or courses of action. The code of the International Federation of Social Workers (1994) and the Norwegian social workers' code (Fellesorganisasjonen for Barnevernpedagoger Socionomer og Vernepleiere (FO), 1998) are good examples of this, very clearly raising questions and outlining potential areas where ethical conflict and dilemmas may arise (for example, between accountability to service users, colleagues, agency or society). So, although such codes contain statements in the form of ethical principles and rules, their purpose is less about enforcing behaviour in accordance with these rules, and more about raising professional awareness about the potential for ethical conflicts, the need to constantly debate and revise the statements in the code and for each practitioner to engage in ethical reflection on individual action.

Codes of ethics as regulatory

Some codes of ethics, however, do have a much more explicit regulatory role in the conduct of professionals, through outlining professional standards to which all workers must conform. We have already noted that some codes of ethics state that breach of their principles, rules or standards will result in disciplinary action by the professional body. In order for such enforced regulation to occur, usually it is necessary for a code to go beyond merely a statement of general ethical principles, and to contain some more detailed ethical and practice rules. It would be hard, for example, to discipline a practitioner for not fighting social injustice wherever it occurs in the world, as the 1991 version of the SSR code seemed to require. The statement quoted earlier from SABSWA ('I believe it is my sacred duty to serve all people') is not well suited to the regulatory function of a code as it is far too general and aspirational. Many of the codes in the social professions do comprise a lot of general ethical principles, interspersed with a few rules. So although a disciplinary function may be indicated, in practice it may be rarely used – as in the case of the British Association of Social Workers' code, for example (see Banks, 1998b).

The American Code, on the other hand, has as one of its explicit purposes the following:

> The Code articulates standards that the social work profession itself can use to assess whether social workers have engaged in unethical conduct. NASW has formal procedures to adjudicate ethics complaints filed against its members. In subscribing to this code, social workers are required to cooperate in its implementation, participate in NASW adjudication proceedings, and abide by any NASW disciplinary rulings or sanctions based on it. (National Association of Social Workers, 1996, p. 2)

At the beginning of the section on ethical standards, it is clearly stated that: 'Some of the standards that follow are enforceable guidelines for professional conduct, and some are aspirational.' The extent to which each standard is enforceable is said to be a matter of professional judgement to be made by those responsible for reviewing alleged violations. The following is an example of what would appear to be an 'enforceable standard' under the heading of 'payment for services':

> Social workers should not solicit a private fee or other remuneration for providing services to clients who are entitled to such available services through the social worker's employer or agency. (National Association of Social Workers, 1996, p. 14)

I would categorise this as a practice rule, whereas the following, under the heading of 'social welfare', is an ethical principle and is clearly 'aspirational', reflecting the stated service ideal of social work:

> Social workers should promote the general welfare of society, from local to global levels, and the development of people, their communities and environments. (National Association of Social Workers, 1996, p. 26)

Although many codes purport to have a regulatory role, by themselves the documents do not lend themselves to this function. For professional bodies to operate a disciplinary function, they must develop implicit and explicit 'case law', which may be based on the code, but goes beyond it and is located in the traditions of the profession as a whole (including the education and professional socialisation of practitioners). Codes can, in fact, be regarded just as much a codification of existing good practice in a profession (Harris, 1994, p. 109) as they are means of enforcing externally defined standards.

The value of codes of ethics

Can professional codes of ethics, comprising such a contradictory mixture of ideals, ethical and practice principles and rules in the form of aspirations, guidance, commands and threats of disciplinary action, really serve any useful function? I have suggested that we need to acknowledge that codes serve a broader purpose than their usual stated aims of protecting service users and guiding practitioners. One of these functions has been identified as part of a move towards professional status, where it is important that a code exists, but not necessarily that it is used. However, I do not want to argue that we should collude with producing a code whose stated purpose bears no relation to its actual purpose, as in the case of the American police code mentioned earlier.

So what role do professional codes of ethics have? If we take an historical/developmental approach to the study of professions, the answer to this question will vary according to the circumstances in which a profession exists in a particular country, in a particular policy and legal framework and a particular time. In the USA, where social work has existed for over a century and there is a very diverse range of social work practice happening in a range of public, voluntary and private sector settings, then it could be argued that a detailed code with regulatory and disciplinary functions is both possible and necessary. Indeed, the code has gradually changed over the years, from a short series of abstract first-person proclamations in the 1960s (Reamer, 1999, p. 44) to the latest version in the form of a set of principles followed by what could almost be described as a 'rule-book'. In the context of youth work in Britain where the code is new, where the range of practice settings is very diverse, and there is no overall professional body, it would be hard to develop a detailed code that would cover all workers in all types of practice. Hence the NYA code is in the form of a set of ethical principles, which serves as a framework, defining the purpose and boundaries of youth work.

In the case of SABSWA, which represents black social workers in South Africa (a sub-group within a profession), then a short, general code may be all that is required to establish professional identity and status. Similarly, in some of the countries in Eastern and Central Europe (for example, Slovakia and the Czech Republic) where the social professions are new or developing, then shorter codes remaining at the level of general principles have been devised (see: Association of Social Workers in the Czech Republic (SSPCR), 1995; Association of Social Workers in the Slovak Republic (ASPS), 1997). Initially, the existence of a code may be more important than the details of its content. In these contexts a code of ethics may have the very important function of maintaining and creating a professional identity, as well as serving the purpose of a publicly declared pledge that the traditional view of professionalism would regard as its hallmark. A statement of general ethical principles, or even a code in the style of the SABSWA code, which stresses the qualities of workers, helps to reinforce an understanding and agreement about the sort of person a professional practitioner is and what she does. It may be fitting for such a code to be aspirational (outlining what social workers hope to become), or educational (raising awareness of ethical issues), and to have a political role in attempting to establish the status and credibility of a professional group.

We have looked at three codes, each taking quite different forms: an oath; a statement of principles; and a statement of principles and rules. Whilst some practitioners complain that oaths and statements of principles are too abstract and idealistic to be of any use to them in professional decision-making, such short and general statements nevertheless avoid the pitfalls of the 'rulebook' approach. Codes

at the level of detail of the NASW document can justifiably be criticised along the lines suggested by Ladd (1998) and Dawson (1994),
as over-prescriptive and appearing to limit the role of professional
judgement in making decisions according to the circumstances of
particular cases. Above all, they encourage a false sense of security
that a code can tell a practitioner how to act. Even if this were desirable, it is impossible to legislate for every eventuality, and professional practitioners need the capacity for ethical reflection and
judgement just as much now as ever. Codes of ethics can certainly
be disingenuous and potentially dangerous, if taken too literally.
However, codes at this level of detail are developing quickly now, as
part of the attempt by professions to demonstrate that they are trustworthy and can engage effectively in self-regulation. But there is
nevertheless a limit to the specificity that can usefully be contained
in codes, which need to apply to all members of a profession doing
very different tasks in different settings. The specific guidelines for
practitioners undertaking particular tasks (such as community care
assessments, reviews of looked-after children or evaluations of
community capacity building), which have recently mushroomed
and are the subject of Chapter 6, have not been couched explicitly in
ethical terms. But they are part of the same trend towards increasing
specificity and prescription, based on the model of professional as
technician.

Concluding comments

We have argued that the form, content and function of codes of
professional ethics changes over time and varies according to place
and circumstances, as the historical/developmental view of the
process of professionalisation would predict. Although they are the
embodiment of the traditional view of professional ethics as outlined
in the Introduction, nevertheless a careful study of recent codes
reveals gestures towards a 'new professionalism' with more stress on
social justice, anti-discriminatory practice and client/user participation than in the earlier shorter documents. Similarly, whilst the core
purpose of codes is clearly to express, reinforce and enhance public
and service user trust in professionals, as codes get longer and more
prescriptive, then the room for trust gets narrower. One feature of
codes of ethics that does not change, however, is their role in

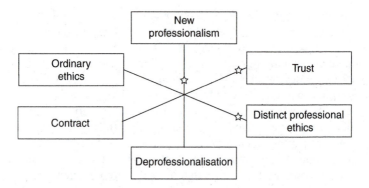

Figure 4.1   Codes of ethics and the key themes in professional ethics

reinforcing the distinctiveness of professional ethics in general (as distinct from the ethics of everyday life) and the distinctiveness of each profession in terms of its core purpose and values. This theme (the distinctiveness of professional values) forms the topic of the next chapter, which focuses on the practice of interprofessional working. In terms of the three axes of changing professional ethics identified in Chapter 2, codes of ethics take positions towards the new professionalism, trust and distinct professional ethics end of the spectra, as shown in Figure 4.1.

5

Practitioner perspectives I: interprofessional working – issues of identity, values and culture

Introduction

In Chapter 2 we explored the extent to which the idea of professional ethics as distinct from the ethics of everyday life makes sense in terms of arguments developed by philosophers. We concluded that while professional ethics must be regarded as derived from ordinary ethics, it does make sense to see professional ethics as distinctive. In this chapter we will explore that idea that each profession has a distinctive set of professional ethics (as espoused and enacted norms) in the context of increasing demands for interprofessional working. This theme will be explored through a case study of an interprofessional service, drawing on conversations with practitioners about their work.

Insofar as interprofessional working entails a blurring of boundaries between professional roles and a commitment on the part of practitioners to new sets of values, rules and procedures defined by a partnership, interagency group or interprofessional team, then this might appear to threaten the notion of distinct professional groups each with their own special sets of guiding ideals, ethical principles and rules. Some of the practitioners interviewed did indeed express such fears about the loss of their professional identities and values, giving examples of specific conflicts and difficulties. On the other hand, insofar as attempts to develop successful interprofessional working have been limited, or encountered serious difficulties and resistance, it has often been suggested in the literature that this is due to 'tribalism' – the unwillingness to give up particular professional ideologies, cultures and values (see, for example, Dalley, 1993; Williamson, 2001, p. 121).

In this chapter we will therefore explore both the implications of interprofessional working for the idea that each profession has a distinctive professional ethics, and the implications of distinctive professional ethics for interprofessional working. This will be achieved in the light of comments made by practitioners in individual interviews and a group discussion on theme of interagency and interprofessional working. In particular this chapter will focus on the views of members of a youth offending and community safety service, which has been chosen as a case study. Where relevant, the comments made by other professionals interviewed for this research (see Appendix for details) on the theme of interagency and interprofessional working will also be included.

The growth of interagency partnerships and multi/interprofessional teams

The exhortation that agencies and professionals employed in the fields of social welfare, justice, environmental services, health and education should work together to improve services has been made over several decades. This has been particularly noticeable in the field of child protection, where a series of tragic deaths of children in the 1970s, 1980s and 1990s led each public inquiry to note the need for greater collaboration between the various agencies involved, especially social services, police and health (see Department of Health, Department for Education and Employment and Home Office, 1999). In hospital settings there is a long tradition of the 'multidisciplinary team', particularly in the fields of mental health, disability and care of older people, comprising consultants, nurses, social workers and various types of therapists (such as physio-, speech and occupational therapists). Recent legislation covering health and social care is driving further shifts towards interagency and interprofessional working in this area, with proposals in the Health and Social Care Act (2001) for the setting up of Care Trusts capable of providing all health and social services for community care purposes.

Indeed, the requirement to establish interagency partnerships and multi-or interprofessional teams and services has gathered momentum at the beginning of the twenty-first century in the context of UK central government policies to 'modernise' public services and develop more effective ways of tackling social exclusion, improving health and educational standards, reducing crime and increasing community safety as discussed in Chapter 1 (see, for example: Department for Education and Employment, 2000; Department of Health, 1998b; Department of the Environment, Transport and the Regions, 1998; Social Exclusion Unit, 1998). These teams and partnerships are now becoming increasingly structured and formal. This may happen through interagency partnerships (such as regeneration partnerships at neighbourhood level, or community safety partnerships at district or borough level) or through the establishment of teams of professionals from several different agencies working together to deliver 'joined up services' or tackle issues in a locality (such as youth offending teams).

The ways in which the agencies and professionals work together in these contexts varies along a continuum of degrees of joint working. A partnership is usually a group of representatives of agencies, organisations or interest groups (sometimes including service users, community members and representatives of private sector organisations) who work together with a common purpose. Many partnerships entail *interagency* collaboration and cooperation at a strategic level, involving information sharing and a reduction in gaps or overlaps in services (see Balloch and Taylor, 2001, for a discussion of a range of types of partnership), whereas in a team setting, professionals work alongside each other at an operational level (see Payne, 2000, for a discussion of a range of types of team). According to Øvretveit *et al.* (1997, p. 5) a team is 'a bounded group of people with a common purpose and a formal or informal organisation'. Carrier and Kendall (1995, p. 10) distinguish *multiprofessional* working, where the traditional forms and divisions of professional knowledge and authority are retained, from *interprofessional*, where there is a willingness to share and give up exclusive claims to specialist knowledge if the needs of service users can be better met by members of other professional groups. Many community-based teams are currently somewhere between multiprofessional and interprofessional, with tensions apparent as they shift along the continuum. The focus of this chapter is interprofessional working. But it is recognised that within teams established with the aim of interprofessional working, much of the actual practice may be at the level of interagency and multiprofessional working.

The term 'disciplinary' rather than 'professional' is often used in the context of teamwork. Although the terms are sometimes used loosely and interchangeably, as Payne (2000, p. 9) points out, they do have slightly different meanings. 'Professional' implies concern for different professional groups, and the functions associated with those groups. 'Disciplinary' refers to the knowledge and skills underlying professional roles. Since the focus of this book is on professions, and the term 'professional' used in this context is broader than 'disciplinary' (as it subsumes the notion of there being specific knowledge underpinning professional roles), I will use it in relation to the teams discussed in this chapter. Payne (2000, p. 9), following Garner and Orelove (1994), introduces the concept of 'transdisciplinary teamwork', which entails the transfer of information, knowledge and skills across disciplinary boundaries, with professionals taking on roles usually associated with another professional group. Payne refers to 'role release' as a situation where team members allow aspects of their primary function to be undertaken by team members from other occupational groups. I will treat this as falling within Carrier and Kendall's broad category of 'interprofessional' working.

Interviews with practitioners

In exploring the themes of interprofessional working and the new accountability in Chapters 5 and 6, the book draws on a group discussion and individual interviews with members of a youth offending and community safety service, and semi-structured, in-depth individual interviews with 32 other practitioners, ranging from directors of services to ground-level staff in both statutory and voluntary sector settings. Group discussions/focus groups were also held with members of a community mental health team and a youth and community service. Interviewees were selected through making requests to organisations for staff willing to discuss issues with me, and through existing contacts. The aim of the interviews was to explore the responses of senior practitioners to changes in the organisation and practice of their work. The interviewees were asked about the nature of their work; their views on changes in their work and the work of the occupational group over the last 10–20 years (specifically asking about interprofessional working and working to procedures, targets and outcomes); and any ethical issues/dilemmas arising in their work.

The interviews were very open-ended, with the interviewer asking questions specifically in relation to what the interviewee raised. A list of the job titles of the practitioners interviewed and the broad themes covered in the interviews is given in the Appendix.

The interviews were tape-recorded and transcribed, and a preliminary analysis undertaken using the qualitative data analysis package, NVivo (see Bazeley and Richards, 2000; Gibbs, 2002). This involved coding sections of the interviews in relation to the broad themes of interest to me (interprofessional working, accountability, dilemmas and challenges) and in relation to specific themes emerging from the data (for example, within the theme of accountability, comments about the use of procedures might be categorised as: 'procedures regarded as promoting equity'; 'procedures as rigid'; 'procedures not followed'). Although the initial open coding of the data followed an approach that might be categorised as a 'grounded theory' methodology (Strauss and Corbin, 1990), the aim of conducting the interviews was not to undertake a systematic research study in its own right, but rather to illuminate the theoretical discussion of the book with insights from accounts of the views and daily work of practitioners. Specifically, in this chapter, the main intention is not to draw out generalisations about interprofessional team-working to add to the already extensive literature on this topic. The accounts given by these practitioners are simply used to explore some of the themes arising in this particular service specifically in relation to interprofessional working and professional ethics. Before looking at these themes, I will briefly describe the youth offending and community safety service.

The youth offending and community safety service: a case study

The youth offending and community safety service covers a population of around 100,000, comprising a large town and its rural hinterland. When setting up the youth offending team (YOT) in 2000 as required by law across England as a result of the Crime and Disorder Act (1998), the partner agencies in the local authority area decided to integrate this with several other services and projects. The YOTs were required to be multi-agency partnerships between the police, social services, health, education and probation with the aim of reducing offending by children and young people. The new service in this particular area also incorporated police and local authority community safety functions, the local authority uniformed wardens, and various substance-abuse and housing workers employed through special projects or the voluntary sector. At the time of the interviews in 2001, all staff were housed together in a building adjacent to the local authority social services department. The service was managed by a head of service, seconded from the social services department, with the youth offending team having its own manager, but integrating its work with other aspects of the service including community safety, street safety, substance misuse, and so on.

The work of the new YOTs is being very closely monitored by the Youth Justice Board, with national systems established for undertaking assessments of young people, and targets set for reductions in youth offending (see Youth Justice Board, 2000 and www.youth-justice-board.gov.uk). The Crime and Disorder Act (1998) created many new powers for the youth courts and local authorities, including new custodial sentences, parenting orders, child curfews and reparation orders. The work previously done by the social services youth justice teams transferred to the YOTs, along with aspects of the functions of the probation service and the police. The inclusion of health and education workers is designed to encourage a more holistic approach to tackling youth crime, as a result of failures identified in the system through earlier research (Audit Commission, 1996). This approach to youth justice has been described as 'corporatism', that is, a centralisation of policy, with increased government intervention, 'with the aim of reducing conflict among professional and other interest groups and encouraging the emergence of a consensus within a coherent and uniform institutional structure' (Smith, 2000, p. 130).

A group discussion was held with eight workers in the youth offending and community safety service, including two police officers, two social workers, a nurse, a probation officer, a neighbourhood warden and an assertive outreach worker (working on an outreach basis with young people). The interviewees were asked to discuss the most important challenges of their work; the pros and cons of working in a multi-agency, interprofessional service; some of the dilemmas they encountered in their work; and what could be done to tackle these. Individual interviews were also held with the head of the service, the YOT manager, community safety coordinator, community safety police inspector, senior neighbourhood warden, prevention coordinator and a social worker on the enforcement side of the work. Although the focus of the book is on the social professions, in exploring this case study on interprofessional working inevitably the viewpoints of other professionals will also be explored.

The practical and ethical benefits of interprofessional working

Since the rationale for developing interprofessional working has been well-rehearsed in the literature and is a generally accepted aim of central and local government policy, not surprisingly the practitioners interviewed described many benefits.

Promoting the welfare of service users: consistency and continuity

The most popular justification for interprofessional working was that if it worked well it resulted in improved services for users. This might occur through: reducing overlap between the services provided by different agencies, greater consistency and continuity of service, improved communication and information sharing between professionals, and the ability to provide a more 'streamlined' and 'seamless' service. The process by which this comes about may be a complex and challenging one, but the respondents were in no doubt that this was being done in the interests of improving outcomes for the people using the services. In ethical terms, this could be regarded as a concern for promoting the welfare of the individual service user, and seen from the perspective of the service as a whole, cumulatively this would be producing a greater amount of welfare or well-being for all service users and their families – which can be interpreted as a utilitarian argument based on the production of good outcomes.

Some of the benefits were viewed as good outcomes both for service users and the wider community or society as a whole. For example, the intensive preventive work the youth offending team is now able to do with young people before they reach what those in the business call 'persistent young offender' status (PYO) was said by several team members to be 'starting to show an effect'. As one worker commented:

> we aren't getting the progression of PYOs. People are starting to realise that there is something else other than continuing along that line, and the intervention this service is putting into that has given them more awareness of the options available to them and also making them more aware of what's going to happen to them if they do continue along that line. And I think that's having an effect.

Although not explicitly stated to be 'good for the young people', the suggestion that they have 'more awareness of the options available to them' implies this is beneficial for them in the long term, as well as being of community benefit in reducing crime.

Promoting community and social welfare: effectiveness and prevention

It was acknowledged, however, by several interviewees that the community safety agenda and the targets to reduce crime had precedence over concern for the welfare and development of individual young people. One youth offending team worker (a qualified social worker, formerly a worker in the youth justice team in social services) who had been off sick for a while, noted the positive results of finding on his return that:

> most of the well-known clients that we've had, with a lengthy criminal history, now are all locked up. So that...the positive thing about that appears to me to be...that all those young people who've offended once or maybe twice, and who we used to kind of have on our back burner,...saying things like we'd love to work with them, but we haven't got time to go back and forwards to court and back and forwards to prison, etc.,...everyone will have a role in this [working with them].

This is part of the new approach to tackling youth crime, brought in by the new legislation and facilitated by the interprofessional approach. Not all team members were unequivocally in favour of this 'tough approach', as we will discuss in the next section. But for some team members this was an indication of the effectiveness of their work. By abandoning the few PYOs, they could give greater attention to more young people who might be more likely to change their behaviour. Again, this can be seen in utilitarian terms as a focus on the greatest good of the greatest number of young people.

Very few respondents simply focused on meeting targets for reducing crime *per se*, as an end in themselves. But given the detailed monitoring and measurement of outputs and outcomes built into the work of youth offending teams across the country, not surprisingly, practitioners also looked to figures relating to re-offending, reduced numbers of court appearances, and so on, to justify the effectiveness of their work. As one youth offending team worker commented after a recent visit to the court:

the clerk of the court has come out and she's said: 'well', she said, 'what's going on up there ... we've only got ten kids, are you trying to do us out of a job?' ... I thought that's nice because they'd acknowledged that, and she'd come out and said it ... that was really good.

This worker's notion of effectiveness is clearly related to the outcomes of a reduction in the number of offenders coming to court.

Several workers mentioned increased funding for their work as one of the advantages of the new interprofessional approach (as a new central government initiative, more resources could be put into preventive work, for example, than might have been the case in a social services youth justice team). Yet it was also mentioned on several occasions that the team was 'under-resourced'. Only one worker (a social worker in the youth offending team) mentioned the possible financial economies of interagency working. In talking about the advantages, he commented: 'it is cheaper in some ways'.

The practical and ethical challenges of interprofessional working

Much more time was spent by these interviewees discussing the challenges and difficulties of interprofessional working. Some of the issues mentioned could be said to be about organisational systems, structures and practical problems, others could be categorised as relating to professional identity, values, cultures and ideological or attitudinal problems. However, while such distinctions may have some analytical utility, in practice all the issues are inter-related. For example, the management systems operating in a social services department may be related to the organisational structure of that agency, but they are not separate from social workers' views of themselves as professionals who work in a certain kind of way. For example, social services operates clear eligibility criteria for services, which reinforces social workers' accounts of themselves as fair-minded. It is impossible to distinguish what may be attributed to a practitioner (by themselves or others) as a professional, from what may be attributed to them as a 'social services employee' or 'health services employee' or a 'voluntary sector employee'. Nevertheless, I will divide this discussion up artificially into the broadly organisational issues and the professional issues, and pay more attention to the latter.

Issues of different systems: hierarchies, procedures and criteria

In all studies of interprofessional and multiprofessional working, some of the main problems reported are around the incompatibility of the managerial structures, procedures and systems operating in the parent agencies employing the practitioners. These create many practical problems, and some ethical dilemmas and problems. They also serve to reinforce differences, and myths about differences, between professionals working for different agencies. For example, several times practitioners from a local authority and voluntary sector background commented on the fact that the police work set hours and are given overtime payments for working beyond these hours. The community safety coordinator (from a local authority background) commented on the 'hierarchical' police structures and also added:

> The thing we laugh about in the office is that the police officers do the shift and that is it. They don't stay back because they don't get paid for it. Whereas some of the local authority people here, what we would do here is we would always stay and do the job until it is done.

This same practitioner went on to discuss her work in conducting a joint 'Best Value' review of community safety with the police service and the challenges this was posing:

> We've got ways in which we do Best Value and the police have got ways in which they do Best Value, and it's: 'do we want two parallel systems or do we want one real joint piece of work...?'

This practitioner did not have a 'professional' background as such. She had a degree and had worked in various local authority departments, developing expertise in auditing. She spoke of 'cultural differences' with the police, commenting that they worked in a different 'style' – with her reference point being her own employing agency (the local authority).

Mismatches in information management systems, and difficulties in accessing different agencies' systems, were also frequently mentioned as causes of frustration and tension.

Issues of professional identity, values and culture

By far the most common types of issues raised in connection with the challenges facing those working in interprofessional settings concerned the threat to, or the obstructive effect of, different professional identities, values and cultures of the practitioners involved. Operating in an interprofessional team can cause the people involved to reflect on their professional identities and values, perhaps to question them, and, above all, to reinforce them. For example, the only qualified nurse in the youth offending team, in the course of an interview and group discussion made several references to his health background. His first comment was:

> The main challenge for me *as a professional coming from a health background*, is actually establishing myself within the framework. Establish that role, without getting away from the fact that, you know, I still want to offer a professional service from a health perspective. (Nurse member of YOT) (my italics)

He spoke of the conflict between what he and the health authority thought he should be doing in a youth offending team and what was expected in the YOT, referring to the potential problems of professionals losing 'part of their *professional identity*'.

Drawing on the interviews with other professionals (not in the youth offending and community safety service) it is interesting to note that a social worker made the following comment as her mental health team was about to become an integrated community mental health team (CMHT) with health colleagues:

> It's been about being really quite frightened about *losing our social work identity*. I think it's about it being eroded, you know, so there's this feeling that if you mix with the 'health lot', *your values will be eroded*. (Social worker in CMHT)

The social work team manager, who had already been managing half her team in an integrated context for a year, commented in relation to maintaining the social work identity:

> I think you have to have very good grounding in social work, as not just as a profession, but as *a value base*, otherwise it's very easy to get sort of sucked into *the dominant culture* which social work is not in an integrated team. (Social work team manager in CMHT)

There are three terms used by these interviewees, which were also used by many others and occur frequently in the literature (see, for example, Irvine, Kerridge, McPhee and Freeman, 2002). These are: 'professional identity'; 'professional values'; and 'professional culture'. The interviewees inevitably use these terms loosely and inconsistently, and are not adopting a particular theoretical stance (at least not consciously anyway). They were not asked to say what they understood by 'culture', 'values' or 'professional identity', and although in some cases the further conversations they have during the interview give some indications, we cannot assume a common understanding of these concepts. These concepts are all essentially contestable in the same way that 'professional ethics' is. The different sociological and philosophical theories of the nature of identity, values and culture separately, and in relation to each other, are legion. So in one sense it would seem not only fruitless but also a mistaken enterprise to attempt to identify these participants' 'lay theories' of culture, identity and values, relate them to relevant sociological theories and attempt to use them to explain their behaviour. As R. Williams (2000, p. 151) points out in his exploration of the concept of identity, this would be to confuse the idiom of the research participants' usage with that of the professional analyst.

Taylor and White (2000, p. 100), discussing professional identity in the health and social care field, suggest that it should be seen as 'a topic to be investigated rather than a resource to be used to explain some factor or other'. This echoes R. Williams's conclusion (2000, p. 147) that rather than attempting to provide general and speculative theories about what identity is and is not, it is preferable to look at 'identity matters as they arise and are dealt with in the socially organised practices of everyday life' (p. 11). Both these approaches reflect the authors' interest in discourse and conversation analysis of verbal interactions in naturally occurring settings. They entail a focus less on what is said (for example, that social work values are different from nursing values) than on how people say things – what they are performing or achieving through their talk (for example the social worker is distinguishing herself from other professionals). This is a useful approach, and has been used to good effect in several studies of the social and health professions (see, for example, Hall, Sarangi and Slembrouck, 1997; Sarangi, 1998). But the interview material presented in this chapter, although some of it was gained through group discussions in an interprofessional setting, as well as individual interviews, is not ideal for this kind of conversation analysis. The approach adopted here, while recognising the value of focusing on how respondents construct professional identity through their talk, will largely be concerned to consider the content of what they say. I will therefore briefly discuss the concepts of professional identity, values and culture in order that some of the theoretical insights may be used to illuminate practitioners' comments, and vice versa.

(1) Professional identity

This term is usually used to refer to people's sense of who they are in their work roles. What account is given of precisely what 'professional identity' comprises and how it is formed will depend on what theoretical position is adopted. There are numerous accounts of the nature of identity in general (see R. Williams, 2000, for a comprehensive overview) of which professional identity can be assumed to be a sub-category. R. Williams (2000, pp. 5–7) outlines Goffman's (1968) threefold distinction between:

- Personal identity – what differentiates each individual person from all others (this may include material such as photographs, other records or mental representations);
- Social identity – those attributes, especially cultural, that individuals share by virtue of a common membership category (this may include a range of cognitive, attitudinal, personal and social features);
- Ego (or felt) identity – the subjective sense of their own situation, continuity and character that individuals come to obtain as a result of their various social experiences. R. Williams (2000, p. 7) calls this a 'subjective and reflexive accomplishment'.

R. Williams suggests that certain treatments of identity may focus more on one understanding than the others, or may indeed subsume one or two into the others. It is important to note that the attributes drawn on in constituting ego identities are not necessarily different from those relating to personal and social identities.

In professional life, social identity is the most commonly used understanding. In the quotation from the social worker above, one reading of the talk of 'losing our social work identity' is to see it as relating to the attributes shared by people in the membership category of 'social worker'. This may include the self and other-ascribed knowledge, values and skills gained through education, training and socialisation into the profession. But arguably, 'ego' or 'felt' identity may also be important for some people. The experience of being a social worker may contribute to part of what an individual thinks about as the deepest and most enduring features of their unique selves. Or, depending on what view one takes of the relationship between professional life and identity, the felt identity may find expression in professional life. Halford and Leonard (1999) discuss the debate over whether work life creates and structures one's identity (see also Freidson, 1994), or whether an individual with a pre-existing identity expresses this in a work situation. They conclude, not surprisingly, that the dichotomy does not make sense, and that both the structural and agentic perspectives are needed to make sense of professional identity.

However, returning to the warnings of R. Williams (2000) and Taylor and White (2000) about using the contested concept of identity to explain conduct, we could instead ask: what is this social worker and the other interviewees doing when they express a fear of losing their professional identity?

(2) Professional values

Although the term 'values' is used very broadly and has many different meanings, 'professional values' commonly tends to be used more specifically to refer to the core ethical principles underpinning the profession, often found in codes of ethics under the heading of 'values'. This would encompass general principles such as: 'promote the individual autonomy of the patient/client/service user'; 'respect the confidentiality of information gained from the service user'. However, the term 'professional values' may sometimes be used more loosely to mean any set of attitudes or beliefs associated with a particular profession (for example, it might be stated that: 'health professionals tend to follow values inherent in the medical model'). Indeed, it may encompass what some people have called 'professional ideology' (see Dalley, 1993), or the general politico-moral beliefs that are said to be commonly held by members of a profession (for example, 'doctors tend to hold values that entail a belief in the moral duty of families to look after their members').

The term 'professional values' or simply 'values' was used frequently by interviewees, particularly when describing conflicts and dilemmas (a clash of professional values can be used to explain a dilemma or problem). Talk of a 'value base', as in the quotation from the team manager of a community mental health team noted above, is common social work terminology to refer to the core values of the profession. But the use of the term 'base' suggests something foundational, at the heart of the profession. The way this team manager uses the expression is somewhat unusual, as she talks about social workers having to have a very good grounding in social work, 'not only as a profession, but also as a value base'. This seems to imply not just that social work is based very firmly on values (values are part of what constitutes social work), but that social work *is* a set of values. And if values lie so much at the heart of social work, then they would also be very important within the social work professional identity for this team manager. Professional values can be regarded as an expression of a profession's service ideal (see Chapter 2 for discussion of the notion of a 'service ideal').

(3) Professional culture

This is another term used frequently in the literature, often rather loosely, to explain some of the barriers to interprofessional working. At first sight, it would would seem to be a sub-category of 'culture', which is often thought of broadly as a common form of life or 'how we associate with each other' (Carrithers, 1992, p. 2). It is a fairly all-embracing concept. According to Anderson and Englehardt (2001, p. 57), it is 'that grand system that provides for, mediates the process of, and is reproduced by human interaction'. They continue (p. 59):

> Culture is something significantly greater than some simplicity of shared values and meanings. Culture involves major systems of ideology and practice that constitute the conditions of our daily affairs.

They identify these systems as: the semiotic (the system of meaning in language and action); epistemic (truth-making); ethical (rights and wrong); aesthetic (beauty); economic (value exchange); political (allocation); and social (self, other and relationships). No culture operates independently of other cultures – indeed, cultures are enmeshed and embedded in each other. They argue against the suggestion that a corporate organisation constitutes a unique culture, suggesting this is a massive error of scale. Organisations 'colour or mark' the cultural systems in which they are embedded. The same could be said of professions (which are forms of organisations). So, for example, professional groups may mark or modify language (the semiotic system) by activating special vocabularies or discourses – professions are often accused of using 'jargon'. This may happen similarly with knowledge and truth-making (what counts as valid knowledge and justification), the ethical system (implicit and explicit codes, policies, rules), the social system (roles, memberships, boundary issues), and so on.

However, this is not necessarily what the various interviewees mean when they use the term 'professional culture'. As with 'professional identity' and 'professional values', referring to 'professional culture' is a way of distinguishing 'us' from 'them'; marking out 'our ways of doing things' (based on values, language, methods of working) from 'their ways of doing things'. Like 'values' the term 'professional culture' tends to be used when speaking of a difference that has engendered a conflict, dilemma or difficulty.

What we do and who we are: issues of professional identity

Two related themes that came up in the discussions with the youth offending and community safety service, which I have construed as being linked to the notion of 'professional identity', were around the distinctiveness of the different professional roles, and about 'who I am in my work role'.

Initially, in the youth offending team, it was decided that there would be an element of generic working in relation to individual young people. So, for example, any of the professionals in the team might take on a referral and undertake the roles and tasks required in initially assessing a young person's situation and behaviour, completing pre-sentence reports for the courts, working with the young person before and after the court appearance and ensuring they complied with their sentences. Previously such tasks would have been carried out by social workers and probation officers. This could be seen as an example of 'role release' mentioned earlier, where aspects of the primary function of one occupational group are undertaken by team members from other occupational groups. However, this was felt to be inappropriate by some members of the team. The nurse in particular felt strongly about the fact that 'people who come in with professional qualifications ... haven't been able to concentrate on their own profession'. He commented in the group discussion:

> I still want to offer a professional service from a health perspective. I think when we initially started...the irony was that we would all be generic workers. That seemed to be a load of rubbish for us to be employed as professionals with experience and skills within a field, and expected all to do the same job. I think we've got away from that to a certain extent, but I think...we've still got a bit of a hangover from the old system, where people wanted to do far too much by themselves without really needing the professionals within the team. You know, I mean, why do something with regards to, say, health and education, when you've got a health and an education worker within the team who was more able to actually do that?

This was elaborated in his individual interview, where he gave the example of being expected to do pre-sentence reports, for which he was not trained: '...you are expected to make recommendations on how to take somebody's life forward and I did not see I had the training to do that'. He commented that because of his professional registration as a nurse he was not prepared to do anything with which he did not feel comfortable or that he did not feel he was competent to do. He suggested that social workers seemed much happier sharing their responsibilities with people not trained to do those duties, whereas:

> as a nurse, I would be appalled if I went into hospital and I was told that, for example, if I had split my head open, that a social worker was going to stitch my head up.... If I was a parent of a young person and I was told a health worker with no qualifications to do a social worker's job was going to be identified as that person's supervising officer, I would take issue with that.

A youth worker interviewed from another youth offending team expressed similar concerns at having to undertake assessments and work with young people within a 12-week period in connection with final warnings. His approach as a youth worker (rather than as youth offending team member) would be entirely different: he would spend longer with those young people who needed more time. He spoke of the 'youth work dilemma' and not being able to justify 'myself to myself' in closing a case after 12 weeks when the young person was not ready. This is discussed further in the next chapter, but indicates that this practitioner had a concept of himself as a youth worker, a notion of what a good youth worker is, and found it hard to compromise this professional identity.

What we believe and how we act: issues of professional values

As noted earlier, it is hard to distinguish issues of values from issues of professional identity and culture. But I have included in this section accounts of particular incidents where values, or what could be construed as value terms (like 'welfare', 'respect' or 'confidentiality' expressed as a guiding principle or belief), were explicitly mentioned.

An example of value conflict centred around understandings of confidentiality was given by the nurse employed in the youth offending team. When team members were asked for examples of ethical dilemmas or problems encountered in their work, he began his account as follows:

> I think *professional ethics comes from my health background*, especially regarding sharing of information. I mean, when I came here I was basically told that all information, which comes from the young person, should be shared with the rest of the team. Now, *professionally*, I can't do that with certain cases. What I need to know *as a professional*, is that the information that they've given me, you know, has some kind of determining factor on their offending behaviour, before I can share that. I mean, as I say, I was told I have to share everything, but as I explained to the team leader, I mean, I'm dealing with issues such as teenage pregnancy, sexual health. Is that really an issue which needs to be shared with every member of the team? It's a case of how far do you take that? (my italics)

He went on to say: 'as an individual professional, you know, I have the right to decide what is best for the interests of that person who I'm dealing with'. He felt that the pressures coming from the team norms were compromising his professional values as a nurse. He elaborated further, describing how all correspondence coming in to any member of the team, unless explicitly marked 'private and confidential', is opened by the administration staff:

> if somebody forgets to put 'private and confidential', that's opened up ... I'm from a background where if something is addressed to you as an individual, unless you've given prior permission, it isn't opened, because that information may be, you know, for you as an individual as opposed to a team.

This nurse is very conscious of himself as a health professional adhering to the value of individual patient confidentiality. He is aware that section 115 of the Crime and Disorder Act (1998) allows information pertinent to criminal activity to be shared between agencies, but does not feel this should be allowed to erode his strongly held commitment to individual patient confidentiality on health matters. Police and even social work members of the team are much more used to the idea of information belonging to a team or agency and do not have such a strict view of individual confidentiality. Similar issues for nursing staff are noted by B. Williams (2000, p. 6) in his preliminary study of YOTs.

Our way of being and doing: issues of professional culture

Under this heading I will explore some of the more general comments made about the different professions' ways of doing things.

Little has been said so far about the views of police officers in the youth offending and community safety service. This is partly because their concerns were not explicitly couched in terms of threats to professional identity and values. Even their examples of 'ethical dilemmas' tended to be about problematic incidents, or examples of 'poor' practice from other agencies or professionals (outside the team), rather than value conflicts. For example, one of the officers described situations where young people fall between the education and social services departments, and the police repeatedly have to pick up the pieces.

The police officers were reported by managers in the service as being initially concerned to 'stay together' – to sit in the same room and not mix with the other professionals. This was expressed by the head of the service as the police being afraid of a 'dilution of police culture', but this was not mentioned by any of the police officers themselves. From the comments made by the police officers themselves and the other interviewees, it would appear that the police officers who joined the service did so because they were actively interested in interprofessional and community-oriented working. They spoke of wanting a 'challenge', 'a change of direction' and a 'different type of work'. Some of their main difficulties and frustrations lay in their relationships with their colleagues based back in the police station, who might perceive them as having taken a soft option and who did not understand the new 'prevention' culture that was operating in the youth offending and community safety context and should also be permeating the police service. They were still locked into the idea of the police role as primarily about detection and enforcement.

The social work and nursing professionals seemed much more concerned about cultural differences within the service, specifically within the youth offending team. One of the social workers described a situation where he felt uncomfortable about writing a reference for a young person without discussing it with the young person first. His team manager told him there was no need. Another social worker endorsed this point and commented on the fact that she had to do things she did not want to do in the youth offending team. This approach was in contrast to the way of working in the social services team in which she used to work:

> Before, we used to all discuss it even in a team meeting. If it was something like, that we didn't want to do, we would have... the manager we used to have, we used to all get together, discuss it and thrash it out, and everybody would agree, so if you weren't happy with something, you'd say it. Now it seems to be, I don't know, 'you will do it because it's the way we work now'.

Further comments were made about how social workers tend to work:

> as a social worker, when we're training, that's trained into you..., you know, you've got to think it through, plan it, you've got to show how you're thinking, and even if it's something whacky, as long as you can provide the thinking round... prove the reading's been done, and the planning is there and you're doing it for the best reason, you're thinking about the welfare, etc., etc. That was always encouraged.

Later one of the social workers made another comment about the way social workers tend to do things in the context of a debate about whether some young people are 'lost causes':

> Many people who are not social workers probably wouldn't believe this,... but... there are... I've seen examples... of schedule one offending adults [people who have committed serious crimes relating to children] working on their offending, on their risk of offending, and it's a risky plan, but there's work done, and they're looking after kids now. They're bringing their kids up. But they may well have committed quite serious

offences in the past. And the same people [people who are not social workers] would originally have thought 'what's the point?' you know, 'you can't turn them around'. But actually there is some examples of some of them turning around, so that's what the social services side of it will say: 'you can't give up on them'.

Several comments were made by those from a social work background about their concern for the welfare of young people. As a social worker commented to her colleague in the group discussion:

I think that's why it's hard for me and you, isn't it? Because we always had that welfare bit as well. We had to look at the welfare and the needs of the child. Now we're told we don't. We just have to look at what the law says, and if it doesn't matter, then it's their job over the road [the social services department], for the welfare and the needs. And I think we find that very hard, because you can't lose that.

Professional values and ethics as obstructive?

One of the questions this chapter set out to explore, which is raised in the literature, is the extent to which attachment to specific professional values obstructs interprofessional working. Carrier and Kendall (1995, p. 18), for example, imply that this is the case, suggesting that calls for interprofessional collaboration are not easily achieved as they require, among other things, 'a shared set of values concerning appropriate responses to shared definitions of need'. Millen and Wallman-Durrant (2001, p. 150), in relation to community mental health teams, note that interprofessional divisions are played out through respective professional attachments to the medical and social models, and this is a 'sterile focus for professional mistrust'. At a general level the difficulties in achieving a shared set of values seems to apply to the service discussed in this chapter. But whilst perceived value differences may initially, or temporarily, disrupt effective team working, their emergence may then force a negotiation between practitioners, who have to explain and justify their positions and listen to those of others. This happened in the youth offending team when the nurse raised issues around the value attached to one-to-one confidentiality between himself and a service user. This process can create a greater awareness amongst team members of what they are doing and why.

A small piece of earlier research I undertook with ten members of a multi-disciplinary hospital-based team also suggests that the different professionals may value each other's expertise and viewpoints (see Banks, 1998a). As one social worker in this team said: 'I see us as partners or pieces of a jigsaw.' Hallet's research on interagency working in the field of child protection revealed high levels of shared similar concerns between the key professions in handling cases of child abuse. She nevertheless questions whether too much consensus is necessarily good, and suggests that disagreement between different professionals may be productive as 'a brake on the coercive power of the state' (Hallet, 1995, p. 331).

Thus the fact that some values or ethical principles may be stressed by one particular profession while others may be shared between different professions may be regarded as a necessary and positive feature of interprofessional working. This is exemplified in a case I encountered in my research with the hospital-based team concerning an elderly patient whose medical treatment was completed. The doctor argued that the patient should go home, in the interests of releasing a bed for another patient. The social worker argued that the patient should remain in hospital because conditions at home were unsatisfactory and the patient had asked to remain in hospital for longer in order to develop her self-confidence and improve her mobility skills. Here the doctor stressed the promotion of general welfare (the greatest good of the greatest number of people) whereas the social worker emphasised the self-determination of the individual client. They could both understand the arguments of the other, but they were prioritising different ethical principles. This ensures that different interests are debated in the course of decision-making. Indeed, when interviewing each member of the team and asking them to identify the values that informed their work, the two doctors included 'concern for how public money is spent' and 'effectiveness and efficiency' amongst their principles. Both social workers mentioned 'respect' for the service user and also included characteristics such as 'trust' and 'care'. It could be argued that a successful interprofessional team holds a blend of shared goals and values alongside a distinctive contribution from each different professional.

It is interesting that in the youth offending team (and the manager of another YOT who was interviewed also gave a similar story), the initial desire to make many of the key roles and tasks (such as writing pre-sentence reports) interchangeable between the different professionals was dropped. This leaves space for a more organic, gradual and flexible system to develop, according to need and levels of trust, as practitioners and their managers get to know each other's competences and predilections, and the team begins to see its work as a whole. For example, the idea of social workers or members of the youth offending team, who are trained counsellors, taking statements from young people instead of the police when particularly sensitive issues are at stake, might initially be resisted when requested. Yet later in a particular case where it seemed appropriate, it might be agreed to. The head of the youth offending and community safety service stated that, while he valued appointing people to posts from no professional background, without the professional baggage (for example, neighbourhood wardens and some other staff without professional qualifications), he did not want to create a specific team culture and commitment solely to the youth offending and community safety service. He recognised that police officers, for example, had to maintain their professional expertise and skills, and would return to the police after five years. He did not want to turn police officers into 'unqualified youth workers' and create an 'homogeneous blob of a new type of profession'.

Comments were made by several interviewees in the youth offending and community safety service about the difficulties of being a single social worker, youth worker or nurse in a workplace – and the sense of losing their professional identity. Fear was expressed by some other interviewees currently working in social services departments, that when care trusts emerge, local authority social services departments may disappear or diminish in importance. Then the social work culture that could thrive in a department full of social workers might get lost. Yet in other professions, it is quite common for an isolated professional to be employed in an organisation – for example, there might be only one accountant or personnel officer in a small agency. Interprofessional working *per se*, provided that the interchangeability of roles and tasks is well-considered, does not necessarily pose a threat to the notion of separate professions each with their codes of ethics. But it does challenge the professions to decide which aspects of their roles and tasks are core, and creates many difficulties and barriers, although most of these can be overcome.

Concluding comments

From exploring just this case study it is not my intention to reach any general conclusions about the interrelationship between professional ethics and interprofessional working – although the issues raised by these practitioners do echo the findings in other research studies and the literature more broadly. What the analysis presented here suggests is that working in an interprofessional setting seems to have stimulated many of the practitioners interviewed to reflect upon their professional values and identities. They have come to see more clearly the nature of their distinctive roles and values in relation to members of other professional groups with whom they have to work very closely. Far from losing their sense of professional identity, for many of these practitioners, working in an interprofessional context may in fact encourage its strengthening, or at least a selective self-attribution of those characteristics felt to be important for their profession. Arguably, a far greater threat to professional identity and values may come from the increasing development of new accountability requirements for all professionals, which impose procedures, targets and outcomes as discussed in the next chapter.

6

Practitioner perspectives II: the new accountability and the ethics of distrust

Introduction

This chapter explores some of the implications for professional ethics of the changes that have been taking place in the organisation and practice of the social professions in the context of moves towards marketisation, privatisation, and increasing managerialism. These changes are located in a context of the restructuring of the 'welfare state', and a questioning of the legitimacy, trustworthiness and effectiveness of professionals as outlined in Chapter 1 (see, for example, Clarke *et al.*, 2000; Exworthy and Halford, 1999; Jones, 2001; Jordan and Jordan, 2000; Lymbery, 2000; O'Neill, 2002b). The discussion draws on semi-structured, in-depth interviews with 32 practitioners.

The focus of this chapter is on just one aspect of what I call the 'new accountability', namely the development of increasingly detailed procedures for doing tasks and the setting of predefined targets or outcomes for work. The increasing demands of internal and external regulation and audit appear to restrict the space for the exercise of professional discretion and the autonomy of professional decision-making. It would seem, therefore, that these trends pose a serious threat to professional ethics, which entails adhering to a set of principles and norms defined by a professional body (as opposed to an employer or auditing agency) and the ability of and opportunity for the individual practitioner to reflect on the ethics of certain choices and make informed decisions.

After briefly discussing what we might mean by 'accountability', 'the new accountability' and 'professional autonomy', I present some of the views of managers and practitioners on the impact of the increasing use of procedures, guidelines, targets and outcomes in their work. In doing this I attempt to relate my interpretation of their comments to relevant ethical theories or approaches to ethics that were summarised in Chapter 3.

Accountability

To be accountable is literally to be liable to be called upon to give an account of what one has done or not done. The account may include all or some of descriptions, explanations, excuses or justifications. Frequently giving an account is associated with the occurrence of a problematic situation and the apportioning of blame. Indeed, Holdsworth (1994, p. 42) defines accountability as 'the obligation to lay oneself open to criticism'. Accountability has always been important for professionals. According to Tadd (1994, p. 88) it is 'the *sine qua non* of any professional group'. But the kind of accountability stressed by professional bodies is that owed to clients or service users. Service to clients is the essence of professional practice; and any professional, whether a doctor, lawyer, or social worker, must be prepared to account for their actions to people using their services. Although we may dispute how well professionals have implemented it, accountability to service users is integral to the core values of the social professions of respecting service users' freedom of choice, promoting their welfare and challenging discrimination and oppression.

In addition to professional accountability to service users, members of the social professions have always had a duty of public accountability to the wider political community (Clark, 2000, pp. 78–9; Pratchett and Wingfield, 1994, p. 9). They often work directly or indirectly for public bodies, with a role to promote the public good by, for example, protecting the vulnerable and treating or controlling dangerous people. Practitioners and their employers are therefore accountable to the public for the effectiveness of the services they deliver. So the notions of professional and public accountability are at the heart of the social professions, and in both areas demands are increasing. The two are interconnected, as employers are introducing quality standards, standardised assessment forms, contracts and complaints procedures partly in response to demands from service users for their rights to more effective services, to participate in decision-making and to complain. But the accountability demands of different parties may also conflict, and one of the themes of my interviews with practitioners is that in striving for organisational and public accountability, the voices, needs and rights of individual service users and their communities may get lost.

The 'new accountability'

> More than ever before, because I've been in social work for a long time, it seems like accountability is very hot on the agenda – demonstrating outcomes and having to have almost number-crunching-type pieces of information that you can give. (Social work team manager, A)

> ... overbearing procedures equate sometimes to, yes, it gives a checklist as to what processes should be followed every time and that can be quite useful in a number of settings, but, it also can be used as a stick to beat up social workers with if a particular procedure hasn't been followed to the letter. (Social work team manager, B)

> One of my clients hung himself in the garage, yesterday afternoon. The first thing I was asked was 'Is the file up to date?' Because it's so important that the file is up to date and that nobody can be held to be responsible. (Senior social worker)

As already indicated, the importance of accountability in professional life is not new, but what is new, as the first quotation above indicates, is an increasing focus on it. This focus is particularly on public accountability requiring the production of quantifiable outputs and outcomes. The procedures mentioned in the second quotation serve a number of purposes, the most obvious of which is to help social workers do a better job (to improve practice). But since they have been developed in a climate of lack of public confidence in professional competence and organisational systems, they are also designed to be used to *show* a good job has been done (according to accepted standards of good practice), and increasingly, through the use of forms, to collect monitoring data for the 'number-crunching exercises'. The last quotation emphasises the link between accountability, responsibility and 'blame' and the importance of being able to demonstrate that all the required procedures have been followed and documented in order not to be blamed for a bad outcome.

What I have called 'the new accountability' is a complex phenomenon, and there are many reasons for what appears to be an almost
obsessive preoccupation with it. For the purposes of this chapter
I will focus on two interlinked manifestations of the 'new accountability' as outlined below, paying most attention to procedures:

(1) *Working to procedures.* A procedure tells the practitioner how to
do a task or set of tasks, or how to manage a situation. Procedures
may outline a set of stages or steps to be undertaken (for example,
'Procedures for family participation in child protection conferences')
or comprise forms that have to be filled in (for example, 'Assessment
report forms for a registered child: First (3 months) review format').
In a social services context, the number of procedures has been
increasing very rapidly – often in direct response to central government legislation or guidance. The child protection procedures were
the first to be developed in any detail in local authorities in the late
1980s (based on Department of Health, 1988), and were a response
to a series of public inquiries relating to child abuse which often
blamed social workers and social services departments for poor
practice and lack of coordination between agencies. Since then the
community care legislation (1990) brought about a massive change
in the way social workers worked with adults, requiring an emphasis
on assessment, care planning, monitoring and reviewing (Department of Health Social Services Inspectorate, 1991). This trend has
continued, so that in one local authority social services department
I visited in 2001, it was said by the person in charge of 'quality documentation' that there were 999 documents on their intranet system
that applied to the social services department. This included policy
documents, guidance and work instructions, as well as procedures.
Whilst it might be expected to find the kinds of documents mentioned
above in connection with child protection, many of the documents
relate to very specific occasions – for example, 'Celebrations/notable
events' (good practice guidelines for day services) or 'Visits by children
to special hospitals' (which lays out how to request and implement
such a visit, as a direct response to a Local Authority Circular). Outside
the statutory sector the proceduralisation has been less heavy, but
has still been required since many voluntary sector organisations have
contracts or service level agreements with statutory bodies and are
required to demonstrate that they have procedures in place.

(2) *Working to pre-defined standards/targets/outputs/outcomes.* How
these operate depends upon the type of work. Standards are criteria

for judging how well something or somebody fits with the accepted norm or what is regarded as good or best practice. They may be set by central government, local authorities or other agencies. For example, in social services departments there are agency-wide 'Quality Protects' standards for children's services, which link specifically to the central government Quality Protects objectives (Department of Health, 1998c). These are standards of which each practitioner and manager needs to be aware and work towards meeting (such as the standards which state that each child should have a care plan and their views should be taken into account). The standards are often embodied in procedures. Many agencies or particular projects set themselves targets/outputs to work towards (for example, 'reduce youth crime by 10%') and set outcomes for their work ('safer, healthier neighbourhoods'). The last two relate to Single Regeneration Budget (SRB) projects, which are required to set their targets, outputs and outcomes in advance, and then report regularly to the funder (in this case the regional development agencies) on whether and to what extent they are being achieved (see, for example, One NorthEast, 1999). This is crucial to enable monitoring of performance, that is, the matching of performance by individuals, agencies or projects to the pre-defined standards, targets/outputs or outcomes.

The reasons for developing these systems for regulating and auditing practice are varied and interlinked, and have changed gradually over time. The following are some of the factors involved:

- *A growing loss of confidence in professional competence and profess-ional ethics*. For example, the reaction to well-publicised incidents of individual and systemic poor practice, malpractice, and unethical practice leads to the response that the only way to ensure good practice is to prescribe how it should be done and to measure it and monitor it in order to improve performance.
- *An ideological attack on professional power and dominance*, leading to a desire to control professional autonomy at the level of pro-fessional groups and individual professionals.
- *The desire and need (practical) for central control at a time of frag-mentation of service delivery* and the mixed economy of welfare. With increasing private and voluntary sector involvement in service provision, there is felt to be a need to establish controls both at the level of central and local government.

- *A high level of concern (moral) with 'equity'*, which is manifesting itself markedly under the New Labour regime in the UK, leading to a desire for standardisation of treatment and outcomes for recipients of services in order to eliminate or reduce 'postcode variability', professional-determined variability, favouritism or negative discrimination.
- *A concern with promoting the rights of individual service users as consumers* to minimum standards of service; to know what to expect; to be able to complain if standards fall below those agreed/advertised; to choose between services (if available).
- *A concern with the rights of taxpayers to value for money* from publicly funded services, and to see and judge performance so that remedial action can be taken to improve 'failing' services.

It needs little argument to show that the elements of the 'new accountability' mentioned above threaten the assumptions traditionally made about professional ethics (see Banks, 1998b; 2001, pp. 135–58) that were listed in the Introduction to this book. To recap, these are:

1. distinct professional groups exist;
2. these groups have distinct sets of values/ethical principles and rules of professional conduct that are broadly accepted;
3. the first loyalty of the professional lies with the client/service user;
4. professional values come before those of the employing agency or society;
5. professionals make ethical judgements on the basis of ethical values, principles and rules accepted by the profession.

In this chapter the last three assumptions are particularly pertinent, in that the demands of employers seem to be taking precedence over the welfare, needs and respect of the service users; agency values, translated into detailed procedures, are dominating professional activity at the expense of professional values relating to respect for service users, confidentiality and so on; and the scope for professional judgement based on expertise and professional values seems to be seriously constrained by the new accountability requirements. These three assumptions all relate to some extent to the concept of 'professional autonomy', often said to be under attack in the new regime.

So before we look at what the practitioners interviewed said about their work and the issues arising for them in relation to our theme of 'the new accountability', we will first consider what is meant by 'professional autonomy'.

Professional autonomy

'Autonomy' literally means 'self-government' and is generally associated with the notion of freedom of choice. The term 'professional autonomy' can be used to refer to:

- *the freedom of the professional group* to determine the framework of principles, standards or desirable character traits in accordance with which their members practice (as opposed to these being defined externally, by, for example, central government or individual employing agencies);
- *the freedom of choice of the individual professional practitioner* to make decisions about how to act. This is usually regarded as being within the framework defined by the professional group, and we often find the term 'discretion' being used in this context. Alternative interpretations of professional autonomy, which see no distinction between the 'personal' and 'professional' spheres, might argue that professional autonomy is about acting in accordance with the practitioner's personally held values or views about what a 'good' person would do.

Clearly a strong professional body, which we might describe as relatively autonomous, and which produces a lot of guidelines and rules of conduct, will limit the personal autonomy of its individual members to make decisions and act in the light of their judgements about the nature of a particular situation or in accordance with their own values. So when the term 'autonomy' is used in the second sense, in relation to individual practitioners, it does not mean freedom to act in accordance with their own personal moral values and judgements about particular situations: it means freedom to act *qua* professional, according to the professionally described norms and standards. Since professionally defined standards tend to be relatively general (they have to apply to practitioners doing very diverse work in a range of settings – private practice as well as organisations in the private, public and voluntary sector), then 'professional autonomy' usually entails professionals having a considerable amount of freedom in interpreting general principles (like, 'respect confidential information') and judging how to apply them in particular cases. However, in most professions the quantity of guidance and number of more detailed rules is getting greater, as our discussion of codes of ethics in Chapter 4 indicated, so the role of professional judgement within professional autonomy may be getting smaller, or at least the limits within which the judgements are made are getting more defined.

Interviews with practitioners

This chapter draws on interviews with 32 practitioners. Generally these were senior practitioners, with professional qualifications and experience in social work, youth and community work. They included: team managers and senior practitioners in local authority social services departments working in the fields of child protection, child care, community care, mental health, initial assessment and the development of policies and procedures; youth workers in youth offending teams; youth and community workers in local authorities and voluntary sector organisations; and community development practitioners and managers working in voluntary sector, local authority and interagency regeneration settings. The selection of the interviewees, the questions asked and analyses undertaken are outlined in Chapter 5, with further details given in the Appendix. As stressed in Chapter 5, the purpose of these interviews was to explore with practitioners their views on the changes in their work, from which I would draw out the ethical implications to add a practice-based perspective to the book.

The new accountability as practically useful and morally good

In speaking of the changes in their work, very few practitioners spoke in terms of the impact on their 'professional autonomy' or 'professional judgement'. Indeed it was largely those who were defending the new accountability from attack that mentioned these terms. For example, a team manager talking about the child protection procedures commented:

> it's a spurious judgement to say that they [child protection procedures] kind of reduced professional autonomy, because I think . . . procedures are simply frameworks for action. Their [social workers'] professional activity is in terms of the engagement with people in terms of communication, in terms of undertaking the assessment, the understanding and applications, the legal context in which you work, the demonstration of a range of skills and intervention techniques that can actually reduce the risk of harm. I mean, the scope within the procedures to actually apply professional knowledge and expertise is very wide. What the procedures to my mind do is create a forum in which that makes sense.

This statement is arguing that the *procedural framework* does not interfere with the *professional activity*. It is interesting in two ways:

1. It does not acknowledge the concept of a *professional framework* to guide professional activity, which may potentially conflict with the procedural framework (defined by the local authority on the basis of central government guidelines);
2. It assumes that the *procedures are only a framework*, or 'forum', implying that they are not particularly detailed or prescriptive, and so leave plenty of space for professional autonomy.

We will come back to how the practitioners who complain about procedures see the 'framework' later. We will now look in more detail at some of the comments made by practitioners who felt the new accountability requirements to be both useful and morally defensible.

Practical arguments: clarity and focus

The drafters of procedures and other documents, and some team managers, tended to regard them as useful and important. An officer in charge of producing and collating all the 'quality documentation' in a social services department stated:

> Procedures and notes of guidance which are clearly written and easily available will enable front line staff to be well informed and deliver high quality services to end users, without encroaching on the professionalism of social workers.

One of the social workers I spoke to, who was a care manager in an assessment and information team (meaning that she dealt with all the initial referrals and requests that came into the social services department) was also very positive about two new sets of procedures that had recently been introduced: the children in need procedures and the eligibility criteria:

> the minute the new procedures [children in need procedures] came in, it was really clear, and I've had no problem since at all. They were the best thing that happened. Clients know exactly what's happening, and where we're coming from.

> we brought in eligibility criteria last year, which I think are important. It clarifies what we're doing, when we do it and who we do it for, which we didn't have...I'm much more confident now in saying to a client that I cannot provide something and why I can't provide it, which I wasn't before.

These comments echo those made by this worker's line manager and the standards and development officer who was involved in developing the children in need procedures: that they provide clarity and focus, and help social workers do their jobs better and more easily. When asked about the changes taking place in social work, the standards and development officer commented positively on 'clarity and transparency in the fact that there are now standards for everything'.

The manager of the assessment and information team recollected previous practice with horror:

> I think going back to when I first did child protection work in the mid-'80s, I think back to some of the practice that went on that was kind of...and it's just horrific to think people could...you know, you could have a meeting about people and they wouldn't even know it was taking place, decisions were made without any kind of consultation with them, you know. So in many respects it's kind of...sociological, societal, cultural change in terms of professions as not being wholly expert, about being open to scrutiny, open to accountability, much more inclusive in the way that information is used and shared.

Ethical arguments: rights, equity, accountability and outcomes

The comment quoted above suggests that in addition to practical arguments relating to clarity and focus there are ethical arguments for regarding aspects of the new accountability positively, which are now summarised.

(1) *The rights of service users* are enhanced. This relates to the rights of service users to know what criteria are being used to judge them, how decisions are made, to involvement in the decision-making and having the information to enable them to complain about poor standards of service. This is emphasised by the following comment made by the standards and development officer: 'Previously people haven't really known what they should get from us and whether they should be satisfied or what have you.'

(2) *Equity in access to services and standards of services delivered* is felt to be very important. As the assessment and information team manager commented in relation to the new eligibility criteria, which were designed to tackle the differences in criteria being used by different sections of the social services department: 'What they've tried to do is create that uniformity and equity of access to services.' He also commented on the most recent restructuring away from area-based management as being 'to do with equity, because it was quite clear different areas had different standards, . . . they were dependent on where you lived'.

(3) *Accountability is enhanced.* Having called the kinds of changes I am looking at the 'new accountability', it may seem somewhat tautological to list 'improved accountability' as one of their positive features. However, it is worth stating that some interviewees mentioned accountability as important and felt that the introduction of procedures, standards, monitoring and so on did genuinely increase the accountability of practitioners, although they did not always specify to whom (service users, employers, government or public, for example). As the same team manager commented:

> looking back over the development of practice over the past 20 years, I would consider it to be on the whole largely a positive development, simply because I think that within that kind of bureaucracy of management, I suppose has become a level of accountability that didn't exist before.

The manager of a large regeneration project (a qualified community worker), when asked about being required to work to targets and monitor outputs for the funders (the regional development agency), said: 'I'm an absolute convert to it', explaining:

> You have to monitor . . . and also in order to claim your money, at least once every three months, you've got to sit down and look at how you're

doing it. Have I met my targets? And then you've got to report to some-body else, and there's some accountability for that.

(4) *A focus on the outcomes of professional intervention* is also thought to be a very positive development. The same regeneration manager spoke in terms of 'needing evidence of progress' and the opportunities that a focus on planning with outputs and outcomes in mind gives for strategic thinking. The standards and development officer felt it was very important to look not just at the process of social work, but at what is being achieved, such as how many times a young person looked after by the local authority has been moved, their educational achievements, and so on:

> I was very excited about Quality Protects when it came in. And I think it still has the ability to improve things in that it does make you focus on whether you're getting the right result, and certainly in the benchmark-ing group that I'm part of....we do have very useful discussions about what's really achieving good outcomes and what practices are working, and which authorities are doing different things.

These ethical arguments are largely from a utilitarian perspective (see Chapter 3). They focus on the promotion of welfare and justice, looking to the outcomes of practice and acting on what seems to produce the greatest amount of good for the greatest number of people (see Banks, 2001, pp. 30–4; Shaw, 1999). The rights of service users that are stressed are more akin to the contract rights of consumers or customers, as opposed to the traditional right to 'respect for persons' (reminiscent of Kantian ethics) based on a trusting relationship with a professional (see Koehn, 1994).

The new accountability as unhelpful and morally dubious

Those managers, document drafters and practitioners who feel the new accountability requirements are generally positive, nevertheless recognise that many practitioners complain and find difficulties with them. For example, they may ignore them, as the quality documenta-tion officer commented: 'I think you've got some team managers who've been here since the year blob and they use the manual to prop the wonky table up.' This implies that there are some team managers and social workers that are resistant to change, perhaps irrationally. A standards and development officer, whose job it is to prepare standards and develop quality in the child care field, spoke about those staff who say: 'I didn't come into social work to fill in forms, sit in front of computers', suggesting that:

> there has got to be a culture change that says actually that's a very import-ant part of the job...and it's not going to go away, and those people just had to go. They had to recognise that the job was not for them any more.

Practical arguments: too many procedures

There may be other reasons, apart from resistance to change, why people are not using the procedures and guidance. Some of the man-agers and practitioners I interviewed who could be described as quite 'modern and go-ahead', still had trouble using them. One of the main issues is that there are too many procedures. As a child care team manager commented: 'I've seen a major shift. I've been totally over-procedure driven. There are just too many procedures.' This team manager went on to give an example of a particular case that had arisen where the local authority shared responsibility for a child with the parent, but the parent was not exercising responsibility. The issue arose as to who within the organisation could give agreement for consent to medical treatment for the child:

> it turned out we were looking at three sets of procedures that all overlapped. That included our 'children in need procedures', our 'children looked after procedures' and our 'children's homes procedures'. It is completely ridicu-lous to think that either as a practitioner, or as an operational manager, that anyone, at any given time, can be aware of everything written in those procedures – when they're just three – when you've got additional proced-ures for child protection, fostering regulations, schedules in the Children Act that you've got to follow, that I would say are a procedure in itself.

The quality documentation officer I interviewed was well aware of these issues. So one response has been to put all the relevant policies, procedures, guidance and work instructions on the local authority intranet system, which means they are all in one place, can be searched easily, and practitioners can be sure that they are looking at the most up-to-date version. Alongside the intranet database has come a new system for reviewing and updating the procedures, whereby the officers in charge of updating are contacted at the appropriate interval and drafts can be exchanged via the intranet. However, this will not help the 'Luddites' identified earlier, as this child care social worker exemplifies:

> *Interviewer:* Yes. Let's go back to these sets of procedures. I was looking at all the books…that are now being recalled, because it's now all on the intranet.
> *Social worker:* Intranet, yes.
> *Interviewer:* And so do you use the intranet to look at them?
> *Social worker:* No. I should do. I should do, and I probably could access them should I need to. I'm not a computer sort of person, and I have no interest sitting playing with the computer. Some people spend all lunch hour…

Furthermore, the intranet system, though helpful in bringing together all the relevant documentation in its most up-to-date form, does not solve the problem of 'procedure overload' – it is just a way of handling even more – especially for those that are responsible for creating and reviewing them.

Both the quality documentation officer and the standards and development officer mentioned earlier were very aware that busy practitioners do not have time to read the procedures, and that many of them are not user-friendly. So another response is to try to make them shorter, more succinct and better laid out. The standards and development officer showed me the latest booklet for 'children in need', explaining how 'the previous procedures had just got ignored' and she has been trying to 'reduce huge tomes down to small booklets that can be used':

> The thing is, I mean, they can put this in their bag and take it out with them. And the standards are on one side of A4 in here…the standards are actually single-sided things.

She commented that she is trying to include things that people can actually use as tools as well, and pointed to a 'nice little grid' that she had devised to help practitioners assess levels of concern about children (mild, moderate and severe). Yet although the new procedures had been introduced a year ago, when asked if people were actually using the grid, she said: 'The problem with anything is actually getting people to change their patterns of practice. So we're not finding people using this grid.'

Practical and ethical arguments: the forms are too prescriptive

Some of the managers and the officers involved in developing the quality documentation believe that some of the resistance to using the procedures and forms stems from a misunderstanding about how to use them. According to the quality documentation officer:

> it's partly really how people see the forms themselves and how they choose to use it, and probably...they see it as the be all and end all. And if they get it out at the beginning, that's the whole rationale for being there. It makes the encounter with the clients something different...

> But we're not asking you to go and say to the client 'Right, I've come to fill a form in.' It should not make any difference to your professional social work face-to-face contact with that client, whether you sort of say at the end of the interview 'I've got to jot a few things down, otherwise I might forget', or whether you take it back to the office and then fill it in, is entirely up to you. But we're not trying to influence that professional relationship. What we're trying to make sure is that you are able to record the information you need, the department gets the information it needs, and at the end of the day the client gets what they need.

However, many social workers recognise, in fact stress, that the forms should not be the 'be all and end all' of an encounter with a client. Indeed they tell of ways they have found of coping with this in their practice, as a care manager told me:

> Well, it depends how you use the forms. You have to do an assessment and you have to put the assessment on the computer...So I tend not to use the form, I just write it in my notebook. So that's the way I've evolved to deal with the fact that the form was not particularly helpful.

But she still talks about covering 'the elements required' – so in that sense her encounter with the service user is partly structured by the information she knows she is required to collect. Although experienced practitioners can be flexible and sensitive, these practitioners still feel the procedures and forms are unduly influencing their work with the service users. One of the features of standardised forms designed to cover everybody's needs and every eventuality is that inevitably questions are asked that are completely irrelevant and inappropriate to the particular people and circumstances with which a social worker is working. This was felt quite strongly by several social workers. Another senior practitioner I interviewed explained why she changed from working with older people at the time when the community care legislation was being introduced in the late 1980s. This practitioner (currently a team manager in a child protection team) refers to the detailed assessment schedules community care managers are required to complete. One of the criticisms of the legislation and the care management approach is that it is not about producing holistic assessments of people's needs, but more concerned with rationing of care services (Stanley, 1999; Taylor and White, 2000, p. 148). The forms focus on 'health, self-care and functional needs', neglecting more personal and individualised aspects:

> *Team manager*: I was very disillusioned with the community care legislation that came in, which I felt very much changed the focus of what we were doing, and got quite upset about that really, as did many of my colleagues. Some of them have stuck with it and learned to live with it, or whatever you do. But I didn't feel it gave me the capacity to do the job properly, and I didn't want to go and see somebody who wanted a day-centre place and ask if they could change a light bulb, you know. It's just...forms...
> *Interviewer*: So the aspects that you didn't like were all the forms...?
> *Team manager*: The forms, that's right. People fitting into boxes. Get to know the people, get to understand them, where they're coming from and then look at what their needs are. Rather than, I felt, foisting on them, fit into this category, or that category, and how much will it cost, was very much the order of the day.

There are several features of this extract that exemplify certain ways of thinking and feeling about the move towards proceduralisation that have ethical implications:

- This practitioner mentions her *feelings*: she got 'upset' about the changes in the work. This suggests that it affected her deeply, perhaps *her sense of who she was*, and certainly her professional identity.
- She says she didn't feel the new community care regime gave her the capacity to do the job properly. This indicates she has a vision of *what the role of a good social worker is/should be*.
- The significance of the next statement, that she 'didn't want to go and see somebody who wanted a day-centre place and ask if they could change a light bulb' embodies a number of issues. It is about the fact that in order to offer someone a day-centre place certain

fixed criteria would be used, which may mean that people who need to have a place in her view, cannot get one. She comments later in the interview about people's emotional needs not being taken into account.

- Further, the fixed criteria for assessing this person's need *will not allow this person to be treated as a whole person, in a very particular context, with very specific and idiosyncratic needs*.
- Using the standard assessment forms may mean having to spend time *asking irrelevant questions, which seem disrespectful to the service user*.
- She *didn't want to be the kind of person* who asked people irrelevant or inappropriate questions and assessed them on standard criteria, fitting them into boxes and foisting them into categories.

These kinds of comments link with approaches to ethics that take as their starting point the role of the good professional, the characteristics she or he should have, placing emphasis on relationships and commitments in particular situations. These are the emphases of virtue ethics, an ethics of proximity, the ethic of care and other 'feminist' or 'existentialist' approaches to ethics as outlined in Chapter 3 under the heading of 'partial situated approaches'.

The team manager mentioned earlier is giving an account of the reasons for her decision to change her area of work that seems to be expressed much more in terms of a personal, situated voice than an impartialist one. Although it may seem as though I am reading a lot into this extract, some of my interpretation comes from later discussions in the interview about how this practitioner views herself and her work. It has also been developed out of comments made by other practitioners, which seem to echo some of these themes. As one social worker commented: 'You can spend so much time ticking boxes that you can actually forget that there's people that need to be helped.'

Ethical arguments: vocation, trust, sensitivity and context

In studying the comments of the managers and workers who expressed unease about the use of procedures, forms and the monitoring of outputs, there were several interrelated themes that they seemed to touch upon. I will outline these below, stressing that the terminology used to identify these themes is mine, and was not used by the workers themselves (who tended to talk in the way the team manager quoted above spoke). These themes relate to concepts of vocation; trust; sensitivity; and particularity/context (which link to a partialist approach to ethics). They are very different from the kinds of themes, and the actual language used, by those (usually, but not always) managers who felt that on balance the development of standards, procedures and so on was generally beneficial. The focus of the latter was on good outcomes; accountability; equity; and service users' rights (which can be linked to an impartialist approach).

(1) Vocation

None of the interviewees actually mentioned the term 'vocation', and the interviews did not specifically ask people why they came into the work (although some people did give this information). Indeed, it seems a rather old-fashioned term to use and also an unrealistic ideal in the current climate of public service work (we may think of the paradigm example of someone being 'called' to the priesthood, for example). However, in talking about their responses to some of the changes taking place in the work, several interviewees made comments suggesting that they felt the ideals of the profession should cohere with their personal values. According to Blum (1994, p. 104), 'an individual with a vocation must believe deeply in the values and ideals of the vocation and must in some way choose or at least affirm them for herself'. Bellah and colleagues (1988, p. 66) distinguish between work as a 'job' (a way of making money and a living, supporting a sense of self defined by economic success and security); a 'career' (which traces progress through life by advancement in an occupation and yields a self defined by prestige, and a sense of expanding power and competency); and 'calling' (where work constitutes a practical ideal of activity and character that makes a person's work morally inseparable from his or her life, and self is subsumed into a community of disciplined practice and sound judgement whose activity has meaning and value in itself, not just in the outputs or profits).

While not wanting to suggest that many social professionals conceive of their work as a vocation in the strongest sense, for some it seemed to be tied up with their sense of self in a slightly stronger way than it would be in a 'career'. For example, a youth worker who had become a manager of a youth offending team (a different team from the one described in Chapter 5) and then decided to quit the job after about a year made the following comment:

> And in one respect, as I say, I'm not particularly proud of the fact that I did kind of jump ship, to excuse the pun, you know. But if I hadn't have, *I think it would have a lasting effect on my own self really.* (my italics)

This worker was not talking about the stress of being a manager, but of the way in which the job demanded that he treated young people. Another youth worker who had joined a youth offending team (and was still working there) gave details of the very detailed forms he was supposed to complete about the young people at the beginning and end of interventions (which should only last 12 weeks) made in connection with final warnings. The forms were essential as they were required by the Youth Justice Board to be entered into the national computerised monitoring system. He made the following comment:

> I'm in very big trouble at the YOT, because I've got cases that are nearly a year old now. And I keep trying to explain, this is about the youth work dilemma thing, I keep trying to explain that I'm about the process of trying to get this young person from here to somewhere. Going in rattling at them for 12 weeks is going just to produce nothing, because when I shut the case and walk away in 12 weeks' time, they will either fall off the perch again and get themselves in trouble and then they've got three offences going to court, and *I can't justify that myself to myself.* (my italics)

This practitioner also refers to 'himself' and implies that he has a view of what good youth work is and of himself as a youth worker. These kinds of comments could be conceptualised as being about 'conscience' or about 'professional identity' as well as 'vocation'. But whatever way they are described, they indicate a sense of a self that is bound up with the job. And aspects of the 'new accountability' seriously offend against this sense of self.

(2) Trust

According to Gambetta (1988, p. 219), 'trusting a person means believing that when offered the chance, he or she is not likely to behave in a way that is damaging to us'. Smith (2001), following

Tonkiss and Passey (1999) and Seligman (1997), distinguishes between confidence in systems and trust in people. Confidence refers to relations that 'are secured by contract or other institutionalised roles', whereas trust serves to guide ethical relations that are not subject to external controls. Trust implies a kind of personal engagement on the basis of which we believe others will not let us down. Smith (2001, p. 293) gives the example of having confidence in an airline company and in the pilot's knowledge and ability to fly the plane, whereas trust lies 'in a belief that the pilot cares about my well-being and that the cabin crew will care enough to help me if the plane crashes'. According to Seligman (1997, quoted in Smith, 2001, p. 291), trust arises in the gaps 'between and around institutional roles'. This view of trust would suggest that as the frameworks of rules, procedures and guidelines get tighter, then the space for trust between professionals and service users gets smaller. If, for example, young people's reoffending behaviour becomes a negative statistic for the agency involved, then the worker may be less willing to take a risk in working with a young person. In the case of child protection, as one social worker commented:

> We're told repeatedly from the director down, if in doubt remove the child. It's easier to defend ourselves by over-reacting than by under-reacting. The message is: 'do it'. It may cause problems, but far better those problems than the child die or injured. The element of risk is lost. You lose a lot of cooperation with parents, a lot of partnership... It [the suspected child abuse] can be just the result of a phonecall and things can't be properly checked out. (Emergency duty team social worker)

Just as the social workers are unable to trust the service users, equally the service users are not willing to trust in the kinds of people (social workers) who behave like this. One child care social worker felt very aggrieved that the priority given to child protection in her team meant that she would often have to drop her 'routine' commitments to young people, which she felt were very important. On the day of the interview, she had planned to take a birthday present up to a children's unit for one of the young women for whom she was the social worker. But she had just received a phone call to say that 'there's a child protection coming in on one of my existing cases' and so that would have to take priority. This theme came up again later, in the context of discussing prioritising her time:

A situation could happen like ... you've got ... little Johnny, for example, [whom] you haven't seen for ages, and you've made an arrangement to go to McDonald's for tea and made arrangements to take him to the park and do something with him. And you know, it's important to him, he hasn't seen you for weeks. And then suddenly child protection or something, somebody downstairs ... what's priority? Why should he be left? You know, you ring up and cancel. [And he thinks] 'well, I'm not important now', because that's taken over.... And I know it's life, but ... it's difficult juggling balls and I think we're quite often on a knife edge.

This social worker wants to be the kind of person who is trustworthy, who keeps her promises and who cares about the young people on her 'caseload'. Part of her role is to develop relationships with the young people who are looked after by the local authority, and the kinds of relationships she is expecting (and some of the young people might be expecting) are trusting relationships, which, as was said earlier, imply a kind of personal engagement on the basis of which people believe others will not let them down. Little Johnny will be let down when she cancels the outing; and although this social worker recognises that 'this is life', and we often do have to respond to urgent needs at the expense of other commitments, she seems to feel particularly powerless – in the hands of 'somebody downstairs' who takes away the possibility of her caring, of being trusted, of being the kind of person who does not let others down. She recognises that the nature of her job, which includes both child care and child protection responsibilities, contains this kind of conflict inherently within it. But it is unsatisfactory, and is the result of a recent reorganisation, which merged these two types of work together.

(3) Sensitivity

Moral sensitivity can be defined as 'the awareness of how our actions affect others', and as such it requires the ability to empathize and imagine ourselves in another person's shoes. I would like to use the term here in a slightly broader sense to include what Blum (1994, pp. 30–61) calls 'moral perception', which involves people seeing various moral features of situations confronting them – which might include noticing someone's discomfort, recognising their hopes, fears, resentments or pain, or seeing a threat or a danger inherent in a situation. As Blum (p. 30) comments: 'one of the most important moral differences between people is between those who miss and those who see various moral features of situations confronting them'. Vetlesen (1994) explores in some depth the nature of moral perception, which he sees as a precondition to making moral judgements. He suggests (p. 6) that the morally relevant features of a situation are 'the features that carry importance for the weal and woe of human beings involved'. He argues that moral perception in turn rests on the faculty of empathy, which is a disposition to develop concern for others. Vetlesen regards empathy as an emotion, but is concerned to distinguish this from a mere feeling (such as an impulse of pity or anger), which is why he calls it a 'faculty'. Like several recent philosophers (see, for example, Blum, 1994; Goldie, 2000; Nussbaum, 2002; Oakley, 1992; Stocker with Hegeman, 1996), he is concerned to rehabilitate the role of emotion in ethics and argues that 'in a distinct emotion there is a blend of affectivity and cognition' (Vetlesen, 1994, p. 78). He distinguishes this from a feeling, which is 'rawer' and has a quality of being so close that the subject is virtually engrossed in it, whereas emotion involves a step back, and 'adds an element of reflection absent in the feeling', signifying a more mature stance towards the object of emotion and a stronger element of interpretation and evaluation. This echoes Blum's (1994, pp. 173–82) account of the 'altruistic emotions' (such as empathy, sympathy and compassion, which are grounded in a concern for the 'weal and woe' of others), which can be distinguished from 'personal feelings' (such as liking and affection, which are grounded in personal, but not necessarily moral, characteristics of the other person).

Echoing the comments made by the team manager who said she did not want to have to ask someone who wanted a day-care place whether he could change a light bulb, a child care social worker gave several instances of situations in which she had felt uncomfortable in following the social services department's procedures. She gave the example of a couple she had to visit and assess in connection with removing a child from a child protection register. The department had had no contact with them for two years, but in order to go through the process of deregistering the child, the social worker had to assess them:

We've got to follow our procedures with no thought as to how the family might perceive the situation.

The department shouldn't expect us to, you know, suddenly to enter into somebody else's life for their own procedures

The social worker giving this account seems to see such situations as representing unwarranted intrusions into people's lives and is sensitive to how this must make them feel. She talks not in terms of abstract moral rights (such as, 'What right do we have to interfere?'), but concern about the family's perceptions when a social worker enters into their lives. She appears to empathise with how the family members must view this intrusion, and therefore perceives the situation as one of moral relevance. The type of moral encounter depicted here is what Hoffman (2000, pp. 3–4) calls the 'transgressor' situation – that is, the social worker sees herself as harming, or about to harm, someone, and the moral issue is: 'does one refrain from harming the other or at least feel guilty afterwards?' From how the social worker continued with her story, it is clear that as she started the process of following the procedures, she felt guilty about what she was doing to the family, and therefore, after a period of six months, and despite the request of a case conference that she continue, she called a halt to the process and went back to the conference and recommended deregistration without further ado.

(4) Particularity and context

This links with the importance of taking into account the particular features of each situation and the people involved in deciding what action is necessary or appropriate. The social worker above judged that there was no need to undertake further visits to assess a family who found her attention intrusive. She gave other examples where the requirements of the forms she had to fill in meant she had to ask unnecessary questions. A social worker may go to visit the family of a young boy because he is having particular problems. But the worker has to ask all the standard questions on the assessment form designed to cover every eventuality:

> You're there probably because he is, you know, taking drugs down the town! And his behaviour's uncontrollable and he's taking all the food out [of] the house. You know what I mean? [And you're asking the question:] 'Does he wet the bed?' Well, you feel stupid, you know.

One of the child care team managers I interviewed was very clear that often it is necessary to override the procedures because of the

particular features of a situation that do not fit the policy or procedures. However, he never 'turned a blind eye', but would ensure that
the reasons for not following a procedure were fully documented.
He gave several examples where decisions had been taken in this
way. He spoke of borderline child protection cases where he would
aim to minimise the harm and intrusion to the family being investigated on the basis of a third-party suspicion:

> If we could identify from the outset that there were certain things we
> didn't need to follow in the interests of that particular case or child,
> then we'd record that in the writing of the strategy minutes. We'd also
> record if there was a feeling of why we wouldn't video interview a
> person who'd made a disclosure when the procedure might say given the
> age of child that'd be the right thing to do...It's about being very
> conscious of the individual needs of the people we're trying to serve.
> I would never override the individual needs of a young person or family
> just because our procedure said at that point that x, y, or z needed to
> happen.
>   Recently we placed an eight-year-old boy in a small children's home.
> Our guidance and procedures say we would never place a child under the
> age of 12 unless there were exceptional circumstances. We recorded reasons
> why the placement was going to be made, we sought approval from both
> service manager level and head of service...and made the placement.
> I would see that as working outside the authority's procedures.

This manager's views about procedures were as follows:

> My preference would be to see a minimisation of procedures. With that it
> brings an ability to actually follow them more appropriately and to have
> an in-built flexibility within there. Because I don't necessarily see that
> huge procedures equals good practice and I've seen a lot of good practice
> take place well outside procedural guidance.

Towards 'good practice': interweaving equity and empathy, or 'just caring'

If we take up this theme of 'good practice', then we may ask: how is it
constructed, how is it achieved and how does it encompass 'ethically
good practice'? The standards and development officer working in
the social services department, whose job it is to develop guidance
and procedures, made this comment:

When you boil it down, and you actually say what are the key processes, and then you say what are the key standards relating to those processes, you come down to just core basic *good practice*, every time. You just come back down to fairly straightforward basic aspects of practice that haven't changed at all, and don't change. And if people were only able to do *good practice*, they would actually fulfil the umpteen different plans and programmes and what have you. But most of the time people are bamboozled by the fact that there's 15 documents, 700 different plans and there's another new initiative on the desk, and . . . but most of the time things . . . there's very little new in anything that's said. (my italics)

The practitioner as designer–tailor

Let us take 'good practice' as practice that meets people's needs, achieves good outcomes, is sensitive and fair. That is, it involves a balance between approaches focusing on both the personal and impersonal; the partial and impartial; and on professional detachment and attention to relationships in a particular context. Trying to ensure good practice with a focus largely on standards, procedures or proformas is inevitably a 'one size fits all' approach. It is like starting with a pattern for a suit, which the practitioner then has to cut to size. The focus of attention is on taking bits of the pre-existing pattern that the practitioner needs, rather than starting with what size the customer is, or what kind of suit she or he wants. The practitioners' skills and creativity as designers or tailors are scarcely utilised, for fear that they will make a mistake, cut too generously or stitch too large (cf. Schön's (1991) notion of 'professional artistry'). Alternatively, to make the same point in a different way, the technicist discourse, the prescribed ways of seeing and doing, leave little space for alternative moral voices of empathy, care, particularity, or, indeed, personal or professional responsibility. The fact that these skills, qualities and voices are being ignored is what some of the practitioners I interviewed objected to, or found hard. As a child care social worker said, quite indignantly, in connection with having to ask whole sets of questions that were irrelevant to the people with whom she was working:

you can go into a family, and I think, I've been working in this business [for a long time] and can more or less suss out what's going on within, say, half an hour, and I think I ask the right questions.

The practitioner as fair assessor

Earlier we mentioned an assessment grid for children in need that had been devised by the standards and development officer quoted above, of which she was quite proud. However, she acknowledged that few people were actually using it. I did discover one person who was using it to good effect, and that was a social worker in the social services department assessment and information team. It fits her role well, which is to assess people quickly and fairly (to screen) and then pass them on to whichever social work team or service they require, if any. Some standard criteria are essential in a role like this, and we noted earlier that this worker reported feeling more confident in her job once the department adopted eligibility criteria for services. She felt happier about what she was doing, and that she was being fair. Yet the child care social worker quoted above was not interested in using the assessment grid. She is an experienced worker; she will develop deeper relationships with people, getting into the details and complexities of their lives as a whole, and the grid does not really help her. For her, the particularities of each family, the context in which they are living and the relationships they have with her and with each other, will be all-important. Different workers doing different kinds of jobs are, not surprisingly, speaking in different 'moral voices' and hence describe and justify their decisions and actions with reference to different types of ethical evaluation.

Balancing equity and empathic care

In the drive for equity and accountability, however, it appears that sensitivity and relationships with individual service users are under-emphasised and the skills and qualities of social professionals in these areas are under-utilised. Inevitably this creates tensions, and raises the question of whether there can be a balance. Can we have equitable services delivered in a caring manner? An example given by a social services team manager in relation to the 'looked-after children' records (a national system developed by the Department of Health) highlights these tensions. He commented that he thinks it is very helpful for records to be kept about young people's lives when they are 'looked after' by the local authority, so that they can refer to them in later life as adults. They have a right to have information about themselves, which, had they been living in their birth family, might have been remembered or recorded by their parents. However, many of the young people themselves do not like making these recordings, which inevitably seem like a chore at the time. So often the social workers do not complete them (claiming that they do not wish to foist the task onto the young people). On the one hand, this could be interpreted as morally reprehensible, ignoring the requirements of the agency, as well as the future good of the young people. Yet, on the other hand, reported as a sensitive gesture on the part of the social workers to how these young people feel now, it could be regarded as exhibiting the moral qualities of empathy, caring, attentiveness and sensitivity. The social workers who have rejected the demands of the recordings obviously frame their accounts and moral evaluations in the latter sense, as we have seen in some of the interviews. This is one way of constructing themselves morally, as empathic, caring and sensitive workers (see Hall *et al.*, 1997, for a discussion of the construction of 'social work stories'). The team manager's arguments for completing the records rest on impartialist concerns about rights and welfare.

In the language of Gilligan, these are different 'moral voices' – two sides of the 'duck-rabbit' figure discussed in Chapter 3. They are both relevant, for neither can offer a complete picture of the ethical domain, but they are incommensurable. How they relate to each other, which voice is dominant in particular types of work and situations and who uses these voices is an important issue (see Hekman, 1995, who argues that there are many moral voices, but for simplicity in this discussion we will stick with two). At the present time, the impartialist voice is dominant, and in order to achieve the impartiality and accountability required, there has been a shift away from the traditional notion of professional ethical principles put into practice by practitioners using a fair degree of autonomy and discretion, towards an emphasis on predefined rule-following and targeting. Whilst in some areas of professional life and in some situations this may be regarded as appropriate, in others it is not. The aspects of being a professional that relate to belonging to an occupational group that has a core purpose or 'service ideal' (such as 'social welfare'), to a notion of 'good practice' as defined by a community of practitioners, to the inclusion of motives, emotions and character traits in ethical evaluations (including care, empathy, compassion, for example), are being undermined. What we are left with are practitioners who are being construed as more akin to technicians or technical experts, rather than reflective, creative, committed professionals.

We noted in Chapter 3 that there are some commentators (for example, McBeath and Webb, 1991) who see this as signalling the end of professional ethics. Yet whilst McBeath and Webb note the stress on the technical elements in the practice of making assessments, calculating risk and monitoring performance, they do not take into account the fact that an important rationale and justification for this technical practice is made in ethical terms. The aim is to promote 'good outcomes' and 'equity' – to work for outcomes for people that improve the quality of the services they receive and hence the quality of their lives and to distribute these outcomes fairly, according to need. These are utilitarian values. Utilitarianism is an ethical theory, which has a view of the nature of right action, which is about promoting good outcomes – 'the greatest good of the greatest number'. These universal values may well contradict some of the individualist and technicist language and practice of the social professions, but they are nevertheless still present in the discourse of the policy-makers and some of the practitioners who defend the new accountability, as the extracts from the practitioner interviews in this chapter have demonstrated.

In response to the critiques made by Bauman (1993, 1995), and others mentioned in Chapter 3, of the impartialist, rational-technical approach being manifested in many organisations that employ professionals and other workers, du Gay (2000, pp. 56–7) argues, using the example of postal workers, in defence of 'bureaucracy':

> Thankfully we do not depend upon the personal moral propensities of our postmen and women to ensure our mail is delivered, but rather on... a set of 'abstract membership rules' that link wage remuneration with a codified set of professional obligations.

Du Gay (p. 59) talks of there being plural spheres of life which give rise to 'quite different ethical personae that are non-reducible' (that is, personal, bureaucratic and so on). Although bureaucracy depersonalises, relies on impartial rules and deals only with parts of people's lives, it has a role and its own set of internally consistent ethical standards. He gives the examples of 'equality before the law' and the notion of 'one person one vote', which rely on depersonalising every facet of a person's life apart from their position as a legal person, or role as a voter, respectively.

So, we may conclude that the rule-governed ethos of the bureaucracy or institution (based on an impartialist, detached approach to ethics) is important, but it is only one aspect of what it means to be ethical in a professional context, as some of our interviewees have suggested. Furthermore, an excess of impersonal rules can inhibit personalised treatment, the taking of personal responsibility for actions, the development and use of moral perception, a sensitivity to context and the motivation and commitment to challenge inhumane or ineffective rules and procedures. Arendt (1963), in studying the testimony of Eichmann in relation to his part in killing the Jews, noted that his actions seemed to spring not from base personal motives or strong ideological convictions, but simply from the following of orders unthinkingly. Vetlesen (1994, pp. 85–125), on the other hand, sees Eichmann's failure not as one of an intellectual deficiency, but as an emotional failure, that is, on the level of moral perception, which is based on the faculty of empathy. Eichmann saw himself as a mere cog in a wheel, a means to someone else's end, and therefore 'as not responsible for the total consequences of his highly specialised and fragmented contribution' (Vetlesen, 1994, pp. 91–2). Although it may seem too easy to cite the holocaust in an argument cautioning against institutionalised rule-following, I will nevertheless end with Vetlesen's comments about Eichmann (p. 111):

> Eichmann failed to exercise judgement, because he robbed himself of the requisite for doing so, namely his autonomy.

Concluding comments

The selections from the interviews with practitioners presented in this chapter suggest that those who are sceptical about the overall contribution of the 'new accountability' to good or ethical practice have a particular view of what good practice comprises. This differs from the vision of good practice of those who view accountability requirements more favourably. Those who regard the 'new accountability' as practically useful and morally good tend to justify their views with reference to utilitarian and rights-based arguments relating to the promotion of good outcomes, the achievement of equity, respecting the consumer rights of service users and the rights of other stakeholders to information and value for money. Those practitioners who view the new accountability requirements as cumbersome, restrictive and morally dubious seem to speak in a different 'moral voice', which can be linked to more personal and situated approaches to ethics, stressing the importance of particular relationships in context, of trust, sensitivity and a sense of 'vocation'. Both 'voices' are part of professional practice, but the new accountability is stressing the former at the expense of the latter.

7

Called to account: the response of the social professions

Introduction

This chapter draws on the previous chapters to offer some tentative conclusions to our exploration of the theme of professional ethics in the context of the changing social professions. It discusses the constantly shifting ground of professional ethics, the ethical challenges faced by practitioners and some of their responses.

The shiftiness of 'professional ethics'

This book set out to explore the implications for professional ethics of certain changes in the organisation and practice of the social professions. To do this we first had to explore the nature of 'professional ethics' – a task that has, in fact, occupied over half of the book. For what counts as 'professional ethics' depends both on our view of professionalism and our view of ethics. Not only does 'professional ethics' have several meanings informed by different theoretical and ideological positions, but 'the behaviour captured by the concept... is itself informed by the concept in question' (MacIntyre, 1973, p. 3). Its meaning is therefore contested and changes as the term is used in different contexts. Indeed, 'professional ethics' falls into the category of what MacIntyre calls an 'essentially contested concept'. Plant (1974) suggests that essentially contested concepts have both descriptive and evaluative meanings. The descriptive meaning describes the relevant features or states of affairs (for example: professional ethics as standards of conduct followed by members of high-status occupations). In fact, essentially contested concepts may have several or

179

many descriptive meanings (for example: professional ethics as the study of standards of conduct; professional ethics as norms and principles defined in professional codes). The evaluative meaning gives the use of the term positive or negative connotations (for example: professional ethics as worthy and a 'good thing').

Plant (1974) and others (see, for example, Butcher, 1993) note the growing use of 'community' in the context of public policy developments, such as 'community care' or 'community policing', which take advantage of the evaluative meaning of 'community', with its cosy and warm connotations. The term 'professional ethics' has not been used in quite the same way, but we are increasingly seeing issues to do with external regulation and control, agency guidelines and procedures included under the heading of 'professional ethics'. This broadening of the use of 'professional ethics' takes advantage of the positive connotations of integrity and responsibility associated with the term.

So, just as 'community' is 'notorious for its shiftiness' (Mayo, 1994, p. 48), so is 'profession', 'ethics' and 'professional ethics'. As the behaviour of professionals changes, so what is encompassed by 'professional ethics' will shift and change; and changing conceptions of professional ethics will in turn feed into changing professional attitudes and behaviour.

The 'new technicians'?

The latter part of the book explored some of the changes taking place in the work of the social professions based on the accounts given by a number of practitioners working in different settings. There is no doubt that some of these changes are having a profound impact on how practitioners view themselves, how they feel they relate to the people with whom they work and how their work is judged by the public. Whether any professions, and specifically the social professions as we currently know them, will continue to exist in the future is a matter of debate. Some have argued that the new discourses of managerialism and the process of managerialisation have brought about a cultural transformation in the public services and created new subjects and identities to replace the traditional 'professional'. Yet as Clarke (1998, p. 242) points out, older discourses linger on, not merely out of nostalgia, but because:

the *specific* practices of welfare provision continue to require particular combinations of skills, competences and orientations which outrun the discourse of business, management and enterprise.

The need for specific expertise in certain areas of work seems unlikely to disappear, but the question remains as to how this expertise is construed and organised, and what this means for the issues that are currently covered under the heading of 'professional ethics'.

Freidson (2001, pp. 197–222), discussing professions in general, argues that the 'assault' on professionalism has been largely in terms of its public credibility. He comments that:

> The assault on professionalism will not in fact seriously weaken the organisation and operation of professional institutions but rather the control over their ends.

This, of course, has profound implications for professional ethics, which have traditionally been based on the notion of a 'service ideal' defined by the professions themselves. According to Freidson, there will be a continuing growth of work that requires quite high levels of skills and competence, but which is performed with much less individual discretion than is the case at present. Freidson calls the practitioners performing these tasks: 'especially privileged technical workers' (p. 209). This trend is already very obvious in the work of many of the professionals interviewed for this book, as exemplified particularly in Chapter 6. Freidson suggests there may be a cadre of professionals whose job it is to develop the myriad of policies, guidelines and procedures, which will then provide quite prescribed or restrictive frameworks for the operational professionals to work within. This does not signify the demise of professionalism, but it certainly does signify a changing conception of the nature of the professional role. It shifts the balance between indeterminacy and technicality so often noted in the literature on the professions (see, for example: Eadie, 2000, p. 170; Hugman, 1998b, p. 181; Jamous and Peloille, 1970; Kirkham, 1998, pp. 123–4). Professional work is said traditionally to have a high ratio of indetermination (knowledge and skills that cannot be contained in rules) to technicality (that part of the work that can be codified in rules/procedures). Recent changes seem to be moving the balance towards technicality, and the question arises as to whether this is morally or practically adequate for the kinds of work that professionals do.

Tronto (2001, p. 189) argues that competence is a key part of professional ethics. However, the notion of professional competence is broader than the narrow technical definition of the knowledge and skills required to fulfil assigned tasks. It also requires the capacity to act in a constantly changing world and to be both cautious and confident about changing conditions (p. 190). Linking her discussion to her earlier work on the ethic of care (see Chapter 3), she argues that the 'competent caregiving' of the professional provides 'something extra' – it goes beyond technical competence. This is because the caregiver is not only the provider of a service, but also the person with knowledge about what constitutes 'good' or 'competent' care in this setting. So professionals have a great deal of discretion over whether to provide 'genuinely' competent care, and a responsibility to assist the client or service user (usually a 'weaker party') on the basis of a trusting relationship. If the focus of attention is too narrowly on technical competence, then the opportunity to care well may be missed. She judges, therefore, that all the moral dimensions of care she identified in her earlier work (attentiveness, responsibility, responsiveness and technical competence) are required for professionally competent care giving. Managers who raise questions of efficiency and issues about motivating workers interfere with the holistic process of care. She suggests that it seems as if the task of the manager is to manage away the 'extra' that marks the moral performance of a professional's work, and that the dispute between professionals and managers is therefore 'a dispute about the capacity of professionals to act ethically' (p. 193). Although we may question Tronto's focus on 'care' as the core of all professional work, her identification of the 'extra' given by professionals is a pertinent point in the context of our discussion.

At a practical level, as Lymbery (2000, p. 134) points out, while managers may control formal aspects of the work they are not able to control what the practitioner does in the face-to-face contact with the service user, nor how they do this. Eadie (2000, p. 170), in discussing changing practice in probation services, refers to May's (1991) concept of the 'implementation gap', where policies are reinterpreted at practitioner level in relation to what is feasible, which is not always the same as what is required by service policy. A significant degree of indeterminacy and ambiguity therefore remains in practice, and indeed, it could be argued that it is vitally important that it does.

The new social professionals

One of the features of the recent changes in the organisation and practice of the social professions has been the addition of managerial responsibilities and tasks to what were formerly practitioner roles. This manifests itself in two ways. Firstly, practitioners have to undertake more administrative work connected with the increased emphasis on assessment, planning, monitoring and so on. Alongside this comes a process of self-monitoring and evaluation, including setting targets and reporting on outcomes. It is expected that work is prioritised and accounted for in relation to a predetermined plan. This links to what Clarke (1998, p. 240) calls a 'dispersed managerial consciousness' whereby the calculative framework of managerialism becomes embedded throughout an organisation. Secondly, and perhaps more significantly, jobs that were formerly regarded and named as professional practitioner roles have been redefined and designated as what might be called 'practitioner-manager' roles. This has been particularly noticeable in the field of community care in social work, where, for example, a post formerly designated as a qualified social work role working with people with disabilities may now have been transformed into a 'care manager'. This involves more responsibility for budgeting, rationing and resource allocation. Similar shifts have taken place in many other occupations, for example youth work. Although traditionally a senior youth worker may often have taken responsibility for the day-to-day management of a building (a youth and community centre), along with part-time and volunteer staff, such a worker now may also be involved managing a devolved budget, developing part of a youth service plan, and participating in several interagency strategic partnerships for tackling youth crime, school exclusion or drugs, for example. This inevitably means the practitioner-manager has to balance a focus on equity in resource distribution and rationing, area or agency-wide outcomes or benefits, alongside an empathic concern for individual service users and participants. Clarke (1998, pp. 240–1) terms this a 'hybrid' form of managing and notes the discomfort of this position, where the tensions between 'service' and 'corporate' concerns and professional and organisational commitments are keenly felt.

At the operational level, as professionally qualified practitioners in the social welfare field take on more of the assessment, monitoring, budgeting and administrative tasks (accountability work), in some areas the in-depth face-to-face work with individual service users is increasingly being done by less qualified or unqualified workers, or volunteers. For example, in the new Connexions service in England, youth workers are taking on the role of 'personal advisers' for young people (see Davies, 2000; Wylie, 2000). Although personal advisers meet young people on a face-to-face basis and work with them on their needs and problems in relation to all aspects of their lives, they have quite a high 'caseload' and their work with young people is closely monitored, recorded and outcomes evaluated. The actual work in depth with a young person may be done much more informally by a volunteer mentor based in a school, or by detached youth workers on the street or in other informal settings. It is these latter types of workers, noted by Jordan and Jordan (2000, p. 37) as 'street workers, support workers and project workers', who will most likely develop the trusting relationships with the young people, and view their work, perhaps, within the framework of what Gilligan (1982) and others have called the 'ethic of care' (as discussed in Chapters 3 and 6), whereas the middle-level professionals will be working within the confines of predetermined monitoring forms and performance criteria, which in their standardisation and uniformity lend themselves to being viewed within the framework of an ethic of justice, in terms of universal rights and fairness.

The picture presented above is, of course, a generalised one. In different areas of the social professions, different trends are at play, with work being organised in various and constantly shifting configurations. It could be argued that practitioners with more 'managerial' roles tend to have responsibilities for the distribution of resources of time and services, so will inevitably be concerned with matters of justice and fairness. They are also responsible for maintaining the overall standards and quality of work, ensuring effectiveness, as well as economic and efficient use of resources. So we would expect them to have a different focus from that of practitioners primarily working face-to-face with individuals and groups. For face-to-face practitioners, matters of care, compassion, empathy, integrity, trust and commitment to relationships with users are felt, acted out and lived through.

Part of the job of the manager is to be 'detached' and 'impartial'. A 'good' manager will recognise the concerns of practitioners about individual people and groups, and expect practitioners to develop trusting, respectful and caring relationships (as appropriate) with the people with whom they work. So managers value and take account of caring and trusting relationships between practitioners and service users, but they also need to retain the broader picture of equity of treatment and the rights of service users in general.

The more face-to-face work practitioners do with the same individuals, families and groups, and the greater the amount of time spent in less formal and unstructured activities, then inevitably the greater the focus on the nature of relationships. This is why the 'ethic of care' has been better developed in the context of nursing than in medicine, for example. The ethic of care also seems very relevant to the work of residential care workers, day-centre workers and some types of youth and community workers who develop sustained and informal relationships with the people in the homes, centres, projects and neighbourhoods where they work. In her study of the day-to-day practice of youth development workers in the USA, Rauner (2000) develops a variation on the ethic of care, which was discussed in Chapter 3 in the section on relationship-based ethics. Issues of universal rights, justice and fairness are not absent from the study. Indeed, such principles were probably part of the rationale for setting up many of the projects Rauner discusses, as well as informing their policies in relation to equal opportunities and so on. But in focusing on the young people's experiences of the projects, their encounters with the workers and the workers' relationships and attitudes towards the young people, then an 'ethic of care' offers a helpful framework for understanding what might be characterised as ethical aspects of the work.

In Chapter 3, I quoted a young person who said in relation to a drop-in centre: 'They let anyone in here, but you are not nobody when you come in' (Rauner, 2000, p. 34). Simplistically, we could say that it was the principles of equality of access and respect for the rights of all (the 'ethic of justice') that let the young person into the project, while it was a concern for particularity, building relationships, empathy, attentiveness and responsiveness (the 'ethic of care') that treated him as 'somebody' once he was inside. The youth development practitioners work within, and believe in, the justice framework (linking to an impartial and detached approach to ethics) as much as their managers, but in accounts of their day-to-day practice, the language and concepts of the ethic of care (reflecting partial and situated approaches to ethics) may be predominant. We might suggest that managers and practitioners may understand and value both frameworks, but the different roles and responsibilities they have mean that they often give accounts of their practice more in terms of one than the other. But as 'dispersed managerial consciousness' and the hybrid practitioner-manager role develops, then professionals may find it challenging to shift between the two.

The ethical challenge for the social professions

So what, we may ask, is the issue? Surely, it is obvious that managers manage, practitioners practice, and there is some overlap between the two? There are two main issues, which this book has raised and explored.

1.   *The approaches to ethics developed in the literature on moral philosophy have not been fine-tuned in their application to professional work*. Often a specific ethical theory or approach, such as principle-based ethics, virtue ethics or an ethic of care, has been advocated for a particular profession (such as medicine, law, nursing or social work) or professions as a whole, assuming that all aspects of the work of all members of a profession are equally amenable to the application of this theory or approach. The fact that the applicability of ethical approaches can vary according to context – which includes details of professionals' roles, the situations in which they find themselves, the agency they work for – may be stated, but not developed.

2.   *Some of the changes in the roles expected of qualified professional practitioners are shifting the balance of their work in ways that make giving an account of their practice in terms of particularity, trust, relationships and care (linking to partial and situated approaches to ethics) less plausible or possible*. Members of the social professions have long worked within an impartialist justice framework, and are experienced in arguing and practising in terms of anti-oppressive practice, equal opportunities and balancing the needs of different service users. But the way in which the justice framework has been fleshed out by employers and government

gives them less room for their own discretion and judgement (based on their particular local knowledge and experience), and requires a greater amount of time, energy and focus to be spent on administration and quality assurance procedures to ensure and demonstrate fairness and to monitor outcomes for individuals and measure results. This distracts them from what some practitioners see as the real needs and real work; it undermines their feeling of autonomy and their sense of themselves as trusted and competent, and above all, it intrudes upon, even redefines, their relationship with the people with whom they are working. It formalises what was hitherto informal and less formal. It pigeonholes, categorises and constrains.

These points relate to our earlier discussion towards the ends of Chapters 3 and 6 about the complementarity, but incommensurability, of impartialist, detached, justice-based accounts, voices or approaches to ethics, and partialist, relationship and care-based approaches. This was depicted in the drawing of the duck-rabbit (Figure 3.1). Whilst both approaches to ethics are important in professional life, the argument of this book has been that an over-emphasis on 'impartialist' and 'justice' approaches narrows the sphere of professional ethics excessively. Vetlesen (1994), in his book on moral perception, argues that what he calls existential-evaluative discourse (the concerned individual's ongoing conversation with, and examination of, herself or himself, which is settled in terms of authenticity) has been separated from moral discourse (public questions of normative rightness, which demand that all parties have an equal say and are settled in terms of their rightness). He is concerned about the narrowing of our moral universe to those things that are universalisable, impartial, impersonal, which tend then to privatise, or regard as merely personal concerns, questions of the good. It is this that we must guard against if the social professions are to maintain their integrity in a climate of challenge and change.

Practitioner responses

What, then, can or should the professional practitioner do in the face of the challenges presented above? It was not conceived as part of the purpose of this book to arrive at prescriptions for those involved in the work of the social professions. Rather, the aim was to examine and explore a number of themes in relation to professional ethics from different perspectives, hoping thereby to shed some light on how we may perceive and understand these issues at the present time. Our exploration might lead us back to our starting point, where we might know the place a little better or differently. Yet perhaps such a philosophical answer is not adequate in a climate where clear action-points and targets are valued. Or perhaps, being less cynical, it is not enough simply to describe and analyse a pervasive and damaging (even if sometimes well-motivated) set of trends. Something must be done. In attempting to answer the question 'what should we do?' I will return to the practitioners' accounts of their work.

Not surprisingly, the diverse range of practitioners interviewed had very varied attitudes towards the work they were currently doing. Some of the differences in attitude might be about 'personality', length of experience or type of job. In considering people's responses to the challenges presented by the increased demands for inter-agency and interprofessional working and the 'new accountability' requirements of the modern management agenda, the following categories were discerned:

- *The new managerial response*. This entails embracing the new demands enthusiastically and relatively uncritically. For example, the manager of a new interagency service reported seeing the task ahead as a welcome challenge, eagerly taking on board the latest government requirements and entering into the competitive spirit of aiming to do well in terms of achieving outputs. A senior practitioner in charge of developing quality documentation in a local authority social services department saw this as a very valuable and worthwhile task, helping to create uniformity and clarity. In this type of response, professional values are subservient to overarching corporate goals and targets of a service.

- *The new professional response*. This involves critically embracing the changes as beneficial on the whole, and using them to improve practice and service delivery. For example, a regeneration manager reported regarding the requirement to specify targets and measure progress regularly as promoting better outcomes for local residents. But he would do this within an explicit framework of community development values, and would challenge systems or modify targets not regarded as useful or worthwhile.

- *Professional entrepreneurial response.* This type of response tends to be most common in the voluntary sector. As with the 'new professional' response, the professional values are still regarded as important, but some 'private sector' approaches may be combined with public service ideals in fund-raising and taking on a constant series of new, short-term projects with very strict requirements for monitoring and accountability. An example of this approach was manifested by two senior managers in medium-sized voluntary organisations, one with a broad social care brief and the other focusing on community development.

- *Reluctant conformity.* This type of response may be more common amongst people at practitioner/senior practitioner level who have been working in the field for some time and who see many of the new requirements as deleterious and/or unnecessary. They may complain to colleagues, but do not take any action, and nevertheless carry on with the work. For example, a senior youth worker reported his serious distaste (with an air of depression) for many of the procedures and policies he was involved in implementing, but seemed to have no avenue for expressing his views constructively.

- *Individual challenge.* This response also involves the belief that many of the new requirements are harmful and unnecessary, but that this does entail taking some action, albeit at an individual level. For example, several face-to-face practitioners in social work, youth work, and community development reported taking a non-conformist stance, deliberately bending or ignoring rules, forms or procedures – consciously and unapologetically.

- *Radical challenge.* This involves openly challenging the need or worth of a particular requirement or way of working, taking a principled stand with managers or policy-makers and arguing a case. One of the youth workers reported in Chapter 6 as working for a youth offending team, who was also active in the Community and Youth Workers' Union, took up some of the issues relating to time-limited working and approaches to young people that contradicted his youth work values. He reported doing this with the intention of moving on anyway.

- *Principled quitting.* This may be the next stage after the radical challenges bear no fruit, or the worker is worn down with the effort of individual challenge and reluctant conformity. The manager of a (different) youth offending team, also from a youth work background, reported in Chapter 6 as 'jumping ship' to retain his integrity, is an example of someone leaving on principled grounds.

What people choose or are able to do depends very much on their individual circumstances, including: their analysis of the situation in which they work, their courage, commitment to certain ideals, the availability of support, their career stage, family circumstances and type of job and employing agency. If readers are looking for lists of recommended actions, then Bottery (1998, p. 146), in concluding his research study of professionals in health and education, recommends three possible responses by public sector professionals to the insidious development of managerialism. These are:

1. Reacting to and criticising legislative change by tackling it at the level of implementation (flexibly and ethically) and describing its human costs (on society generally, not just professionals).
2. Launching critical attacks upon the very basis of change, including critiques of quasi-markets and central control; pointing out deficiencies in economic assumptions underpinning many reforms; describing the disadvantages of the new public management.
3. Rethinking the basis of professional practice, and re-engineering this to take account of previous criticisms and future societal developments.

Bottery (1998, pp. 162–74) develops a redefinition of the role of the professional, stressing involvement in 'citizenship education', which involves viewing the nature of the professional role not only within individual organisations, but in a societal context, as a focus for the promotion of collective life and social cohesion. This ties in with the aspects of the 'new professionalism', linked to anti-oppressive practice, being promoted for social work (see Dominelli, 2002) and the active citizenship and community participation themes in current government policies which open up opportunities in particular for informal education professionals such as youth workers and community development practitioners.

Perhaps the most positive steps that can be taken by beleaguered professionals are to critique policies and engage in dialogue with each other (making alliances within and between occupational groups), service users, policy-makers and the public. Clarke (1998, p. 248) notes the strands of collegiality (horizontal links) and cosmo-politanism attached to professionalism. This gives professional prac-titioners a reference point beyond the organisations for which they work and the national policies of countries in which they are based, and runs counter to hierarchical and centralising organisational regimes. The retention and strengthening of this collegiality and cosmopolitanism, exemplified in the many national and inter-national professional associations and trade unions, is an important tactic for professional practitioners in the current climate. It is also important to note that there is a significant number of practitioners who, in Clarke's (1998, p. 245) analysis of the discourse of manager-ialism, 'do not believe a word of it':

> What has been most striking about the impact of managerialism is its ability to produce behavioural compliance at the same time as inducing scepticism, cynicism and disbelief. For many people working in social welfare the problem about the discourse is not that it constructs them as subjects, but that they find it offensively transparent (or transparently offensive).

Concluding comments

Professions in general, and the social professions in particular, are in a state of change, with some commentators predicting their demise and others their transformation. We have argued that to talk of the 'demise' of professions may be too extreme, but what we are witness-ing is nevertheless a transformation. One of the questions this book aimed to explore was what the changes in the social professions might mean for the traditional view of the nature and role of profes-sional ethics. To conclude the book, we will review the key assump-tions of the traditional view of professional ethics outlined in the Introduction.

1. *Distinct professional groups exist.* This is still the case, although more flexibility is encouraged, through the push for interprofes-sional and 'joined-up' working, as discussed in Chapter 5. Although there is some blurring of the boundaries of different occupational groups, it is likely, however, that the need for distinct technical

skills and knowledge will mean that a division of labour remains, but with more permeable boundaries in some areas – particularly in the social professions, where there is quite wide scope for cross-cutting work to tackle intractable social problems.

2.   *These groups have distinct sets of values and rules of professional conduct that are broadly accepted.* If it is the technical skills that are valued, the need for a distinct set of professional values may be questioned. According to the arguments presented in Chapter 2, it is the service ideal (on which these professional values are based) that grounds professional ethics, based on relationships of trust. If the quality and standards of service are ensured by a contract relationship, then we do not need trust and we do not need the professional pledge to serve clients/service users according to a service ideal. The kinds of compromises taking place between the traditional view and the new version of professional ethics are exemplified by some of the recent codes of professional ethics as discussed in Chapter 4. Codes of ethics, which were originally designed as 'oaths', now comprise many more rules. New regulatory bodies established for social care work in the UK are developing codes of conduct with clear disciplinary functions. But, can the 'contract' model actually deliver what is required in terms of public welfare services? Does the new managerial approach actually result in 'better services'? This is a hard question to answer, as in the past many of the outputs and outcomes have not been measured. Furthermore, many other factors influence the outcomes achieved, including levels of poverty, unemployment, the state of the school system or policing. So it is impossible to say that since new procedures or standards were adopted, then services to the public have actually improved. Mere league tables, 'clear-up rates' or speed of answering phone calls tell us very little. At present the 'trust' and 'contract' models appear to be operating simultaneously. As argued in Chapter 6, it will be important not to allow the trust model to slip away, as contract is not sufficient for people-oriented services. The recent discourse of 'relational contracts' (Newman, 2000) in the context of purchaser–provider relationships in public services is an interesting shift along the trust–contract axis presented in Chapter 2.

3.   *The first loyalty of the professional lies with the client/patient/service user.* This is not straightforwardly the case. As argued in Chapter 6, there has always been a complex system of accountability operating

in the public services, and the primacy of managers, employers and central government has developed over time. However, the message of this book is that the balance between conflicting accountability requirements must be constantly kept in mind, and the service user must be firmly kept in central view as a real person, as shown in Chapter 6. The new agenda on public participation gives more primacy to user/citizen/community participation (as opposed to the defining of clients' needs by professionals). If professionals can build new alliances with users and participants, then there is scope to reclaim this position.

4. *Professional values come before those of the employing agency or society.* As our discussions in Chapters 5 and 6 show, the primacy of professional values is being challenged. But as professional codes of ethics get longer, and regulatory bodies develop sets of values and codes, then the distinction between professional values and agency/societal values is less clear-cut. But what is clear is that some notion of independent professional values may be important in guarding against the danger of the dominance of outcome-focused practice based on utilitarian principles. But the 'professional values' will need to be developed to take full account of user definitions of needs and the complexity and diversity of 'social problems'.

5. *Professionals make ethical judgements on the basis of ethical principles and rules accepted by the profession.* This book has explored aspects of the claim that professional autonomy is being restricted – especially through the prescribing or restricting of professionals' action and behaviour by employers or central government policies and guidelines. But again, this development should not prevent professionals from reserving the right to make their own judgements, particularly when the scope of the rules or the prescriptions of the employing agency do not cover particular cases. There is a need for flexibility and creativity, and, rather ironically, 'innovation' in public services is being sought, alongside adherence to rules, procedures and the reaching of predefined standards. If this flexibility can be capitalised upon, building on the notion of partnership with users and residents, then there may be scope to challenge the iron grip of managerialist standardisation.

Although the credibility of professions in general, and social professions in particular, has been partially undermined and their distinctiveness and independence threatened, their expertise, holistic competence and trustworthiness are still required. There is room in the gaps between contracts for trust; in the spaces between the regulations for judgement and discretion; and between prescribed targets for creativity and flexibility. As ever, there are contradictions in government policies, where the discourse of 'innovation' in public services is developing alongside the continued drive for increased accountability. As Newman (2000, p. 49) points out: 'Innovation in public services is a more difficult concept [than in the business sector] because the requirements of control and accountability place constraints on risk taking and entrepreneurial action.' Yet the fact that it is being talked about and sought – although often seemingly as an end in itself (regardless of the substance of the innovation) – does leave some room for manoeuvre, although perhaps more in the fields of youth work and community work than in social work.

The everyday meetings between professional practitioners and service users/participants compel empathy and compassion; their circumstances call for an appreciation of uniqueness and complexity. Practitioner interventions cannot be reduced to measuring someone's ability to change a light bulb or assessing 'community capacity' on a 10-point scale. It is only because professional practitioners are highly skilled, flexible and reflective that they succeed in their work. Prescription and measurement may be superimposed – but they do not touch the heart of the work. It could be argued that professional ethics and the ability to make sensitive judgements lies at the heart of the work, and requires that practitioners are able to balance the competing demands of professional work, including care, education, liberation and control. Although these demands may surface in new guises, through new discourses of modernisation and transformation, they have been ever-present in the work of the social professions and are still there. Balances may shift, and new actors or 'stakeholders' may become dominant. The ground of professional ethics may be shifting, and the 'value base' may seem less of a firm foundation than in the past. But this exploration of the shifting ground of professional ethics so far has not signalled a revolution on the scale of an earthquake, signifying the end of ethics, the end of social work or the end of youth and community work. It is rather a series of tremors, rocking the foundations, requiring some rebuilding and restructuring, but based on the solid traditions of the past, constantly evolving and changing.

Appendix: details of interviewees and interviews

1. Individual interviewees working in the fields of social work, youth and community work

Area of work	Gender	Job role	Professional background	Sector	Specialism
1. Social services	Male	Service manager	Community and youth work	Statutory	Prevention
2. Youth work	Male	Youth worker	Youth work (non qual.)	Voluntary	Work with young people
3. Social services	Male	Social worker/ care manager	Social work	Statutory	Learning disabilities
4. Community development	Female	Community resource centre manager	Librarianship	Voluntary/ Community	Community work
5. Social services	Male	Director	Social work	Statutory	Social services
6. Regeneration	Male	Director	Community work	Partnership	Regeneration
7. Regeneration	Female	Community worker	Business	Voluntary	Community development
8. Social services	Female	Team manager	Social work	Statutory	Child care
9. Youth work	Female	Youth worker	Community and youth work	Statutory	Youth work
10. Social services	Female	Team manager	Social work	Statutory	Child care
11. Social services	Female	Service manager	Social work	Statutory	Quality documentation
12. Social services	Male	Senior social worker	Social work	Statutory	Child care
13. Youth offending	Male	Youth worker, seconded to YOT	Community and youth work	Statutory	Youth offending

14. **Social services**	Female	Standards and development officer	Social work	Statutory	Standards development
15. **Social services**	Female	Social worker/ children and families	Social work	Statutory	Children and families
16. **Community development**	Female	Director	Voluntary sector	Voluntary	Rural community development
17. **Community work**	Female	Senior community support worker	Community work	Statutory	Community development
18. **Social services**	Female	Social worker/ care manager	Social work	Statutory	Physical disability
19. **Social services**	Female	Team manager	Occupational therapy	Statutory	Physical disability
20. **Social services**	Female	Social worker/ care manager	Nursing	Statutory	Physical disability
21. **Social services**	Male	Service manager	Social work	Statutory	Social services
22. **Generic social care and community**	Male	Development director	Social worker	Voluntary	Management
23. **Social services**	Female	Manager	Social work	Statutory	Child care-reviews/ case conferences
24. **Youth work**	Male	Youth worker, independent access project	Community and youth work	Statutory	Young people with special needs
25. **Social services**	Male	Senior social worker	Social work	Statutory	Children and families/mental health
26. **Community work**	Male	Service manager	Social work/ Community dev.	Statutory	Community development
27. **Youth work**	Male	Youth and community worker	Community and youth work	Statutory	Youth and community work
28. **Social services**	Female	Team manager, mental health	Social work	Statutory	Community mental health
29. **Social services**	Male	Team manager	Social work	Statutory	Child care
30. **Social services**	Male	Social worker/ emergency duty	Social work	Statutory	Emergency duty
31. **Social services**	Female	Social worker/ assessment and info.	Social work	Statutory	Assessment and Info.
32. **Community work**	Male	Community support unit manager	Community and youth work	Statutory	Community development

2. Individual interviewees in the case study youth offending and community safety service

Area of work	Gender	Job role	Professional background	Sector	Specialism
33. **Youth offending**	Male	Health officer	Mental health nurse	Interagency service	Health/ youth offending
34. **Youth offending**	Female	YOT team manager	Social work	Interagency service	Youth offending
35. **Community safety**	Male	Police inspector, community safety	Police	Interagency service	Community safety
36. **Youth offending**	Male	YOT officer (enforcement)	Social work	Interagency service	Youth offending
37. **Substance misuse/HIV prevention**	Female	Prevention coordinator	Counselling	Interagency service	Substance misuse/HIV prevention
38. **Community safety**	Female	Community safety coordinator	Degree, experience in local authorities	Interagency service	Community safety
39. **Youth offending**	Male	Assertive outreach worker	Army	Interagency service	Youth offending
40. **Neighbourhood warden**	Male	Senior uniformed warden	None	Interagency service	Neighbourhood warden

3. Participants in the group discussion with case study youth offending and community safety service

1. Police Inspector, Community Safety (police background)
2. Youth Offending Officer (enforcement, social work background)
3. Youth Offending Officer (prevention, social work background)
4. Health Officer (nursing background)
5. Senior Neighbourhood Warden (first job)
6. Youth Offending Officer (enforcement, probation background)
7. Police Sergeant, Community Safety (police background)
8. Assertive Outreach Worker (previous experience in the army)

4. Broad areas of questioning in group discussion with case study youth offending and community safety service

1. What have been the most important challenges you have faced since working here?
2. What are some of the pros and cons of working in multi-agency, inter-professional service?
3. What are some of the ethical dilemmas/problems you encounter in your work?
4. What can be done to help you tackle these dilemmas/problems?

5. Broad themes for questions in individual interviews

1. What is your job title and what is the nature of your job?
2. When did you qualify and what other jobs have you done?
3. What do you think are some of the biggest changes in [area of work] over the last 10–15 years?
4. Follow up comments made, and then check out views on: inter-professional working, working to procedures and targets, specialisation, short-term project work, and any issues specific to their jobs.
5. How have these affected you?
6. Have any of these changes raised ethical issues for you?
7. What are some of the commonest ethical dilemmas in your work?
8. Can you describe a particular situation/incident that raised difficult ethical issues for you?
9. Do you have any dealings with professional bodies or any other organisation that provides guidance, advice, professional information in your field of work?

References

Abbott, P. and Meerabeau, L. (1998) 'Professionals, Professionalisation and the Caring Professions', in P. Abbott and L. Meerabeau (eds), *The Sociology of the Caring Professions*, 2nd edn, London, UCL Press, pp. 1–19.

Addelson, K. (1994) *Moral Passages: Towards a Collectivist Moral Theory*, New York and London, Routledge.

Airaksinen, T. (1994) 'Service and Science in Professional Life', in R. Chadwick (ed.), *Ethics and the Professions*, Aldershot, Avebury, pp. 1–13.

Allmark, P. (1995) 'Can There Be an Ethics of Care?', *Journal of Medical Ethics*, vol. 21, pp. 19–24.

Anderson, J. and Englehardt, E. (2001) *The Organizational Self and Ethical Conduct: Sunlit Virtue and Shadowed Resistance*, Forth Worth, Texas, Harcourt College Publishers.

Arendt, H. (1963) *Eichmann in Jerusalem*, New York, Viking.

Aristotle (1954) *The Nichomachean Ethics of Aristotle*, translated by Sir David Ross, London, Oxford University Press.

Arras, J. (1991) 'Getting Down to Cases: The Revival of Casuistry in Bio-ethics', *Journal of Medicine and Philosophy*, vol. 16, pp. 31–3.

Ashworth, M. (1984) *The Oxford House in Bethnel Green. 100 Years of Work in the Community*, London, Oxford House.

Association of Social Workers in the Czech Republic (SSPCR) (1995) *Ethical Code of Social Workers in the Czech Republic*, Prague, SSPCR.

Association of Social Workers in the Slovak Republic (ASPS) (1997) *The Code of Ethics for Social Workers in Slovakia*, Bratislava, ASPS.

Audit Commission (1996) *Misspent Youth: Young People and Crime*, London, Audit Commission.

Baier, A. (1985) *Postures of the Mind: Essays on Mind and Morals*, Minneapolis, Minneapolis University Press.

Baier, A. (1986) 'Trust and Anti-Trust', *Ethics*, vol. 96, pp. 231–60.

Bailey, R. and Brake, M. (eds) (1975) *Radical Social Work*, Edward Arnold, London.

Baldock, P. (1974) *Community Work and Social Work*, London, Routledge & Kegan Paul.

Balloch, S. and Taylor, M. (eds) (2001) *Partnership Working: Policy and Practice*, The Policy Press, Bristol.

Banks, S. (1996) 'Youth Work, Informal Education and Professionalisation: The Issues in the 1990s', *Youth and Policy*, no. 54, pp. 13–25.

Banks, S. (1998a) 'Codes of Ethics and Ethical Conduct: A View from the Caring Professions', *Public Money and Management*, vol. 18, no. 1, pp. 27–30.

Banks, S. (1998b) 'Professional Ethics in Social Work – What Future?', *British Journal of Social Work*, vol. 28, pp. 213–31.

Banks, S. (1999a) 'Ethics and the Youth Worker', in S. Banks (ed.), *Ethical Issues in Youth Work*, London, Routledge, pp. 3–20.

Banks, S. (1999b) 'Etica in frammneti? I valori del servizio sociale in tempi di radicale cambiamento' (Ethics in fragments? Social work values in a state of change), in P. Donati and F. Folgerhaiter (eds), *Gli operatori sociali nel welfare mix. Privatizzazione, pluralizzazione dei soggetti erogatori, managerialismo: il futuro del servizio sociale?*, Trento, Italy, Erikson, pp. 145–68.

Banks, S. (2000) 'Report to National Youth Agency on Ethics in Youth Work' (unpublished), Durham, University of Durham.

Banks, S. (2001) *Ethics and Values in Social Work*, 2nd edn, Basingstoke, Palgrave.

Banks, S. (2002) 'Professional Values and Accountabilities', in R. Adams, L. Dominelli and M. Payne (eds), *Critical Practice in Social Work*, Basingstoke, Palgrave, pp. 28–37.

Baron, M. (1995) *Kantian Ethics Almost Without Apology*, Ithaca, New York, Cornell University Press.

Batten, T. (1967) *The Non-Directive Approach to Group and Community Work*, Oxford, Oxford University Press.

Bauman, Z. (1993) *Postmodern Ethics*, Oxford, Blackwell.

Bauman, Z. (1994) 'Morality without Ethics', *Theory, Culture & Society*, vol. 11, pp. 1–34.

Bauman, Z. (1995) *Life in Fragments: Essays in Postmodern Morality*, Oxford, Blackwell.

Bauman, Z. (1997) 'Morality Begins at Home – or: Can There Be a Levinasian Macro-Ethics?', in H. Jodalen and A. Vetlesen (eds), *Closeness: An Ethics*, Oslo, Scandinavian University Press, pp. 218–44.

Bazeley, P. and Richards, L. (2000) *The NVivo Qualitative Project Book*, London, Sage.

Beauchamp, T. (1996) 'The Role of Principles in Practical Ethics', in L. Sumner and J. Boyle (eds), *Philosophical Perspectives on Bioethics*, Toronto, University of Toronto Press, pp. 79–95.

Beauchamp, T. and Childress, J. (1994) *Principles of Biomedical Ethics*, 4th edn, Oxford and New York, Oxford University Press.

Bellah, R., Masden, R., Sullivan, W., Swidler, A. and Tipton, S. (1988) *Habits of the Heart: Middle America Observed*, London, Century Hutchinson.

Benhabib, S. (1992) *Situating the Self: Gender, Community, and Postmodernism in Contemporary Ethics*, Cambridge, Polity Press.

Bernstein, E. and Gilligan, C. (1990) 'Unfairness and Not Listening: Converging Themes in Emma Willard Girls' Development', in C. Gilligan, N. Lyons and T. Hanmer (eds), *Making Connections*, Cambridge, Mass., Harvard University Press, pp. 147–61.

Blaug, R. (1995) 'Distortion of the Face to Face: Communicative Reason and Social Work Practice', *British Journal of Social Work*, vol. 25, pp. 423–39.

Blindenbacher, R. (1999) 'The Task Dilemma in Human Service Organizations and Its Impact on Efficacy', *European Journal of Social Work*, vol. 2, no. 2, pp. 131–8.

Blum, L. (1994) *Moral Perception and Particularity*, Cambridge, Cambridge University Press.

Bond, T. (2000) *Standards and Ethics for Counselling in Action*, 2nd edn, London, Sage.

Bottery, M. (1998) *Professionals and Policy: Management Strategy in a Competitive World*, London, Cassell.

Bouquet, B. (1999) 'De l'éthique personelle à une éthique professionelle', *EMPAN*, no. 36, pp. 27–33.

Bowden, P. (1997) *Caring: Gender Sensitive Ethics*, London, Routledge.

Bradshaw, P. (1996) 'Yes! There is an Ethics of Care: An Answer for Peter Allmark', *Journal of Medical Ethics*, vol. 22, pp. 8–12.

Brandt, R. (1976) 'The Concept of Welfare', in N. Timms and D. Watson (eds), *Talking about Welfare: Readings in Philosophy and Social Policy*, London, Routledge & Kegan Paul, pp. 64–87.

Briskman, L. and Noble, C. (1999) 'Social Work Ethics: Embracing Diversity?', in B. Pease and J. Fook (eds), *Transforming Social Work Practice: Postmodern Critical Perspectives*, London, Routledge, pp. 57–69.

Burrage, M. (1990) 'Introduction: The Professions in Sociology and History', in M. Burrage and R. Torstendahl (eds), *Professions in Theory and History: Rethinking the Study of the Professions*, London, Sage, pp. 1–23.

Butcher, H. (1993) 'Introduction: Some Examples and Definitions', in H. Butcher, A. Glen, P. Henderson and J. Smith (eds), *Community and Public Policy*, London, Pluto Press, pp. 3–21.

Caputo, J. (2000) 'The End of Ethics', in H. LaFollette (ed.), *The Blackwell Guide to Ethical Theory*, Oxford, Blackwell, pp. 111–28.

Carrier, J. and Kendall, I. (1995) 'Professionalism and Interprofessionalism in Health and Community Care: Some Theoretical Issues', in P. Owens, J. Carrier and J. Horder (eds), *Interprofessional Issues in Community and Primary Health Care*, Basingstoke, Macmillan, pp. 9–36.

Carrithers, M. (1992) *Why Humans Have Cultures: Explaining Anthropology and Social Diversity*, Oxford, Oxford University Press.

Carr-Saunders, A. (1955) 'Metropolitan Conditions and Traditional Professional Relationships', in A.M. Fisher (ed.), *The Metropolis in Modern Life*, Garden City, New York, Rooksbury.

Carr-Saunders, A. and Wilson, P. (1933) *The Professions*, London, Oxford University Press.

Carter, H. and Ward, D. (2002) 'Britain's worst serial killer: 215 dead but we still don't know why', *The Guardian*, 20th July, Manchester, p. 1.

Central Council for Education and Training in Social Work (1995) *Assuring Quality in the Diploma in Social Work – 1: Rules and Requirements for the DipSW*, London, CCETSW.

Chadwick, R. and Levitt, M. (1997) 'Professions in Crisis: The Ethical Response', in J. Scally (ed.), *Ethics in Crisis?*, Dublin, Veritas, pp. 55–65.

Clark, C. (2000) *Social Work Ethics: Politics, Principles and Practice*, Basingstoke, Macmillan.

Clarke, J. (1995) 'After Social Work?', in N. Parton (ed.), *Social Theory, Social Change and Social Work*, London, Routledge, pp. 36–60.

Clarke, J. (1998) 'Managerialism and Social Welfare', in P. Abbott and L. Meerabeau (eds), *The Sociology of the Caring Professions*, 2nd edn, London, UCL Press, pp. 234–54.

Clarke, J., Gewirtz, S. and McLaughlin, E. (2000) 'Reinventing the Welfare State', in J. Clarke, S. Gewirtz and E. McLaughlin (eds), *New Managerialism, New Welfare?*, Buckingham, Open University Press, pp. 1–26.

Clifford, D. (2002) 'Resolving Uncertainties? The Contribution of Some Recent Feminist Ethical Theory to the Social Professions', *European Journal of Social Work*, vol. 5, no. 1, pp. 31–41.

Collins, R. (1990) 'Market Closure and the Conflict Theory of the Professions', in M. Burrage and R. Torstendahl (eds), *Professions in Theory and History: Rethinking the Study of the Professions*, London, Sage, pp. 24–44.

Corrigan, P. and Leonard, P. (1978) *Social Work Practice under Capitalism: A Marxist Approach*, London, Macmillan.

Crisp, R. (ed.) (1996) *How Should One Live? Essays on the Virtues*, Oxford, Oxford University Press.

Crisp, R. and Slote, M. (eds) (1997) *Virtue Ethics*, Oxford, Oxford University Press.

Dalley, G. (1993) 'Professional Ideology or Organisational Tribalism? The Health Service–Social Work Divide', in J. Walmsley, J. Reynolds, P. Shakespeare and R. Woolfe (eds), *Health, Welfare and Practice: Reflecting on Roles and Relationships*, London, Sage, pp. 32–9.

Daniels, N. (1996) 'Wide Reflective Equilibrium in Practice', in L. Sumner and J. Boyle (eds), *Philosophical Prespectives on Bioethics*, Toronto, University of Toronto Press, pp. 96–114.

Davies, B. (1988) 'Professionalism or Trade Unionism? The Search for a Collective Identity', in T. Jeffs and M. Smith (eds), *Welfare and Youth Work Practice*, Basingstoke, Macmillan, pp. 200–14.

Davies, B. (1999a) *From Voluntaryism to Welfare State: A History of the Youth Service in England. Volume 1, 1939–1979*, Leicester, Youth Work Press.

Davies, B. (1999b) *From Thatcherism to New Labour: A History of the Youth Service in England, Volume 2, 1979–1999*, Leicester, Youth Work Press.

Davies, B. (2000) 'Connecting with Connexions – Some Lessons from Youth Service History', http://www.nya.org.uk/connex-TFC-less-hist-exec-sum.htm, 04.05.01.

Davis, M. (1999) *Ethics and the University*, London, Routledge.

Dawson, A. (1994) 'Professional Codes of Practice and Ethical Conduct', *Journal of Applied Philosophy*, vol. 11, no. 2, pp. 125–33.

Dean, J. (1995) 'Discourse in Different Voices', in J. Meehan (ed.), *Feminists Read Habermas: Gendering the Subject of Discourse*, New York and London, Routledge, pp. 205–30.

Department for Education and Employment (2000) *Connexions: The Best Start in Life for Every Young Person*, London, Department for Education and Employment.

Department for Education and Employment (2001) *Transforming Youth Work: Developing Youth Work for Young People*, London, Department for Education and Employment.

Department of Health (1988) *Protecting Children: A Guide for Social Workers Undertaking a Comprehensive Assessment*, London, HMSO.

Department of Health (1998a) *Modernising Social Services: Promoting Independence, Improving Protection, Raising Standards*, London, The Stationery Office.

Department of Health (1998b) *Partnership in Action: New Opportunities for Joint Working Between Health and Social Services*, London, The Stationery Office.

Department of Health (1998c) *Quality Protects: Framework for Action and Objectives for Social Services for Children*, London, Stationery Office.

Department of Health Social Services Inspectorate (1991) *Care Management and Assessment: Practitioners' Guide*, London, HMSO.

Department of Health, Department for Education and Employment and Home Office (1999) *Working Together to Safeguard Children*, London, HMSO.

Department of the Environment, Transport and the Regions (1998) *Modernising Local Government: Local Democracy and Community Leadership*, London, DETR.

Department of Trade and Industry (1998) *Our Competitive Future: Building the Knowledge Driven Economy*, London, The Stationery Office.

Dominelli, L. (1996) 'Deprofessionalising Social Work: Anti-Oppressive Practice, Competencies and Postmodernism', *British Journal of Social Work*, vol. 26, pp. 153–75.

Dominelli, L. (2002) *Anti Oppressive Social Work Theory and Practice*, Basingstoke, Palgrave Macmillan.

Downie, R. and Jodalen, H. (1997) '"I-Thou" and "Doctor–Patient": A Relationship Examined', in H. Jodalen and A. Vetlesen (eds), *Closeness: An Ethics*, Oslo, Scandinavian University Press, pp. 129–41.

Downie, R. and Telfer, E. (1980) *Caring and Curing*, London, Methuen.

du Gay, P. (2000) *In Praise of Bureaucracy: Weber, Organisation, Ethics*, London, Sage.

Dunleavy, P. and Hood, C. (1994) 'From Old Public Administration to New Public Management', *Public Money and Management*, vol. 14, no. 3, pp. 9–16.

Dworkin, R. (1977) *Taking Rights Seriously*, Cambridge, Mass., Harvard University Press.

Eadie, T. (2000) 'From Befriending to Punishing: Changing Boundaries in the Probation Service', in N. Malin (ed.), *Professionalism, Boundaries and the Workplace*, London, Routledge, pp. 161–77.

Edgar, A. (1994a) 'Narrating Social Work', in R. Chadwick (ed.), *Ethics and the Professions*, Aldershot, Avebury, pp. 125–35.

Edgar, A. (1994b) 'The Value of Codes of Conduct', in G. Hunt (ed.), *Ethical Issues in Nursing*, London, Routledge, pp. 148–63.

Etzioni, A. (1969) *The Semi-Professions and Their Organisation*, New York, Free Press.

Etzioni, A. (ed.) (1995a) *New Communitarian Thinking: Persons, Virtues, Institutions, and Communities*, Charlottesville, USA, University Press of Virginia.

Etzioni, A. (1995b) *The Spirit of Community*, London, Fontana.

Exworthy, M. and Halford, S. (eds) (1999) *Professionals and the New Managerialism in the Public Sector*, Buckingham, Open University Press.

Federation of Community Work Training Groups (2002) 'Review of National Occupational Standards in Community Work', http://www.community learning.org.uk, 29.03.02.

Fellesorganisasjonen for Barnevernpedagoger Socionomer og Vernepleiere (FO) (1998) *Professional Ethical Principles and Guidelines*, Oslo, FO.

Flynn, N. (2000) 'Managerialism and Public Services: Some International Trends', in J. Clarke, S. Gewirtz and E. McLaughlin (eds), *New Managerialism, New Welfare?*, London, Open University/Sage, pp. 27–44.

Foot, P. (1978) *Virtues and Vices*, Oxford, Oxford University Press.

Freedman, M. (1975) *Lawyers' Ethics in an Adversary System*, Indianapolis, Bobbs-Merrill.

Freidson, E. (1983) 'The Theory of Professions: State of the Art', in R. Dingwall and P. Lewis (ed.), *The Sociology of the Professions: Lawyers, Doctors and Others*, Basingstoke, Macmillan, pp. 19–37.

Freidson, E. (1994) *Professionalism Reborn: Theory, Prophecy and Policy*, Oxford, Polity Press.

Freidson, E. (2001) *Professionalism: The Third Logic*, Cambridge, Polity Press.

Gambetta, D. (1988) 'Can We Trust Trust', in A. Gambetta (ed.), *Trust: Making and Breaking Cooperative Relations*, London, Basil Blackwell.

Garner, H. and Orelove, F. (1994) *Teamwork in Human Services: Models and Applications Across the Life Span*, Newton, Massachussets, Butterworth-Heinemann.

General Social Care Council, http://www.gscc.org.uk.

Gibbs, G. (2002) *Qualitative Data Analysis: Explorations with NVivo*, Buckingham, Open University Press.

Giddens, A. (1998) *The Third Way: The Renewal of Social Democracy*, Cambridge, Polity Press.

Gilligan, C. (1982) *In a Different Voice: Psychological Theory and Women's Development*, Cambridge, Mass., Harvard University Press.

Gilligan, C. (1988) 'Adolescent Development Reconsidered', in C. Gilligan, J. Ward, C. Taylor and B. Bardige (eds), *Mapping the Moral Domain: A Contribution of Women's Thinking to Psychological Theory and Education*, Cambridge, Mass., Harvard University Press, pp. i–xxxix.

Gilligan, C., Lyons, N. and Hamner, T. (eds) (1990) *Making Connections*, Cambridge, Mass., Harvard University Press.

Gilligan, C., Rogers, A. and Brown, L. (1990) 'Epilogue', in C. Gilligan, N. Lyons and T. Hanmer (eds), *Making Connections*, Cambridge, Mass., Harvard University Press, pp. 314–34.

Gilligan, C., Ward, J., Taylor, J. and Bardridge, B. (eds) (1988) *Mapping the Moral Domain: A Contribution of Women's Thinking to Psychological Theory and Education*, Cambridge, Mass., Harvard University Press.

Goetschius, G. (1969) *Working with Community Groups: Using Community Development as a Method of Social Work*, London, Routledge & Kegan Paul.

Goffman, E. (1968) *Stigma: Notes on the Management of Spoiled Identity*, Harmondsworth, Penguin.

Goldie, P. (2000) *The Emotions: A Philosophical Exploration*, Oxford, Oxford University Press.

Goldman, A. (1980) *The Moral Foundations of Professional Ethics*, Totowa, New Jersey, Rowman & Littlefield.

Green, J. and Chapman, A. (1992) 'The Community Development Project: Lessons for Today', *Community Development Journal*, vol. 27, no. 3, pp. 242–58.

Greenwood, E. (1957) 'Attributes of a Profession', *Social Work*, vol. 2, no. 3, pp. 44–55.

Gulbenkian Study Group (1968) *Community Work and Social Change*, London, Longman.

Habermas, J. (1984) *Theory of Communicative Action. Volume 1: Reason and the Rationaliastion of Society*, translated by T. McCarthy, London, Heinemann.

Habermas, J. (1987) *Theory of Communicative Action. Volume 2: Lifeworld and System: A Critique of Functionalist Reason*, translated by T. McCarthy, Cambridge, Polity Press.

Habermas, J. (1988) 'Law and Morality', translated by K. Baynes, in S. McMurren (ed.), *The Tanner Lectures on Human Values*, Salt Lake City, Salt Lake City University Press, pp. 217–79.

Habermas, J. (1990) *Moral Consciousness and Communicative Action*, translated by C. Lenhardt and S. Nicholsen, Cambridge, Mass., MIT Press.

Hadley, R. and Clough, R. (1997) *Care in Chaos: Frustration and Challenge in Community Care*, London, Cassell.

Haimes, E. (2002) 'What Can the Social Sciences Contribute to the Study of Ethics? Theoretical, Empirical and Substantive Considerations', *Bio-ethics*, vol. 16, no. 2, pp. 89–113.

Halford, S. and Leonard, P. (1999) 'New Identities? Professionalism, Managerialism and the Construction of Self', in M. Exworthy and S. Halford (eds), *Professionals and the New Managerialism in the Public Sector*, Milton Keynes, Open University Press, pp. 102–20.

Hall, C., Sarangi, S. and Slembrouck, S. (1997) 'Moral Construction in Social Work Discourse', in B.-L. Gunnarsson, P. Linell and B. Nordberg (eds), *The Construction of Professional Discourse*, London, Longman, pp. 265–91.

Hallet, C. (1995) *Interagency Coordination in Child Protection*, London, Her Majesty's Stationery office.

Hand, S. (ed.) (1989) *The Levinas Reader*, Oxford, Blackwell.

Hanford, L. (1994) 'Nursing and the Concept of Care: An Appraisal of Noddings' Theory', in G. Hunt (ed.), *Ethical Issues in Nursing*, London, Routledge, pp. 181–97.

Hare, R. (1981) *Moral Thinking*, Oxford, Oxford University Press.

Harris, N. (1994) 'Professional Codes and Kantian Duties', in R. Chadwick (ed.), *Ethics and the Professions*, Aldershot, Avebury, pp. 104–15.

Harris, V. (ed.) (2001) *Community Work Skills Manual*, Association of Community Workers and Community Work Training Company, Newcastle.

Harrison, S. and Pollitt, C. (1994) *Controlling Health Professionals*, Buckingham, Open University Press.

Häyry, H. and Häyry, M. (1998) 'Applied Philosophy at the Turn of the Millennium', in O. Leaman (ed.), *The Future of Philosophy: Towards the Twenty-First Century*, London, Routledge, pp. 90–104.

Hekman, S. (1995) *Moral Voices, Moral Selves: Carol Gilligan and Feminist Moral Theory*, Cambridge, Polity Press.

Held, V. (1993) *Feminist Morality: Transforming Culture, Society and Politics*, Chicago, University of Chicago Press.

Henderson, P. and Salmon, H. (1998) *Signposts to Local Democracy. Local Governance, Communitarianism and Community Development*, London, Community Development Foundation.

Hippocratic Oath (c. 420 BC), in I. Thompson, K. Melia and K. Boyd (eds), *Nursing Ethics*, (2000) 4th edn, Edinburgh, Churchill Livingstone, p. 339.

Hoffman, M. (2000) *Empathy and Moral Development*, Cambridge, Cambridge University Press.

Holdsworth, D. (1994) 'Accountability and the Obligation to Lay Oneself Open to Criticism', in R. Chadwick (ed.), *Ethics and the Professions*, Aldershot, Avebury, pp. 42–57.

Horne, M. (1999) *Values in Social Work*, 2nd edn, Aldershot, Wildwood House.

Howe, D. (1995) *Social Work and the University*, Department of Social Studies Occasional Paper No 4, Dublin, University of Dublin, Trinity College.

Hudson, B. (2000) 'Conclusion: "Modernising Social Services" – A Blueprint for the New Millenium?', in B. Hudson (ed.), *The Changing Role of Social Care*, London, Jessica Kingsley, pp. 219–38.

Hugman, R. (1998a) *Social Welfare and Social Value: The Role of Caring Professions*, Basingstoke, Macmillan.

Hugman, R. (1998b) 'Social Work and De-Professionalisation', in P. Abbott and L. Meerabeau (eds), *The Sociology of the Caring Professions*, 2nd edn, London, UCL Press, pp. 178–98.

Hursthouse, R. (1999) *On Virtue Ethics*, Oxford, Oxford University Press.

Husband, C. (1995) 'The Morally Active Practitioner and the Ethics of Anti-Racist Social Work', in R. Hugman and D. Smith (eds), *Ethical Issues in Social Work*, London, Routledge, pp. 84–103.

International Federation of Social Workers (1994) 'The Ethics of Social Work – Principles and Standards', http://www.ifsw.org/publications/4.4.pub.html, 10.05.02.

Irvine, R., Kerridge, I., McPhee, J. and Freeman, S. (2002) 'Interprofessionalism and Ethics: Consensus or Clash of Cultures', *Journal of Interprofessional Care*, vol. 16, no. 3, pp. 199–210.

Jamous, H. and Peloille, B. (1970) 'Professions or Self-Perpetuating Systems? Changes in the French University-Hospital System', in J. Jackson (ed.), *Professions and Professionalisation*, Cambridge, Cambridge University Press, pp. 111–52.

Jeffs, T. (1979) *Young People and the Youth Service*, London, Routledge & Kegan Paul.

Jeffs, T. (2001) ' "Something to Give and Much to Learn": Settlements and Youth Work', in T. Jeffs and R. Gilchrist (eds), *Settlements, Social Change and Community Action*, London, Jessica Kingsley, pp. 152–72.

Johnson, C. (2001) 'Strength in Community: Historical Development of Settlements Internationally', in R. Gilchrist and T. Jeffs (eds), *Settlements, Social Change and Community Action: Good Neighbours*, London, Jessica Kingsley, pp. 69–91.

Johnson, T. (1972) *Professions and Power*, London, Macmillan.

Johnson, T. (1984) 'Professionalism: Occupation or Ideology?', in S. Goodlad (ed.), *Education for the Professions: Quis custodiet . . . ?*, Guildford, SRHE & NFER-Nelson, pp. 17–25.

Jones, C. (2001) 'Voices from the Front Line: State Social Workers and New Labour', *British Journal of Social Work*, vol. 31, pp. 547–62.

Jonsen, A. (1996) 'Morally Appreciated Circumstances: A Theoretical Problem for Casuistry', in L. Sumner and J. Boyle (eds), *Philosophical Perspectives on Bioethics*, Toronto, Toronto University Press, pp. 37–49.

Jonsen, A. and Toulmin, S. (1988) *The Abuse of Casuistry: A History of Moral Reasoning*, Berkeley, University of California Press.

Jordan, B. and Jordan, C. (2000) *Social Work and the Third Way: Tough Love as Social Policy*, London, Sage.

Kant, I. (1964) *Groundwork of the Metaphysics of Morals*, New York, Harper Row.

Kirkham, M. (1998) 'Professionalization: Dilemmas for Midwifery', in P. Abbott and L. Meerabeau (eds), *The Sociology of the Caring Professions*, London, UCL Press, pp. 123–58.

Kittay, E. (1999) *Love's Labour: Essays on Women, Equality, and Dependency*, New York and London, Routledge.

Koehn, D. (1994) *The Ground of Professional Ethics*, London, Routledge.

Koehn, D. (1998) *Rethinking Feminist Ethics: Care, Trust and Empathy*, London, Routledge.

Kohlberg, L. (1981) *Essays on Moral Development: Volume 1, The Philosophy of Moral Development: Moral Stages and the Idea of Justice*, New York, Harper Row.

Kuczewski, M. (1997) *Fragmentation and Consensus: Communitarian and Casuist Bioethics*, Washington, Georgetown University Press.

Kuhn, T. (1970) *The Structure of Scientific Revolutions*, 2nd edn, Chicago, Chicago University Press.

Kymlicka, W. (1996) 'Moral Philosophy and Public Policy: The Case of New Reproductive Technologies', in L. Sumner and J. Boyle (eds), *Philosophical Perspectives on Bioethics*, Toronto, University of Toronto Press, pp. 244–71.

Ladd, J. (1998) 'The Quest for a Code of Ethics: An Intellectual and Moral Confusion', in P. Vesilund and A. Gunn (eds), *Engineering, Ethics and the Environment*, Cambridge, Cambridge University Press, pp. 210–18.

Langan, M. (2000) 'Social Services: Managing the Third Way', in J. Clarke, S. Gewirtz and E. McLaughlin (eds), *New Managerialism, New Welfare?*, London, Sage/Open University Press, pp. 152–68.

Larson, M.S. (1977) *The Rise of Professionalism: A Sociological Analysis*, Berkeley, CA, University of California Press.

Lash, S. (1996) 'Postmodern Ethics: The Missing Ground', *Theory, Culture & Society: Explorations in Critical Social Science*, vol. 13, no. 2, pp. 91–104.

Leonard, P. (1995) 'Postmodernism, Socialism and Social Welfare', *Journal of Progressive Human Services*, vol. 6, pp. 3–19.

Leonard, P. (1997) *Postmodern Welfare: Reconstructing an Emancipatory Project*, London, Sage.

Levinas, E. (1989) 'Ethics as First Philosophy', translated by Seán Hand, in S. Hand (ed.), *The Levinas Reader*, Oxford, Blackwell, pp. 75–87.

Levinas, E. (1997) 'On Buber, Marcel, and Philosophy', in H. Jodalen and A. Vetlesen (eds), *Closeness: An Ethics*, Oslo, Scandinavian University Press, pp. 27–44.

Llewelyn, J. (1995) *Emmanuel Levinas: The Genealogy of Ethics*, London, Routledge.

Lorenz, W. (2001) 'Social Work Responses to "New Labour" in Continental European Countries', *British Journal of Social Work*, vol. 31, pp. 595–609.

Lorenz, W. and Seibel, F. (1998) *Erasmus-Evaluation Conference – Social Professions for a Social Europe, Koblenz 1999, National Reports*, CD Rom, Version 3/05.08.98. edn, Koblenz, European Centre for Community Education.

Lorenz, W. and Seibel, F. (1999) 'European Educational Exchanges in the Social Professions – The ECSPRESS Experience', in E. Marynowicz-Hetka, A. Wagner and J. Piekarski (eds), *European Dimensions in Training and Practice of the Social Professions*, Katowice, Poland, Slask, pp. 315–41.

Lymbery, M. (2000) 'The Retreat from Professionalism: From Social Worker to Care Manager', in N. Malin (ed.), *Professionalism, Boundaries and the Workplace*, London, Routledge, pp. 123–38.

Lyotard, J.-F. (1984) *The Postmodern Condition: A Report on Knowledge* (trans G. Bennington and B. Maasumi), Manchester, Manchester University Press.

MacIntyre, A. (1973) 'The Essential Contestability of Some Social Concepts', *Ethics*, vol. 84, no. 1, pp. 1–21.

MacIntyre, A. (1981) *After Virtue: A Study in Moral Theory*, 1st edn, London, Duckworth.

MacIntyre, A. (1985) *After Virtue: A Study in Moral Theory*, 2nd edn, London, Duckworth.

Manning, R. (1992) *Speaking from the Heart: A Feminist Perspective on Ethics*, Lanham, Maryland, Rowman & Littlefield.

Marshall, T. (1976) 'The Right to Welfare', in N. Timms and D. Watson (eds), *Talking about Welfare: Readings in Philosophy and Social Policy*, London, Routledge & Kegan Paul, pp. 51–63.

Matthews, J. and Kimmis, J. (2001) 'Development of the English Settlement Movement', in T. Jeffs and R. Gilchrist (eds), *Settlements, Social Change and Community Action: Good Neighbours*, London, Jessica Kinglsey, pp. 54–68.

May, T. (1991) *Probation: Politics, Policy and Practice*, Buckingham, Open University Press.

May, T. (1996) *Situating Social Theory*, Buckingham, Open University Press.

Mayo, M. (1994) *Communities and Caring: The Mixed Economy of Welfare*, Basingstoke, Macmillan.

Mayo, M. and Taylor, M. (2001) 'Partnerships and Power in Community Regeneration', in S. Balloch and M. Taylor (ed.), *Partnership Working: Policy and Practice*, Bristol, The Policy Press, pp. 39–56.

McBeath, G. and Webb, S. (1991) 'Social Work, Modernity and Post Modernity', *Sociological Review*, vol. 39, no. 4, pp. 745–62.

Merton, B. (2001) *'So What's New?': Innovation in Youth Work*, Leicester, National Youth Agency.

Meyers, D. (1994) *Subjection and Subjectivity: Psychoanalytic Feminism and Moral Philosophy*, London and New York, Routledge.

Mill, J.S. (1972) *Utilitarianism, On Liberty, and Considerations on Representative Government*, London, Dent.

Millen, J. and Wallman-Durrant, L. (2001) 'Multi-Disciplinary Partnership in a Community Mental Health Team', in V. White and J. Harris (eds), *Developing Good Practice in Community Care: Partnership and Participation*, London, Jessica Kingsley, pp. 149–73.

Millerson, G. (1964) *The Qualifying Associations: A Study in Professionalisation*, London, Routledge & Kegan Paul.

Milner, J. (2001) *Women and Social Work: Narrative Approaches*, Basingstoke, Palgrave.

Milson-Fairbairn Report (1969) *Youth and Community Work in the '70s*, London, HMSO.

Moody-Adams, M. (1991) 'Gender and the Complexity of Moral Voices', in C. Card (ed.), *Feminist Ethics*, Lawrence, Kansas, University Press of Kansas, pp. 195–212.

Mulhall, S. and Swift, A. (1992) *Liberals and Communitarians*, Oxford, Blackwell.

Nagel, T. (1986) *The View from Nowhere*, New York and Oxford, Oxford University Press.

National Association of Social Workers (1996) *Code of Ethics*, Washington, NASW.

National Youth Agency (2001) *Ethical Conduct in Youth Work: A Statement of Values and Principles from the National Youth Agency*, Leicester, National Youth Agency.

Nelson, H. (1997) 'Introduction: How to Do Things with Stories', in H. Nelson (ed.), *Stories and Their Limits: Narrative Approaches to Bioethics*, New York and London, Routledge, pp. vii–xx.

New Zealand Association of Social Workers (1993) *Code of Ethics*, Dunedin, NZASW.

Newman, J. (2000) 'Beyond the New Public Management? Modernizing Public Services', in J. Clarke, S. Gewirtz and E. McLaughlin (eds), *New Managerialism, New Welfare?*, London, Open University/Sage, pp. 45–61.

Noddings, N. (1984) *Caring: A Feminine Approach to Ethics and Moral Education*, Berkeley and Los Angeles, University of California Press.

Norman, R. (1998) *The Moral Philosophers*, 2nd edn, Oxford, Oxford University Press.

Nozick, R. (1974) *Anarchy, State and Utopia*, Oxford, Blackwell.

Nussbaum, M. (1986) *The Fragility of Goodness*, New York, Cambridge University Press.

Nussbaum, M. (1992) 'Virtue Revived', *The Times Literary Supplement*, 3 July, pp. 9–11.

Nussbaum, M. (2002) *Upheavals of Thought: The Intelligence of Emotions*, Cambridge, Cambridge University Press.

Oakley, J. (1992) *Morality and the Emotions*, London, Routledge.

Oakley, J. and Cocking, D. (2001) *Virtue Ethics and Professional Roles*, Cambridge, Cambridge University Press.

One NorthEast (1999) *Single Regeneration Budget Bidding Guidelines Round 6: A Guide for Partnerships*, Newcastle, One NorthEast.

O'Neill, O. (1996) *Towards Justice and Virtue: A Constructive Account of Practical Reasoning*, Cambridge, Cambridge University Press.

O'Neill, O. (2002a) *Autonomy and Trust in Bioethics*, Cambridge, Cambridge University Press.

O'Neill, O. (2002b) *A Question of Trust*, Cambridge, Cambridge University Press.

Osborne, T. (1998) 'Constructionism, Authority and the Ethical Life', in I. Velody and R. Williams (eds), *The Politics of Constructionism*, London, Sage, pp. 221–34.

Øvretveit, J., Mathias, P. and Thompson, T. (1997) 'Introduction', in J. Øvretveit, P. Mathias and T. Thompson (eds), *Interprofessional Working for Health and Social Care*, Basingstoke, Macmillan, pp. 1–8.

Parkin, F. (1974) *The Social Analysis of Class Structure*, London, Tavistock.

Parkin, F. (1979) *Marxism and Class Theory*, London, Routledge & Kegan Paul.

Parrott, L. (1999) *Social Work and Social Care*, Eastbourne, The Gildridge Press.

Parsons, T. (1939) 'The Professions and Social Structure', *Social Forces*, vol. 17, pp. 457–67.

Parton, N. and O' Byrne, P. (2000) *Constructive Social Work: Towards a New Practice*, Basingstoke, Macmillan.

Payne, M. (1995) 'The End of British Social Work', *Professional Social Work*, vol. 5.

Payne, M. (1996) *What is Professional Social Work?*, Birmingham, Venture Press.

Payne, M. (2000) *Teamwork in Multiprofessional Care*, Basingstoke, Macmillan.

Perkin, H. (1969) *Key Profession: The History of the Association of University Teachers*, London, Routledge & Kegan Paul.

Picht, W. (1914) *Toynbee Hall and the English Settlement Movement*, London, G. Bell & Sons.

Plant, R. (1974) *Community and Ideology*, London, Routledge & Kegan Paul.

Poole, R. (1991) *Morality and Modernity*, London, Routledge.

Popple, K. (1995) *Analysing Community Work: Its Theory and Practice*, Buckingham, Open University Press.

Pratchett, L. and Wingfield, M. (1994) *The Public Service Ethos in Local Government*, London, Commission for Local Democracy and Institute of Chartered Secretaries and Adminstrators.

Rao, N. (2000) *Reviving Local Democracy: New Labour, New Politics*, Bristol, The Policy Press.

Rauner, D. (2000) *They Still Pick Me Up When I Fall: The Role of Caring in Youth Development and Community Life*, New York, Columbia University Press.

Rawls, J. (1973) *A Theory of Justice*, Oxford, Oxford University Press.

Rawls, J. (1993) *Political Liberalism*, New York, Columbia University Press.

Reamer, F. (1990) *Ethical Dilemmas in Social Service*, 2nd edn, New York, Columbia University Press.

Reamer, F. (1999) *Social Work Values and Ethics*, 2nd edn, New York, Columbia University Press.

Rhodes, M. (1986) *Ethical Dilemmas in Social Work Practice*, Boston, Mass., Routledge & Kegan Paul.

Rice, D. (1975) 'The Code: A Voice for Approval', *Social Work Today*, 18 October, p. 381.

Ronnby, A. (1993) 'The Carer Society and Ethics', unpublished paper, Östersund, Department of Social Work and Humanities, Mid-Sweden University.

Rosenau, P. (1992) *Postmodernism and the Social Sciences: Insights, Inroads and Intrusions*, Princeton, Princeton University Press.

Rossiter, A., Prilleltensky, I. and Walsh-Bowers, R. (2000) 'A Postmodern Perspective on Professional Ethics', in B. Fawcett, B. Featherstone, J. Fook and A. Rossiter (eds), *Postmodern Feminist Perspectives: Practice and Research in Social Work*, London, Routledge, pp. 83–103.

Royal Institute of British Architects (1997) *Code of Professional Conduct*, London, RIBA.

Royal Town Planning Institute (1997) *Code of Professional Conduct*, London, RTPI.

Sandel, M. (1998) *Liberalism and the Limits of Justice*, 2nd edn, Cambridge, Cambridge University Press.

Sarangi, S. (1998) 'Interprofessional Case Construction in Social Work: The Evidential Status of Information and its Reportability', *Text*, vol. 18, no. 2, pp. 241–70.

Schön, D. (1991) *The Reflective Practitioner: How Professionals Think in Action* (first pub. 1983) paperback edn, Aldershot, Avebury/Ashgate.

Schön, D. (1992) 'The Crisis of Professional Knowledge and the Pursuit of an Epistemology of Practice', *Journal of Interprofessional Care*, vol. 6, no. 1, pp. 49–63.

Seebohm Report (1968) *Report of the Committee on Local Authority and Allied Personal Social Services*, London, HMSO.

Seligman, A. (1997) *The Problem of Trust*, Princeton, Princeton University Press.

Sevenhuisen, S. (1998) *Citizenship and the Ethics of Care: Feminist Considerations on Justice, Morality and Politics*, London, Routledge.

Shaw, W. (1999) *Contemporary Ethics: Taking Account of Utilitarianism*, Oxford, Blackwell.

Siegrist, H. (1994) 'The Professions, State and Government in Theory and History', in T. Becher (ed.), *Governments and Professional Education*, Buckingham, SRHE and Open University Press, pp. 3–20.

Sites, W. (1998) 'Communitarian Theory and Community Development in the United States', *Community Development Journal*, vol. 33, no. 1, pp. 57–65.

Slote, M. (2000) 'Virtue Ethics', in H. LaFollette (ed.), *The Blackwell Guide to Ethical Theory*, Oxford, Blackwell, pp. 325–47.

Slote, M. (2001) *Motives from Morals*, Oxford, Oxford University Press.

Smith, C. (2001) 'Trust and Confidence: Possibilities for Social Work in "High Modernity"', *British Journal of Social Work*, vol. 31, pp. 287–305.

Smith, D. (2000) 'Corporatism and the New Youth Justice', in B. Goldson (ed.), *The New Youth Justice*, Lyme Regis, Russell House, pp. 129–43.

Smith, M. (1965) *Professional Education for Social Work in Britain*, London, George Allen & Unwin.

Smith, M.K. (1988) *Developing Youth Work: Informal Education, Mutual Aid and Popular Practice*, Milton Keynes, Open University Press.

Smith, M.K. (2003) 'The End of Youth Work?', *Young People Now*, 5–11 February, p. 15.

Social Exclusion Unit (1998) *Bringing Britain Together: A National Strategy for Neighbourhood Renewal*, London, Cabinet Office.

Social Exclusion Unit (2001) *A New Commitment to Neighbourhood Renewal: National Strategy Action Plan*, London, Cabinet Office.

Soper, K. (1993) 'Postmodernism, Subjectivity and the Question of Value', in J. Squires (ed.), *Principled Positions: Postmodernism and the Rediscovery of Value*, London, Lawrence & Wishart, pp. 17–30.

Sorell, T. (2000) *Moral Theory and Anomaly*, Oxford, Blackwell.

South African Black Social Workers' Association (no date, received 1999) *Code of Ethics*, South Africa, SABSWA.

Stanley, N. (1999) 'User – Practitioner Transactions in the New Culture of Community Care', *British Journal of Social Work*, vol. 29, no. 3, pp. 417–36.

Statman, D. (1997) 'Introduction to Virtue Ethics', in D. Statman (ed.), *Virtue Ethics: A Critical Reader*, Edinburgh, Edinburgh University Press, pp. 3–41.

Stocker, M. with Hegeman, E. (1996) *Valuing Emotions*, Cambridge, Cambridge University Press.

Strauss, A. and Corbin, J. (1990) *Basics of Qualitative Research: Grounded Theory Procedures and Techniques*, London, Sage.

Swedish Union of Social Workers' Personnel and Public Administrators (SSR) (1991) *Guidelines for Professional Ethics in Social Work*, Stockholm, SSR.

Tadd, W. (1994) 'Accountability and Nursing', in R. Chadwick (ed.), *Ethics and the Professions*, Aldershot, Avebury, pp. 88–103.

Tam, H. (1998) *Communitarianism: A New Agenda for Politics and Citizenship*, Basingstoke, Macmillan.

Taylor, C. (1989) *Sources of the Self: The Making of Modern Identity*, Cambridge, Cambridge University Press.

Taylor, C. and White, S. (2000) *Practising Reflexivity in Health and Welfare*, Buckingham, Open University Press.

The New Shorter Oxford English Dictionary (1993), Oxford, Clarendon Press.

The Oxford House in Bethnel Green 1884–1948 (1948), London, T. Brakell Ltd.

Thomas, D. (1983) *The Making of Community Work*, London, Allen & Unwin.

Thomason, G. (1969) *The Professional Approach to Community Work*, London, Sands & Co.

Thompson, N. (1992) *Existentialism and Social Work*, Aldershot, Hants, Avebury.

Timms, N. (1983) *Social Work Values: An Enquiry*, London, Routledge & Kegan Paul.

Tonkiss, F. and Passey, A. (1999) 'Trust, Confidence and Voluntary Organisations: Between Values and Institutions', *Sociology*, vol. 33, no. 2, pp. 257–76.

Torstendahl, R. (1990) 'Essential Properties, Strategic Aims and Historical Development: Three Approaches to Theories of Professionalism', in M. Burrage and R. Torstendahl (eds), *Professions in Theory and History: Rethinking the Study of the Professions*, London, Sage, pp. 44–61.

Torstendahl, R. and Burrage, M. (eds) (1990) *The Formation of Professions: Knowledge, State and Strategy*, London, Sage.

Toulmin, S. (1987) 'The National Commission on Human Experimentation: Procedures and Outcomes', in H. Englehardt and A. Caplan (eds), *Scientific Controversies; Case Studies In the Resolution of Disputes in Science and Technology*, New York, Cambridge University Press, pp. 599–614.

Tronto, J. (1993) *Moral Boundaries: A Political Argument for an Ethic of Care*, London, Routledge.

Tronto, J. (2001) 'Does Managing Professionals Affect Professional Ethics? Competence, Autonomy and Care', in P. DesAutels and J. Waugh (eds), *Feminists Doing Ethics*, Lanham, Maryland, Rowman & Littlefield, pp. 187–202.

Veatch, R. (1981) *A Theory of Medical Ethics*, New York, Basic Books.

Vetlesen, A. (1994) *Perception, Empathy and Judgment: An Inquiry into the Preconditions of Moral Performance*, University Park, Pennsylvania, The Pennsylvania State University Press.

Vetlesen, A. (1997) 'Introducing an Ethics of Proximity', in H. Jodalen and A. Vetleson (eds), *Closeness: An Ethics*, Oslo, Scandinavian University Press, pp. 1–19.

Walker, M. (1998) *Moral Understandings: A Feminist Study in Ethics*, New York, Routledge.

Walker, M. (2001) 'Seeing Power in Morality: A Proposal for Feminist Naturalism in Ethics', in P. DesAutels and J. Waugh (eds), *Feminists Doing Ethics*, Lanham, Maryland, Rowman & Littlefield, pp. 3–14.

Walzer, M. (1983) *Spheres of Justice*, New York, Basic Books.

Weeks, J. (1993) 'Rediscovering Values', in J. Squires (ed.), *Principled Positions: Postmodernism and the Rediscovery of Value*, London, Lawrence & Wishart, pp. 189–209.

Weeks, J. (1995) *Invented Moralities: Sexual Values in an Age of Uncertainty*, Cambridge, Polity Press.

Wellcome News (2000) 'Mad, Bad or Ill? New Insights into Antisocial Behaviour', no. 25, pp. 20–1.

Wilding, P. (1982) *Professional Power and Social Welfare*, London, Routledge & Kegan Paul.

Wilensky, H. (1964) 'The Professionalization of Everyone', *American Journal of Sociology*, vol. 70, pp. 142–6.

Williams, B. (1985) *Ethics and the Limits of Philosophy*, London, Fontana Paperbacks and William Collins.

Williams, B. (2000) 'Youth Offending Teams and Partnerships', in G. Mair and R. Tarling (eds), *The British Criminology Conference: Selected Proceedings. Volume 3. Papers from the British Society of Criminology Conference, Liverpool, July 1999*, Loughborough, http://www.lboro.ac.uk/departments/ss/bsc/bccsp/vol03/williams.html, pp. 1–14.

Williams, R. (2000) *Making Identity Matter: Identity, Society and Social Interaction*, Durham, sociologypress.

Williamson, V. (2001) 'The Potential of Project Status to Support Partnerships', in S. Balloch and M. Taylor (eds), *Partnership Working: Policy and Practice*, Bristol, The Policy Press, pp. 117–42.

Wilmot, S. (1997) *The Ethics of Community Care*, London, Cassell.

Winkler, E. (1996) 'Moral Philosophy and Bioethics: Contextualism versus the Paradigm Theory', in L. Sumner and J. Boyle (eds), *Philosophical Perspectives on Bioethics*, Toronto, University of Toronto Press, pp. 50–77.

Wittgenstein, L. (1972) *Philosophical Investigations*, translated by G.E.M. Anscombe, 3rd edn, Oxford, Blackwell.

Wylie, T. (2000) *Connexions: The Implications for LEAs' Work with Young People*, London, The Education Network/National Youth Agency.

Young, I. (1993) 'Together in Difference: Transforming the Logic of Group Political Conflict', in J. Squires (ed.), *Principled Positions: Postmodernism and the Rediscovery of Value*, London, Lawrence & Wishart, pp. 121–50.

Younghusband, E. (1959) *Report of the Working Party on Social Workers in Local Authority Health and Welfare Services*, London, HMSO.

Younghusband, E. (1981) *The Newest Profession: A Short History of Social Work*, Sutton, Surrey, IPC Business Press Ltd.

Youth Justice Board (2000) *Youth Justice Board: Review of the Year 1999–2000*, London, Youth Justice Board.

Zussman, R. (2000) 'The Contributions of Sociology to Medical Ethics', *Hastings Center Report*, January–February, pp. 7–11.

Index

postmodernism 84–5, 92, 94–5;
application of 95–6; constructive
social work approach 96; and
consumer responsiveness 96;
and end of ethics 95; and ethics
of reconstruction 98; political
97–8; sceptical/affirmative 95;
and uncertainty 96–7
power 97, 153
practitioner–manager role 183–4
principle-based ethics 66, 100, 107;
concept 78; contractarian
78–9; dominance of 79–80;
Kantian–utilitarian approach 78
principles 50, 83, 84, 109, 110, 112,
114, 119, 189–90, 193
procedures 134, 152, 157–8, 161–2,
171–2
profession 180; approaches to 18; as
contested concept 18; definition
of 21; definitions of 17–18;
essentialist approach 19–20, 60;
historical/developmental approach
21–3; ideal/typical 23–5; strategic
approach 20–1
professional culture 134–7; concept
139; our way of being/doing 143–5;
use of term 139–40
professional ethics 47, 125; acceptance
of rules/values of conduct 192;
assumptions 191–3; central to
success of practitioners 194;
changes in 194; and changing
social professions 7–8; cynical
view of 52; distinction with
ordinary ethics 60–3; espoused/
enacted 50, 61, 62, 64; essentialist/
traditionalist view 51–2; ethical
theory 6–7; existence of distinct
groups 191–2; explorations of
8–10; judgements based on
principles/rules accepted by
profession 193; legitimacy
of 51–3; as living a life of its
own 70; loyalty to client/patient
user/service user 192–3; nature
of 3–4; as obstructive 145–7;
outline 10–15; as part of moral
philosophy/social sciences 71–4;
philosophical perspectives 11–12;
possible end of 176; and the
professions 5–6; the same as
ordinary ethics 63–5; shiftiness

of 179–80; as special 65–8; as
special norms 49–51; strategic/
cynical view 52–3; themes 4–8,
69; as topic of concern 1; and
trust 58–60, 68; understanding of
term 49–51; values come before
employing agency/society 193
professional identity 134–7, 164,
167, 180; concept 137; personal,
social, ego 137–8; what we
do/who we are 140–2
professional practice 13; future
of 15–16; practitioner
perspectives 14–15
professional project 43
professional values 134–7, 154;
concept 138; conflict 142; as
obstructive 145–7; use of term
138–9; what we believe/how we
act 142–3
professionalism, ambivalence towards
36–7; assault on 181; as body of
knowledge/skill officially
recognised 42; bureaucratic
authoritarian model 22–3;
changing nature of 68–9, 181;
and concept of closure 20–1;
deprofessionalising 37, 43–4; as
evolving notion 45; as ideology
serving some transcendent value
43; implementation gap 182;
and managerialism in public
services 37–42; move toward
technicality 181–2; new 42–5;
as occupationally controlled
division of labour 42; as
occupationally controlled labour
market 42–3; as occupationally
controlled training programme
43; post-revolutionary
liberal-democratic model 23;
public trust in 58–60; and
reprofessionalisation 44;
traditional corporate/weak state
model 22; trait theory 19–20, 52
professionals, as advocates of clients'
welfare 65–6; autonomy of 155–6;
balance of duty to client/other
stakeholders 66–7; competence
of 182; entrepreneurial response
189; and ethic of care/justice 184,
185–6; and face-to-face encounters
184, 185; hybrid role 183–4;

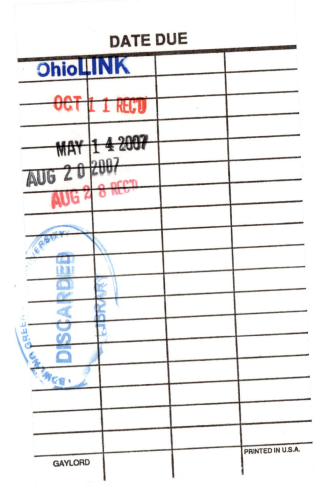